L. M. MONTGOMERY'S
"EMILY OF NEW MOON"

Children's Literature Association Series

L. M. MONTGOMERY'S "EMILY OF NEW MOON"

A Children's Classic at 100

Edited by Yan Du
and Joe Sutliff Sanders

University Press of Mississippi / Jackson

The University Press of Mississippi is the scholarly publishing agency of
the Mississippi Institutions of Higher Learning: Alcorn State University,
Delta State University, Jackson State University, Mississippi State University,
Mississippi University for Women, Mississippi Valley State University,
University of Mississippi, and University of Southern Mississippi.

www.upress.state.ms.us

The University Press of Mississippi is a member
of the Association of University Presses.

Any discriminatory or derogatory language or hate speech regarding race,
ethnicity, religion, sex, gender, class, national origin, age, or disability
that has been retained or appears in elided form is in no way
an endorsement of the use of such language outside a scholarly context.

Copyright © 2024 by Yan Du and Joe Sutliff Sanders
All rights reserved

∞

Library of Congress Cataloging-in-Publication Data

Names: Du, Yan (Children's author), editor. | Sanders, Joe Sutliff, editor.

Title: L. M. Montgomery's "Emily of New Moon" : a children's classic at 100 /
Yan Du, Joe Sutliff Sanders.
Other titles: Children's Literature Association series.
Description: Jackson : University Press of Mississippi, 2024. |
Series: Children's literature association series | Includes bibliographical
references and index.
Identifiers: LCCN 2023056008 (print) | LCCN 2023056009 (ebook) |
ISBN 9781496852496 (hardback) | ISBN 9781496852502 (trade paperback) |
ISBN 9781496852526 (epub) | ISBN 9781496852519 (epub) | ISBN 9781496852533 (pdf) |
ISBN 9781496852540 (pdf)
Subjects: LCSH: Montgomery, L. M. (Lucy Maud), 1874–1942. Emily of New Moon. |
Montgomery, L. M. (Lucy Maud), 1874–1942—Criticism and interpretation. |
Canadian literature—20th century. | Children's stories, Canadian—History and criticism. |
Children—Books and reading—Canada—History—20th century. | Orphans in literature.
Classification: LCC PR9199.3.M6 E45 2024 (print) | LCC PR9199.3.M6 (ebook) |
DDC 813/.52—dc23/eng/20240215
LC record available at https://lccn.loc.gov/2023056008
LC ebook record available at https://lccn.loc.gov/2023056009

British Library Cataloging-in-Publication Data available

CONTENTS

Introduction 3
Yan Du and Joe Sutliff Sanders

Part One: Literary Resonances

Chapter 1. Warring with Failure: *Emily's Quest* and the Victorian Past . . 23
Kate Lawson

Chapter 2. Exile and Instrumentality in the Emily Books 38
Jessica Wen Hui Lim

Chapter 3. Emily Byrd Starr Meets Brené Brown:
"Braving the Wilderness" and Achieving "True Belonging" 54
Lesley D. Clement

Part Two: Emily's Things

Chapter 4. Everyday Objects: Material Culture in the Emily Trilogy . . . 71
Allison McBain Hudson

Chapter 5. "Something Incalculably Precious":
Diary Writing in *Emily of New Moon* 87
Lindsey McMaster

Part Three: Gender

Chapter 6. The Japanese Reception
of the Emily Trilogy through Translation 105
Yoshiko Akamatsu

Chapter 7. Claiming and Reclaiming the Maternal:
Mothering and Mothers in the Emily Books 130
Rita Bode

Chapter 8. "A Ghost You Can *Feel* and *Hear* but Never *See*":
Queer Hauntings in *Emily of New Moon* 144
Katharine Slater

Part Four: Time

Chapter 9. The Romance of History in the Emily Novels 161
E. Holly Pike

Chapter 10. Encroaching Darkness:
L. M. Montgomery's Books about Emily. 175
Carol L. Beran

Chapter 11. Reading Emily out of Time and Place:
Breaking Chronology and Space 189
Margaret Steffler

Chapter 12. Emily's Afterlives: Trauma, Repetition,
and (Re)Reading in *Emily of New Moon* and *Russian Doll*. 203
Anastasia Ulanowicz

About the Contributors 219

Index 223

L. M. MONTGOMERY'S
"EMILY OF NEW MOON"

INTRODUCTION

YAN DU AND JOE SUTLIFF SANDERS

> I wonder if, a hundred years from now, anybody will win a victory over anything because of something *I* left or did. It is an *inspiring thought*.
> (EMILY CLIMBS 9)

At the time in her life when Lucy Maud Montgomery wrote *Emily of New Moon*, she was a very different person from the woman who wrote her first and most famous novel, *Anne of Green Gables*. Montgomery was known around the world, married with children, and financially successful. She approached her career as a writer with confidence and a skill for juggling responsibilities and public faces that she had learned through necessity. This was also, however, a time of dark trial for Montgomery, as she struggled with her husband's insecurities, the role she had to play as minister's wife in a community not always given to kindness, and multiple legal battles. Most famous among these would be her protracted battles with Louis Coues Page, the American publisher of the Anne books. By 1917, Montgomery approached her fight with Page with, as Mary Henley Rubio put it in her biography of the author, "no small amount of residual anger" (*Lucy Maud Montgomery* 225). In the years leading up to the writing of *Emily*, Montgomery "lived in a constant state of tension" (235), further compounded by a local lawsuit resulting from an automobile accident. This case, Rubio explains, "poisoned the community atmosphere," and it was in exactly this atmosphere that Montgomery wrote *Emily of New Moon*, beginning two months after the accident and concluding shortly before the trial (252).

Emily provided not a break with the past but a pivotal renegotiation with it for Montgomery. As Elizabeth Waterston observes, Montgomery had begun revisiting and reinscribing her past journals in 1919, and it is within those "early jottings" that she "recognized the gem of a new kind of story" (113). By August 1920, Montgomery was tired of her most famous creation. Upon completing the manuscript for *Rilla of Ingleside*, a book focusing on Anne's daughter, Montgomery recorded in her journal that "I am done with Anne forever—I swear it as a dark and deadly vow." Emily offered an opportunity to take on a new character, leaving behind the series at the heart of the endless legal battles with Page. "I want to create a new heroine now," Montgomery wrote; "she is already in embryo in my mind—she has been christened for years. Her name is 'Emily.' She has black hair and purplish gray eyes. I want to tell folks about *her*" (qtd. in Rubio, *Lucy Maud Montgomery* 289). Rubio remarks that "'Anne' had begun to feel like an incubus that hung around her neck, thanks largely to Page" (289). Still, Emily also allowed Montgomery a chance to return to a domestic realism with which she was comfortable and a formula with which she had already had success. Emily also enabled a frank, even therapeutic reengagement with Montgomery's own girlhood. In the author's journals, Rubio finds,

> Maud acknowledges that Emily's inner life is partly hers—a rare admission. Maud details the psychological hardships that Emily suffers in a restricted, contained, and confined life, drawing heavily from her own memories. Heir to the entire clan's criticism, Emily longs for her dead father's unconditional love, and she suffers terribly from her clan's ridicule of her writing ambitions. (291)

As a professional writer who emerged from familial trauma and a deeply damaged father-daughter relationship, Emily represented to Montgomery a chance to renegotiate her childhood, professional career, and personal relationships. Such renegotiation is reflected, too, in Montgomery's elaborate revisions of the Emily manuscripts. Since the creation of Emily parallels with Montgomery's busy dive into her past, the manuscript bore the mark of the author's changing mindset. Elizabeth Rollins Epperly observes that Montgomery made relatively dense revisions in sections regarding Emily's letters to her father, which coincide with the author's reshaping of her childhood in her journals ("L. M. Montgomery's Manuscript Revisions" 234). Already a rigorous reviser of her previous novels such as those in the Anne series, revising the Emily books seems to yield a special opportunity, one that allows the author to navigate the porous boundaries between past and present, life and writing, public and private.

As such, our collection of essays on *Emily of New Moon* and its two sequels means to us something very similar to what Emily meant to Montgomery.

Yan's experience with the trilogy echoes other self-identifying writers who saw themselves in Emily. But something in Emily spoke to Yan personally, in ways that also had to do with her family history. Like Emily, Yan's grandmother and great-grandmother lived in a time when women's voices were not valued. They were oral storytellers and chroniclers of family life, but unlike Emily, they could not write them down because they were weighed down by the dozens of children they gave birth to or by their lack of access to literacy education.

Yan grew up inheriting her grandmothers' keen sensibility for stories, and she saw in Emily the unspoken, uncharted imagination of her ancestors, the tenacity that carried forth acts of storytelling despite life's constant vagaries. Interestingly, Yan did not discover the books until she was in her twenties, when she was searching for primary texts for her dissertation. She had read *Anne* voraciously as a child but did not know *Emily*, since the translation did not exist then. The encounter with *Emily* after a lapse of almost a decade felt like a destined event, at a time when Yan was just beginning to understand the significance of her identity as a writer, a calling that she could not resist, like Emily.

The trilogy also came to Yan as she was searching for a way to talk about the relationship between girls and writing, a hackneyed and classic topic but one that perplexes her endlessly. Why is it that girls, past and present, are drawn to writing? What does it mean to be caught in that (sometimes) alienating vision of creativity and trials of emergent authorship but also somehow finding one's place, one's belonging in that process? The Emily trilogy seems like a perfect starting point to tap into these questions and provide a space for a critical negotiation that will never end. Indeed, when Yan and Joe were working together on Yan's doctoral thesis, every time the topic of *Emily of New Moon* (1923) came up in that work, we became so distracted with all the interesting things that could be said about it that we had trouble getting back to work on the thesis. Like the quartet of friends at the center of L. M. Montgomery's trilogy about Emily, Yan and Joe come from very different backgrounds. Also like Ilse, Teddy, and Perry, we found our way to the purple-eyed orphan in very different ways, but our lives have been altered by her: in fact, Joe's doctoral thesis also focused on *Emily*, indeed began because he couldn't stop thinking about the book, so our professional identities have been shaped by this girl who became a professional writer because she could no sooner stop writing than she could stop being herself.

The origins of the book, then, echo Emily's story and its significance to its author, but our collection in its emerging form is also profoundly similar to Emily. Some years ago, Joe taught a graduate seminar on turn-of-the-century orphan girl novels, drawing on his monograph (which, as further evidence of the importance of Emily in his life, came from his thesis) about those stories, and he discovered to his embarrassment that he had misunderstood something fundamental about them all along. First reading them almost a hundred years after they had been written, Joe had assumed that the books were set in the time in which they were published, but in fact these books were routinely set before the birth of the girls who initially consumed them, frequently in the time of the *grandmothers* of those first readers. Perhaps most readers would have come to that realization earlier, though it is noteworthy that at least one other specialist, Peter Hunt, regards the slip of time between publication and setting as a discovery, in his short essay on *The Secret Garden* (1911) (68).[1]

But what a strange thing, that books published in a very modern, forward-looking period would routinely look back. Stranger yet that the books in this orphan girl tradition were frequently bestsellers at the turn into the twentieth century. These years were exactly the same period in which, for example, the Stratemeyer Syndicate was publishing massively popular books about children who were using the latest technology to explore the deep sea (*The Rival Ocean Divers*, 1905), race motorcycles and automobiles (*The Motor Boys*, with three volumes published in 1905 alone, and *The Motor Girls*, with ten volumes between 1910 and 1917), and produce films (*The Moving Picture Girls* in seven volumes between 1914 and 1916).[2] These years overlap with the period of modernism, with abundant experiments in art, architecture, law, and even animation. That novels about the recent past found publication, let alone international audiences, is a puzzle.

It is not, however, at all out of keeping with Emily herself. Emily Byrd Starr embodies this contradiction between the forward-looking and the nostalgic. She is herself a professional woman writer making a steady living doing something that was traditionally men's work, writing in a realist tradition more associated with masculinity, and publishing in the New York marketplace. She is also, however, deeply happy with the old-fashioned elements of life at New Moon: the candles, the potato pot, skimming of the milk, the flooring, the wallpaper, and every other traditional aspect of life that her aunts follow with Murray sobriety. And of course, Emily chooses to stay in Prince Edward Island, in this old-fashioned place, rather than join the modern world of New York, struggling on the one hand against the small-mindedness of her neighbors and advocating on the other for the staid romance of the Victorians.

The authors in this collection are like Emily. We are situated in a reading position that is contemporary, and we are going to have questions for and objections to the trilogy that come from that position. We also, however, love these books and cannot separate our emotional connection to them from our critical reading of them now. Comfortingly, that sense of being on the cusp has been part of the history of the novels since their very gestation; indeed, the author herself had a similar relationship with these books. Lucy Maud Montgomery loved the first book but anticipated disappointment with the next books even before the first was published. On February 15, 1922, she wrote in her diary,

> Today I finished *Emily of New Moon*, after six months writing. It is the best book I have ever written—and I have had more intense pleasure in writing it than any of the others—not even excepting *Green Gables*. I have *lived* it, and I hated to pen the last line and write *finis*. Of course, I'll have to write several sequels but they will be more or less hackwork I fear. They cannot be to me what this book has been. (qtd. in Rubio and Waterston 39)

What the trilogy "has been" to us is a complicated story, as we think about the versions of ourselves who first read the books, the versions who read them now, and the versions who will read them and return to the snapshot of Emily criticism that we are able to capture in this collection. And of course, our contributions in this volume of new scholarship are shot through with insights lent to us by preceding work.

EMILY OF NEW MOON: CRITICAL RECEPTION AND SCHOLARSHIP

Critical discussion on the Emily trilogy did not fully begin to take shape until the 1970s. In 1967, Sheila Egoff's comprehensive review of Canadian children's literature, *Republic of Childhood: Critical Guide to Canadian Children's Literature*, mentioned *Anne of Green Gables* only in passing and made no reference to the Emily books. In autumn 1975, however, John R. Sorfleet's edited issue on Montgomery appeared in the *Canadian Children's Literature* journal, carrying an assembled group of specialized articles on the renowned author's life and works. In this issue, Emily is repeatedly evoked as a memorable character alongside Anne, Pat, Marigold, and Jane, while Ann S. Cowan explains the books' quality as a *Künstlerroman*. In the decades that followed, Emily criticism blossomed into multiple directions, some of them anticipated in these first efforts.

A key strategy of scholars from the 1980s and into the new millennium has been to put the Emily trilogy in dialogue with other texts. T. D. MacLulich's 1985 essay, for example, situates Emily in the nineteenth-century juvenile tradition that descended from Louisa May Alcott's *Little Women* ("L. M. Montgomery and the Literary Heroine"). Following MacLulich, children's literature scholars have analyzed *Emily* by aligning it with different literary or generic traditions within (predominantly) girls' fiction. Joe Sutliff Sanders invites us to consider Montgomery's work more specifically within the sentimental domestic tradition that gave way to orphan girl narratives in the latter half of the nineteenth century. Sanders demonstrates how *Emily of New Moon* embodies a moving away from modes of sentimental discipline that had characterized earlier North American orphan girl protagonists. Hilary Emmett takes up where Sanders left off by expanding his identification of how the mode of sentimental discipline in the novel has been revised. Drawing from Sara Ahmed's work about willfulness as a concept and discussing *Emily of New Moon* alongside a group of texts from across the Anglo world, Emmett reveals that the book serves as one of the "nodes in a complex transatlantic and transhemispheric network" of girls' texts where willful heroines are shown to negotiate—and resist—their place within the structure of sentimental education (213). While Emmett takes Sanders's work further via an extended exploration of girls' responses to sentimental strategies, Jane Suzanne Carroll brings the focus back to Emily's role as an orphan girl that embodies the marginal and liminal qualities of orphaned female protagonists in the long nineteenth century.

Apart from its participation within the nineteenth- and early twentieth-century girls' narratives of sentimental discipline and orphanhood, the trilogy also, as Michelle Smith et al. demonstrate, signifies within the context of colonial girls' experience of modernity. According to Smith and her collaborators, the novels represent the modern girl in the tradition of early twentieth-century colonial girls' print culture, especially through the development of her writing career and her clearheaded decision about her marriage choices. Engaging with a strand of debates on children's literature and legal justice, Kate Sutherland additionally considers how Emily's story reflects Thomas C. Klein's observations of children's texts privileging natural law, a higher conception of justice based on universal moral truths about humanity, over positive law, and a set of rules and conventions constructed by humans.

The trilogy's classic status among the tradition of girls' authorship in children's literature has also been observed by Dawn Sardella-Ayres and Claudia Mills, whose analyses outline the narrative patterns that shape the young female writers' literary apprenticeship and romantic choices and the implications that her choices may have on her readers. Other scholars read Emily's creative talent in terms of the literary traditions in which she participates as a budding poet. Margaret Steffler sees Emily as a Romantic child and believes that the Wordsworthian values of artistic creativity and imagination alive in Emily benefit the Canadian community. Alicia Pollard, on the other hand, connects Emily with Percy Bysshe Shelley, noting that her journey is punctuated by antirevelation that takes her from rapture into despair. Shelley's mysticism appeals to Emily's curiosity for the mysterious and the dark, elevating the young poet into experiences of the Romantic sublime. Brenton D. G. Dickieson delves more specifically into Emily's Wordsworthian-informed flash, discussing its effects and essence in relation to C. S. Lewis, another renowned author of widely known books that children love, specifically his philosophical reasoning on *sehnsucht* (longing).

Emily's Romantic poetic sensibilities naturally invite additional critical interest with regard to her interactions with nature. Readers have variously adopted concepts from ecocriticism, theology, and spirituality. Elizabeth Rollins Epperly, for instance, refers to the ecocritical concept of "dwelling," which she reads as a process, a state of being, a place (*"Emily's Quest"*). Unlike the ethereal experiences of beauty suggested by Emily's subliminal encounters, "dwelling" anticipates a relationship with nature punctuated by harmonious interdependence, "a life-sustaining engagement" that manifests in daily embodied experiences of pain, loss, and joy (220). Other discussions center on Emily's appreciation of the spiritual dimensions nature opens (Catherine Posey), including her pagan imagination (Kirstie Blair and William V. Thompson) and her investment in a form of feminine spirituality (Kathleen Anne Miller). Emily's figure as both a maturing young woman deeply shaped by nature as daily sustenance and a pagan girl who develops an otherworldly kinship with nature reveals how Montgomery's portrayal of girlhood, nature, and spirituality not only draws on traditions of Romantic epiphanic modes but also involves a revisionist approach toward the culture of conventional religious mores and paganism linked with ancient legends and nature worship.

The Emily trilogy's significance in several ongoing strands of children's literature criticism, however, does not eclipse its uniqueness as a series that had most often been associated with Montgomery's attempt at writing something completely different from the more idyllic Anne series. MacLulich reveals the curious crossover quality of the novels, stating that *Anne of Green Gables* belongs more firmly to the children's canon while *Emily of New Moon* showed the author "aspir[ing] to higher things" ("L. M. Montgomery and the Literary Heroine" 12). Subsequent Montgomery scholars repeatedly returned to the trilogy's crossover potential, especially in regard to how it characterizes Montgomery's darker style and her fascination with "a psychological study" of her coming-of-age characters.

Since the late 1990s, critics have identified the trilogy's abundant gothic undertones. Some (Lorna Drew, Kathleen Ann Miller) point out the trilogy's intertextual links with classic gothic narratives such as Ann Radcliffe's *Mysteries of Udolpho* and Charlotte Brontë's *Jane Eyre*, highlighting the (female) gothic tropes that contribute to the novels' complex gender politics. Many of these earlier readings illuminate how gothicized effects in the novels rupture the patriarchal narrative logic (Drew) and reveal the repressed, the traumatic, and the unruly. Kate Lawson ("Adolescence") and Lindsey McMaster examine elements of the gothic through Emily's negotiation of a rebellious maternal inheritance and the repressive patriarchal influence in the clan, all of which return to traumatize the family in uncanny ways. In another article, Lawson traces Montgomery's own fascination with the idea of Freudian uncanny to examine Emily's main psychic episodes across the three installments ("The 'Disappointed' House"). Soon after, she discovers that Montgomery's use of the gothic mode in *Emily Climbs*, particularly the idea of subliminal awareness, allows the author to rupture "the disciplinary system that enjoins the adolescent girl to situate her desires in the home" ("The Alien at Home" 156)—an observation echoed by gender literary theorists such as G. A. Woods. Their line of inquiry, again, uncovers Montgomery's skillful probing of gender relations and adolescent psychosexual development through a powerful "Gothic backstory" (McMaster 66). Reading Emily's gothic elements through Montgomery's Leaskdale journals (referring to the journals she kept during the period after she moved to Leaskdale in 1911), Natalie Forest more recently suggests that Montgomery's psychological experiences at Leaskdale were translated into her journals and fiction, so that her works, especially the Emily trilogy, can be read as an extension of her own "private gothic reality" (178).

While the gothic has been a potent tool for framing Emily's transgressive and traumatic sexual maturity process and psychic development, Irene Gammel reminds us to look at aspects where we can read the heroine's sexuality not only via the gothic but also through female embodiment. Her analysis, rooted in feminist body theory and a feminist historical approach, shows that Emily's sexuality is represented as a locus for eroticized pleasure and for negotiating contesting social expectations ("The Eros of Childhood"; "'My Secret Garden'"). Gammel's claim that Emily embodies "the desires and pleasures of a healthy and strong Canadian girl" prepares later scholars for interpreting the trilogy's representations of adolescent female bodily growth, specifically in terms of their health ("The Eros of Childhood" 114). Susan Meyer traces turn-of-the-century changes in health discourse as well as Montgomery's response to them, foregrounding the author's association of fresh air metaphors and outdoor activities with Emily's physical and creative vitality. Jenn Macquarrie, on the other hand, borrows from theories in contemporary dance, particularly the dance philosophies of Isadora Duncan, to think about how Montgomery constructs natural movement and how Emily's health is framed in relation to the language of dance.

As Montgomery's most autobiographical work, the trilogy has long drawn critical attention in terms of how it reflects the author's own life, career, narrative strategies, and views on literature and writing as a (Canadian) woman. Scholarship in this respect has often been borrowed from gynocriticism and biographical accounts. Earlier studies include Judith Miller's comments on the novels' characteristic portrayal of a female artist, followed by Thomas E. Tausky's 1983 biocritical study of the entire series, as well as MacLulich's 1985 contribution ("L. M. Montgomery's Portraits"). During the late 1980s, critical debates started to benefit from the publication of Montgomery's *Selected Journals*, giving rise to a host of more nuanced debates regarding how Emily carries Montgomery's fictional agenda aimed at exposing the tensions between the female writer's life and art and the difficulty for her to find a voice (Epperly, *Fragrance*). Ian Menzies and Mary Rubio ("Subverting") both cite Emily as an example of Montgomery's subversive strategy, the former focusing on symbolic codes and archetypal patterns in Emily's *Künstler* quest and the latter explaining how Montgomery undermines expectations of the formulaic romance genre through narrative techniques, intertextual discourse, and a complication of happy endings. Other scholars identify the perilous nature of romantic relationships in Emily's artistic maturation to comment on Montgomery's critique of conventional romance rhetoric (Marie Campbell) and her exploration of a female artist's preservation of her creative vitality (Sardella-Ayres, Gabriella Åhmansson). Later criticism shifted slightly toward Montgomery's depiction of Emily as a Canadian writer (E. Holly Pike, Faye Hammill). These studies interpret the significance of the trilogy in regionalist and national perspectives, extrapolating how it reflects the author's career and her views on the Canadian literary scene.

The past few years have witnessed an overall reappraisal and reevaluation of the trilogy: new critical perspectives have been introduced and previously overlooked issues redressed. Attention has been given to secondary or tertiary characters—often men and boys—revealing Montgomery's complex representations of boyhood and masculinity (see Bode, "Vulnerable Situations"). Meanwhile, critics have drawn from cultural studies, such as

Pike's 2020 analysis that relies on insights from material culture to examine Emily's gradual understanding of material books and manuscripts as potential commodities for possible commercialization and consumption. Lesley D. Clement's illustrated essay traces Montgomery's reliance on visualization to construct Emily as a woman and artist, paying attention to "the cultural 'traces,'" particularly images and portraits, that train Emily to interrogate ways of seeing, not seeing, being seen, and not being seen. Attention has also been paid to Montgomery's allocations of time and space. Epperly revisits her reading of Emily's creative experiences in terms of time, especially its unique fluidity as "engaged energy" ("Reading Time"), while Rebecca Thompson utilizes Bachelard's space theory to interrogate Emily's appropriation and ownership of spaces imbued with patriarchal influence.

Apart from adopting refreshed lenses to interpreting old materials, critics have also turned their interest back to the trilogy's adaptation and reception. Previously, scholars have commented on the CBC TV adaptation of Emily, especially its melodramatic functions (Christopher Gittings) and the complexities involved in representing Emily's sexual pleasures and transgressions in a televised medium (Gammel, "The Eros of Childhood"). Andrea McKenzie was the first to explore the visual rhetoric of the Emily trilogy's cover images from the mid-1920s to the late 1950s in Europe and North America, arguing that the different cover illustrations reflect how cultural values of young girls' authorship are inscribed visually. Yet these earlier studies did not touch on aspects of reader response and translation, and it was only recently that scholars reconsidered the series' transnational appeal and addressed these gaps. Laura Leden studies the abridgement and purification strategies of several Swedish and Finnish translations of the Emily books, highlighting what has been lost in the translations and how the translated versions respond to the generic conventions of girls' fiction and/or the strictures of addressing a child audience ("Reading as Empowerment"; "Emily Byrd Starr Conventionalized"; "For Children Only"; "Girls' Classics"). Diving into the archives of C. W. K. Gleerup, the first publisher of Montgomery's Anne and Emily books in Sweden, Åsa Warnqvist discloses the publisher's potent influence in shaping Swedish translations of Emily. Vappu Kannas's research concerns the reader reception of the Emily books in the Finnish context, explicating the trilogy's potential for empowering readers through building a dialogic relationship with the books throughout their lives.

Following the resurgence of new critical innovations surrounding the trilogy, this collection, too, aims to uncover new patterns in a familiar fabric of text. In many respects, the original chapters in this collection embody not only an effort to renegotiate with the past but also to represent the contributors' progressed and evolving thinking on Montgomery's centennial piece, offering a kaleidoscopic lens to an enduring classic.

THE CHAPTERS

Our collection similarly renegotiates our relationship with the past, specifically our perspectives on *Emily of New Moon* and its two sequels a century after they came into the world. Part One focuses on the literary resonances of the Emily books, including the inheritances under which Emily and her author labored, the inspirations Emily drew, and the long literary history in which she came to participate, in some cases a history beyond that which Montgomery could have seen herself. Kate Lawson's chapter, "Warring with Failure: *Emily's Quest* and the Victorian Past," builds a theory for understanding literary failure. She draws on Emily's perceptions of her own shortcomings, Montgomery's infamously conflicted feelings about the quality of the trilogy, and the traditions of sequels that Montgomery received from her Victorian predecessors. Lawson provides a refreshing understanding of failure as potentially energizing, thereby offering an importantly different perspective on what Emily and Montgomery considered to be their own literary failings.

In "Exile and Instrumentality in the Emily Books," Jessica Wen Hui Lim returns to one of the most cherished observations about the Emily books, namely their debt to Wordsworth, particularly through Emily's flash. By way of a careful and personal reexamination of the subtlest nuances of Wordsworth's "flash that has revealed / The invisible world," Lim argues for a new understanding of Emily's flash through a more precise understanding of Wordsworth. Lim demonstrates that an inevitable element of Emily's Romantic insight is displacement, alienation from exactly the elements of companionship and belonging that she most desires, adding a new dimension to one of the most familiar ways of reading the trilogy.

Finally, Lesley D. Clement's "Emily Byrd Starr Meets Brené Brown: 'Braving the Wilderness' and Achieving 'True Belonging'" applies the theories of Brené Brown to Emily to understand what it means to belong. Beginning with the concept borrowed from Toni Morrison that "you are only free when you realize you belong no place—you belong every place—no place at all," Clement examines how the main quartet of friends in the Emily books find their place in the physical and constructed worlds of Edwardian Prince Edward Island. As with Lim's chapter, Clement's essay explores a kind of spiritual dilemma, as Montgomery's characters must work through the fate of never belonging and the desire for true belonging.

Our second section turns to the objects of Emily's life, including the material goods that interact with her emerging character and the private things of her most guarded thoughts. Allison McBain Hudson, in "Everyday Objects: Material Culture in the Emily Trilogy," asks us to give up a traditional strategy of reading so that we may discover an understanding of the trilogy that has been in front of us all along. Rather than reading the objects of Emily's life as symbolic, Hudson encourages us to think about how Emily's life is shaped by the fact that in the diegetic space, these things *are things*. Rather than conceiving of objects as imaginary constructs, she suggests how encountering the embodied elements of Emily's imagined world illuminates the materiality of this fictional life.

Lindsey McMaster examines those objects with which Emily is most closely associated: the papers, letters, and journals that she produces. In "'Something Incalculably Precious': Diary Writing in *Emily of New Moon*," McMaster considers Emily's writing as an especially rich and provocative space from which to understand the mysteries that haunt Emily's existence and that invite the reader to probe the boundaries of the public and private. For Emily, as for Montgomery, journal writing served multiple purposes, and Emily's writing for herself provides an opportunity to think about what elements of privacy might be inherently less than private.

This section also highlights an underexamined point of disagreement between Emily scholars over the decades, namely, how to read Teddy Kent. For Hudson, Teddy represents an opportunity to understand what true connection between human beings must be. For McMaster, Teddy is a reminder of the many varieties of childhood pain. Across our collection as a whole, Teddy's meaning will change many times, perhaps indicating that the next wave of Emily scholarship should attend more closely to him.

Part Three considers the discourses of gender that surround and shoot through the Emily trilogy, shaping Emily's imaginary experiences and the lived experiences of Emily that the novels have generated in the century following publication. Yoshiko Akamatsu opens this section with "The Japanese Reception of the Emily Trilogy through Translation." This essay, based on Akamatsu's own experiences serving as a translator and consultant for the adaptation of the Emily books to Japanese audiences, explores how the meaning of the series in Japan has been negotiated over time. Especially important to these insights are the implications of the trilogy and its adaptations for professional women and the girls who dream of becoming them.

Rita Bode embarks on a similarly subtle quest in "Claiming and Reclaiming the Maternal: Mothering and Mothers in the Emily Books." Bode uses

Montgomery's own loss of and longing for a certain kind of maternal force in her life to open up the barely spoken longings of the novel. From this starting place, she reinvents our understanding of what mothers might be and how they might be valued in Emily's story.

Katharine Slater's "'A Ghost You Can *Feel* and *Hear* but Never *See*': Queer Hauntings in *Emily of New Moon*" closes the section by arguing that the ghosts that haunt the Emily books are more than spectral. A nonnormative queerness also pervades the story, provoking dissonances between what is desired and what is required, offering a sense of unhappiness that highlights the gap between the heteronormative structures of early-century Prince Edward Island and the gendered identities that resist. The chapters in this section also bring forward a theme that is important throughout the collection: empathy. Empathy comes into focus through the relevance of Emily to contemporary women writers, mothers both fictional and biographical, and all those who have experienced loss.

The final section turns to an inevitably appropriate theme as we meditate on a century of Emily: time. History and a sense of the past inform not only our own reading of the novels but also the path that Emily must climb. Still, as the chapters in this section argue, the flow of history is something with which we can engage critically, something that might not be as irresistible as we have come to think. E. Holly Pike begins this section with "The Romance of History in the Emily Novels." Here, Pike explores one of the most consistent sources of conflict in the trilogy, namely the pressure of the past on the present, as Emily struggles with the traditions, sins, joys, and grievances of the many people she counts as ancestors. Pike offers an overlooked model for the trilogy's understanding of history, a model that structures and illuminates Emily's own understanding of the history that she must negotiate.

Carol L. Beran's "Encroaching Darkness: L. M. Montgomery's Books about Emily" argues for a biographical understanding of Montgomery's history as a writer that pinpoints her changes from her most famous book to the book on which we focus here. With careful attention to the personal and national changes and traumas between the publication of the first Anne book and the beginning of the Emily series, Beran explains the darkness that weaves through the latter series as not simply a tonal shift but an authentic expression of an author who continued to struggle with grief.

Margaret Steffler follows with "Reading Emily Out of Time and Place: Breaking Chronology and Space." Here, Steffler takes a refreshingly personal and reflective approach to both the trilogy and Steffler's own previous experiences of it. Whereas her previous readings have relied on a sense of how things grow and move forward, this reading posits that the Emily books may best be understood by refusing to consider them in the safe, linear structure in which they are offered to us. The result is an analysis that challenges our long-held assumptions about the story and opens new ways of reading historical fiction in general.

Anastasia Ulanowicz closes our collection with "Emily's Afterlives: Trauma, Repetition, and (Re)Reading in *Emily of New Moon* and *Russian Doll*," a consideration of Emily prompted by the cycles of trauma and rereading in the time loop television series *Russian Doll*. More than a comparison between the two texts, Ulanowicz's analysis models a meditation on reading, rereading, and not-reading, on how any text must be repeatedly reapproached from different points in our lives to be understood, if only fleetingly.

NOTES

1. Sandra Dinter, however, recognizes easily that *The Secret Garden* must be set in the Victorian era, possibly several generations before readers could have picked up a first edition of Frances Hodgson Burnett's novel.

2. It is perhaps also worth noting that Montgomery wrote another novel, *The Blue Castle*, in the midst of composing the Emily trilogy, and *The Blue Castle* has a fondness for motor cars and frustration with tradition decidedly out of place in the Emily books.

WORKS CITED

Åhmansson, Gabriella. "The Survival of the Artist: L. M. Montgomery and the Attempted Murder of Emily Byrd Starr." *Literary Responses to Arctic Canada: Proceedings from the Third International Conference of the Nordic Association for Canadian Studies, University of Oslo, 1990*, edited by Jørn Carlsen, Nordic Association for Canadian Studies / L'Association nordique d'études canadiennes, 1993, pp. 185–92.

Blair, Kirstie, and William V. Thompson. "The Mood of the Golden Age: Paganism, Ecotheology and the Wild Woods in L. M. Montgomery's *Anne* and *Emily* Series." *Literature and Theology*, vol. 30, no. 2, 2016, pp. 131–47. https://doi.org/10.1093/litthe/frw017.

Bode, Rita. "Vulnerable Situations: Boys and Boyhood in the Emily Books." *Children and Childhoods in L. M. Montgomery: Continuing Conversations*, edited by Rita Bode, Lesley D. Clement, E. Holly Pike, and Margaret Steffler, McGill-Queen's UP, 2022, pp. 68–90.

Campbell, Marie. "Wedding Bells and Death Knells: The Writer as Bride in the *Emily* Trilogy." *Harvesting Thistles: The Textual Garden of L. M. Montgomery; Essays on Her Novels and Journals*, edited by Mary Henley Rubio, Canadian Children's Press, 1994, pp. 137–45.

Carroll, Jane Suzanne. "Girlhood and Space in Nineteenth-Century Orphan Literature." *Rereading Orphanhood: Texts, Inheritance, Kin*, edited by Diane Warren and Laura Peters, Edinburgh UP, 2020, pp. 186–205.

Clement, Lesley D. "Visual Culture, Storytelling, and Becoming Emily: An Illustrated Essay." *Journal of L. M. Montgomery Studies*, 2020 Vision Forum. https://journaloflmmontgomerystudies.ca/vision-forum/becoming-emily-illustrated-essay.

Cowan, Ann S. "Canadian Writers: Lucy Maud and Emily Byrd." *L. M. Montgomery Issue*, special issue of *Canadian Children's Literature / Littérature canadienne pour la jeunesse*, edited by John R. Sorfleet, vol. 1, no. 3, Autumn 1975, pp. 42–49. https://ccl-lcj.ca/index.php/ccl-lcj/article/view/1215.

Dickieson, Brenton D. G. "C. S. Lewis's Theory of Sehnsucht and L. M. Montgomery's Flash: Vocation and the Numinous." *The Faithful Imagination: Papers from the 2018 Frances White Ewbank Colloquium on C. S. Lewis and Friends*, edited by Joe Ricke and Ashley Chu, Winged Lion Press, 2019, pp. 144–65.

Dinter, Sandra. "Spatial Inscriptions of Childhood: Transformations of the Victorian Garden in *The Secret Garden*, *Tom's Midnight Garden*, and *The Poison Garden*." *Children's Literature Association Quarterly*, vol. 40 no. 3, 2015, p. 217–37. Project MUSE, https://doi.org/10.1353/chq.2015.0030.

Drew, Lorna. "The Emily Connection: Ann Radcliffe, L. M. Montgomery and 'the Female Gothic.'" *Canadian Children's Literature / Littérature canadienne pour la jeunesse*, no. 77, Spring 1995, pp. 19–32. https://ccl-lcj.ca/index.php/ccl-lcj/article/view/4663.

Egoff, Sheila. *The Republic of Childhood: A Critical Guide to Canadian Children's Literature in English*. Oxford UP, 1967.

Emmett, Hilary. "The 'Willful' Girl in the Anglo-World: Sentimental Heroines and Wild Colonial Girls, 1872–1923." *Children, Childhood and Youth in the British World*, edited by Shirleene Robinson and Simon Sleight, Palgrave Macmillan, 2016. pp. 201–17.

Epperly, Elizabeth Rollins. "*Emily's Quest*: L. M. Montgomery's Green Alternative to Despair and War?" *L. M. Montgomery and War*, edited by Andrea McKenzie and Jane Ledwell, McGill-Queen's UP, 2017, pp. 214–33.

Epperly, Elizabeth Rollins. *The Fragrance of Sweet-Grass: L. M. Montgomery's Heroines and the Pursuit of Romance*. U of Toronto P, 1992.

Epperly, Elizabeth Rollins. "L. M. Montgomery's Manuscript Revisions" (originally published 1995). *The L. M. Montgomery Reader Volume Two: A Critical Heritage*, edited by Benjamin Lefebvre, U of Toronto P, 2014, pp. 228–35.

Epperly, Elizabeth Rollins. "Reading Time: L. M. Montgomery and the 'Alembic of Fiction.'" *L. M. Montgomery and Reading*, special collection of *Journal of L. M. Montgomery Studies*, edited by Emily Woster and Kate Scarth, 5 June 2019.

Forest, Natalie. "(Re)Locating Montgomery: Prince Edward Island Romance to Southern Ontario Gothic." *L. M. Montgomery's Rainbow Valleys: The Ontario Years, 1911–1961*, edited by Lesley D. Clement and Rita Bode, McGill-Queen's UP, 2015, pp. 166–83.

Gammel, Irene. "The Eros of Childhood and Early Adolescence in Girl Series: L. M. Montgomery's *Emily* Trilogy." *Windows and Words: A Look at Canadian Children's Literature in English*, edited by Aïda Hudson and Susan-Ann Cooper, U of Ottawa P, 2003, pp. 97–118.

Gammel, Irene. "'My Secret Garden': Dis/Pleasure in L. M. Montgomery and F. P. Grove." *English Studies in Canada*, vol. 25, no. 1, March 1999, pp. 39–65. https://doi.org/10.1353/esc.1999.0037.

Gittings, Christopher. "Re-Visioning *Emily of New Moon*: Family Melodrama for the Nation." *L. M. Montgomery and Popular Culture*, special issue of *Canadian Children's Literature / Littérature canadienne pour la jeunesse*, vol. 24, no. 91–92, Fall–Winter 1998, pp. 22–35. https://ccl-lcj.ca/index.php/ccl-lcj/article/view/4491.

Hammill, Faye. *Literary Culture and Female Authorship in Canada 1760-2000*. Brill, 2003.

Hunt, Peter. "How Did Mary Get to Misslethwaite Manor?" *How Did Long John Silver Lose His Leg? And Twenty-Six Other Mysteries of Children's Literature*, edited by Dennis Butts and Peter Hunt, Luttleworth Press, 2013, pp. 65–69.

Kannas, Vappu. "'Emily Equals Childhood and Youth and First Love': Finnish Readers and L. M. Montgomery's *Anne* and *Emily* Books." *Reading Today*, edited by Heta Pyrhönen and Janna Kantola, UCL Press, 2018, pp. 118–31.

Lawson, Kate. "Adolescence and the Trauma of Maternal Inheritance in L. M. Montgomery's *Emily of New Moon*." *Canadian Children's Literature/Littérature canadienne pour la jeunesse*, no. 94, Summer 1999, pp. 21–41. https://ccl-lcj.ca/index.php/ccl-lcj/article/view/4575.

Lawson, Kate. "The Alien at Home: Hearing Voices in L. M. Montgomery's *Emily Climbs* and F. W. H. Myers." *Gothic Studies*, vol. 4, no. 2, 2002, pp. 155–66. https://doi.org/10.7227/GS.4.2.6.

Lawson, Kate. "The 'Disappointed' House: Trance, Loss, and the Uncanny in L. M. Montgomery's *Emily* Trilogy." *Children's Literature*, vol. 29, 2001, pp. 71–90. https://doi.org/10.1353/chl.0.0800.

Leden, Laura. "Emily Byrd Starr Conventionalized: Omissions of Nature Descriptions in the Swedish Translation of L. M. Montgomery's *Emily* Trilogy." *The Looking Glass: New Perspectives on Children's Literature*, vol. 18, no. 2, 2015. https://ojs.latrobe.edu.au/ojs/index.php/tlg/article/view/652.

Leden, Laura. "For Children Only: Abridgement of Crossover Characteristics in the Finnish Translation of L. M. Montgomery's Emily Trilogy." *Translating Boundaries: Constraints, Limits, Opportunities*, edited by Stefanie Barschdorf and Dora Renna, Ibidem, 2018, pp. 121–43.

Leden, Laura. "Girls' Classics and Constraints in Translation: A Case Study of Purifying Adaptation in the Swedish Translation of L. M. Montgomery's *Emily of New Moon*." *Barnboken: Journal of Children's Literature Research*, vol. 42, 2019, pp. 1–22. https://doi.org/10.14811/clr.v42i0.377.

Leden, Laura. "Reading as Empowerment: Lost in the Swedish Translations of L. M. Montgomery's Emily Books." *L. M. Montgomery and Reading*, special collection of *Journal of L. M. Montgomery Studies*, edited by Emily Woster and Kate Scarth, 28 April 2021. https://doi.org/10.32393/jlmms/2021.0011.

MacLulich, T. D. "L. M. Montgomery and the Literary Heroine: Jo, Rebecca, Anne, and Emily." *Canadian Children's Literature / Littérature canadienne pour la jeunesse*, no. 37, 1985, pp. 5–17. https://ccl-lcj.ca/index.php/ccl-lcj/article/view/1822.

MacLulich, T. D. "L. M. Montgomery's Portraits of the Artist: Realism, Idealism, and the Domestic Imagination." *English Studies in Canada*, vol. 11, no. 4, December 1985, pp. 459–73. https://doi.org/10.1353/esc.1985.0056.

Macquarrie, Jenn. "Growing Up in Nature: Health and Adolescent Dance in L. M. Montgomery's *Emily* Series." Adolescence in Canadian Literature, special section of *Studies in Canadian Literature / Études en littérature Canadienne*, edited by Heather Snell, Heidi Butler, John Clement Ball, and Jennifer Andrews, vol. 36, no. 1, 2011, pp. 34–50. https://journals.lib.unb.ca/index.php/SCL/article/view/18627.

McKenzie, Andrea. "Writing in Pictures: International Images of Emily." *Making Avonlea: L. M. Montgomery and Popular Culture*, edited by Irene Gammel, U of Toronto P, 2002, pp. 99–113.

McMaster, Lindsey. "The 'Murray Look': Trauma as Family Legacy in L. M. Montgomery's *Emily of New Moon* Trilogy." *Canadian Children's Literature / Littérature canadienne pour la jeunesse*, vol. 34, no. 2, Fall 2008, pp. 50–74. https://ccl-lcj.ca/index.php/ccl-lcj/article/view/4922.

Menzies, Ian. "The Moral of the Rose: L. M. Montgomery's *Emily*." *Canadian Children's Literature / Littérature canadienne pour la jeunesse*, no. 65, 1992, pp. 48–61. https://ccl-lcj.ca/index.php/ccl-lcj/article/view/4744.

Meyer, Susan. "The Fresh-Air Controversy, Health, and Art in L. M. Montgomery's *Emily* Novels." *Storm and Dissonance: L. M. Montgomery and Conflict*, edited by Jean Mitchell, Cambridge Scholars Publishing, 2008, pp. 209–20.

Miller, Judith. "Montgomery's Emily: Voices and Silences." *Studies in Canadian Literature*, vol. 9, no. 2, 1984, pp. 158–68. https://journals.lib.unb.ca/index.php/SCL/article/view/8013.

Miller, Judith. "The Writer-as-a-Young-Woman and Her Family: Montgomery's *Emily*." *New Quarterly*, vol. 7, no. 1–2, Spring–Summer 1987, pp. 301–19.

Miller, Kathleen Ann. "Haunted Heroines: The Gothic Imagination and the Female *Bildungsromane* of Jane Austen, Charlotte Brontë, and L. M. Montgomery." *Lion and the Unicorn*, vol. 34, no. 2, April 2010, pp. 125–47. https://doi.org/10.1353/uni.0.0502.

Miller, Kathleen Ann. "Transfiguring the Divine: L. M. Montgomery's Emily Trilogy and the Quest towards a Feminine Spirituality." *L. M. Montgomery's Interior and Exterior Landscapes*, special issue of *CREArTA*, edited by Rosemary Ross Johnston, vol. 5, 2005, pp. 144–57.

Mills, Claudia. "The Ethics of the Author/Audience Relationship in Children's Fiction." *Children's Literature Association Quarterly*, vol. 22, no. 4, 1997, pp. 181–87. https://doi.org/10.1353/chq.0.1249.

Pike, E. Holly. "Reading the Book as Object and Thing in L. M. Montgomery's Emily Series." *L. M. Montgomery and Reading*, special collection of *Journal of L. M. Montgomery Studies*, edited by Emily Woster and Kate Scarth, 15 Dec. 2020. https://doi.org/10.32393/jlmms/2021.0003.

Pike, E. Holly. "(Re)Producing Canadian Literature: L. M. Montgomery's Emily Novels." *L. M. Montgomery and Canadian Culture*, edited by Irene Gammel and Elizabeth Epperly, U of Toronto P, 1999, pp. 64–76.

Pollard, Alicia. "Wordsworth's Light and Shelley's Shadow: Revelation in L. M. Montgomery's Anne and Emily Series." *L. M. Montgomery and Vision*, special collection of *Journal of L. M. Montgomery Studies*, edited by Lesley D. Clement and Tara K. Parmiter, 3 Aug. 2021. https://journaloflmmontgomerystudies.ca/vision/Pollard/Wordsworths-Light-and-Shellys-Shadow.

Posey, Catherine. "Ethereal Etchings: Connecting with the Natural World in Lucy Maud Montgomery's *Anne of Green Gables* (1908), *Emily of New Moon* (1923), and *Magic for Marigold* (1929)." *Knowing Their Place? Identity and Space in Children's Literature*, edited by Terri Doughty and Dawn Thompson, Cambridge Scholars Publishing, 2011, pp. 95–108.

Rubio, Mary. *Lucy Maud Montgomery: The Gift of Wings*. Anchor Canada, 2008.

Rubio, Mary. "Subverting the Trite: L. M. Montgomery's 'Room of Her Own.'" *Canadian Children's Literature / Littérature Canadienne pour la jeunesse*, no. 65, 1992, pp. 6–39. https://ccl-lcj.ca/index.php/ccl-lcj/article/view/4740.

Rubio, Mary, and Elizabeth Waterston. *The Selected Journals of L. M. Montgomery Volume III: 1921–1929*. Oxford UP, 1992.

Sanders, Joe Sutliff. *Disciplining Girls: Understanding the Origins of the Classic Orphan Girl Story*. Johns Hopkins UP, 2011.

Sardella-Ayres, Dawn. "Under the Umbrella: The Author-Heroine's Love Triangle." *Canadian Children's Literature / Littérature Canadienne pour la jeunesse*, no. 105–6, Spring-Summer 2002, pp. 100–113. https://ccl-lcj.ca/index.php/ccl-lcj/article/view/3849.

Smith, Michelle, et al., *From Colonial to Modern: Transnational Girlhood in Canadian, Australian, and New Zealand Literature, 1840–1940*. U of Toronto P, 2018.

Steffler, Margaret. "Brian O'Connal and Emily Byrd Starr: The Inheritors of Wordsworth's 'Gentle Breeze.'" *Windows and Words: A Look at Canadian Children's Literature in English*, edited by Aïda Hudson and Susan-Ann Cooper, U of Ottawa P, 2003, pp. 87–96.

Sutherland, Kate. "The Education of Emily: Tempering a Force of Nature through Lessons in Law." *L. M. Montgomery and the Matter of Nature(s)*, edited by Rita Bode and Jean Mitchell, McGill-Queen's UP, 2018, pp. 128–40.

Tausky, Thomas E. "L. M. Montgomery and 'The Alpine Path, So Hard, So Steep.'" *Canadian Children's Literature / Littérature canadienne pour la jeunesse*, no. 30, 1983, pp. 5–20. https://ccl-lcj.ca/index.php/ccl-lcj/article/view/1679.

Thompson, Rebecca J. "'That House Belongs to Me': The Appropriation of Patriarchal Space in L. M. Montgomery's *Emily* Trilogy." *L. M. Montgomery and Gender*, edited by E. Holly Pike and Laura M. Robinson, McGill-Queen's UP, 2021, pp. 152–72.

Warnqvist, Åsa. "'Don't Be Too Upset with Your Unchivalrous Publisher': Translator-Publisher Interactions in the Swedish Translations of L. M. Montgomery's Anne and Emily Books." *Barnboken: Journal of Children's Literature Research*, vol. 42, 2019. https://doi.org/10.14811/clr.v42i0.449.

Waterston, Elizabeth. *Magic Island: The Fictions of L. M. Montgomery*. Oxford UP, 2008.

Woods, G. A. "The (W)rite of Passage: From Childhood to Womanhood in Lucy Maud Montgomery's Emily Novels." *Gender and Narrativity*, edited by Barry Rutland, Carleton UP, 1997, pp. 147–58.

Part One

Literary Resonances

Chapter 1

WARRING WITH FAILURE

Emily's Quest and the Victorian Past

KATE LAWSON

L. M. Montgomery's assessment of her final Emily novel, *Emily's Quest*, in November 1926 is bleak: "It is no good. How could it be?" (*Journals* 3: 313). Almost three years earlier, in January 1924, she offers a similar, if less damning, critique of the second novel in the series, *Emily Climbs*:

> Of course *Emily II* isn't half as good as *New Moon*. . . . One can write of children as they are; so my books of children are always good; but when you come to write of the "miss" you have to depict a sweet, insipid young thing—really a child grown older—to whom the basic realities of life and reactions to them are quite unknown. (*Journals* 3: 157)

Montgomery's explanation for the failures of *Emily Climbs*—arguably applicable to *Emily's Quest* as well—is rooted in the very genre to which Montgomery dedicates herself: realist narratives of growth and development.

Her fictional ethos rests on accurate and moving representations of children growing up, but the Bildungsroman typically ends in the protagonist's adulthood, not the life of "a child grown older." *Jane Eyre* and *David Copperfield*, to take two classic examples, ultimately represent the personal, sexual, and professional maturity of their central characters, their accommodations to an adult world replete with disappointment, loss, freedom, and entanglement with the needs of others.[1] Alternatively, Montgomery's defensive "you have to depict a sweet, insipid young thing" could gesture to children's literature as the relevant genre and the concomitant demands of a child readership. This genre would limit representations of what the opening paragraphs of *Emily's Quest* make clear, that Emily is now "considered grownup" (7). Admittedly the generic constraints of children's literature are subject to debate, and, as Jacqueline Rose provocatively argues, the very category of "Children's Fiction" may be "impossible."[2] Whatever the genre, Montgomery's expressed dilemma is clear: she needs to write about a "grownup" but also needs to ensure that "the basic realities of [adult] life" remain "quite unknown" and unrepresented in incident, character, and affect. The effects of this dilemma are clear. As P. K. Page suggests, if readers experience the three Emily novels as "one long book which begins magically," then "it becomes thinner, offers us less" as it draws to a close (240).[3]

Montgomery's gloomy assessment that *Emily's Quest* "is no good" is mirrored in the novel itself when Emily experiences a sick sense of professional failure as a novelist. She decides to stop writing novels because, she says, quoting Bliss Carman's "A Song before Sailing," she is "Too sick at heart to war / With failure any more" (156, ll. 7–8). Yet in fact, Emily persists in writing, and Montgomery does too, waging her own "war / With failure" in the face of her damning verdict of *Emily's Quest*. As T. D. MacLulich writes, Montgomery was both "a more committed and a more serious writer than is generally recognized" and was "hindered ... from consistently attaining the level of excellence she exhibits in her best work" (459). Montgomery's own evaluation of the decline of the Emily series as serious and engaging fiction provides a window into her analysis of the novelistic enterprise generally and of the forces that might prevent a consistent "level of excellence."

A second indirect self-evaluation by Montgomery is arguably provided in her unsentimental musings on Charlotte Brontë's early death. She writes in her journal in October 1924 that Charlotte Brontë's "genius ... had a narrow range and I think it had reached its limit" by the time of her death; "She could not have gone on forever writing *Jane Eyre*s and *Villette*s and there was nothing in her life and experience to fit her for writing anything else" (3: 204). While this claim about Brontë hardly seems valid, it is suggestive about Montgomery's sense of her own novelistic "range" and on "[going] on forever writing" novels (in her case) in a series.

In October 1924, she was still near the beginning of what was to be a two-year-long struggle to complete the final Emily novel.[4] She may well have been asking herself what "range" *she* had exhibited in *Anne of Green Gables, Anne of Avonlea, Anne of the Island, Anne's House of Dreams, Rainbow Valley,* and *Rilla of Ingleside*. Or *she* may have felt doomed to "[go] on forever writing" about Anne and Emily because "there was nothing in her life and experience to fit her for writing anything else." The problem of a "narrow range" is particularly acute in a series; writing *could* "[go] on forever" in sequel after sequel, following established characters and plots and eschewing new topics and fresh explorations.[5]

A different Victorian novelist, Anthony Trollope with his Barsetshire and Palliser series, provides a relevant example of how early episodes tend to determine or delimit later ones. As D. A. Miller writes, Trollope's series are characterized by "a highly developed system of familiarizations," and readers fall "into the usual appreciation of [Trollope's] appreciation of the usual"; the result is a "banality" that that author "relentlessly cultivates" (107, 108). In struggling to complete the Emily series, Montgomery may well have been wrestling with the "banality" of an Emily caught in a familiar plot and setting and maturing from a child into "a child grown older." The effect, as Benjamin Lefebvre observes, is that the final novel "avoids . . . romantic tension . . . and delays the 'inevitable' dénouement as long as possible," until the "inevitable" can no longer be avoided and Emily, eventually, marries Teddy (132).[6] Indeed, Teddy epitomizes the banality of *Emily's Quest*; readers may well sympathize with Ilse's comment: "Sometimes he bores me—really. Although I was so sure he wouldn't" (*Quest* 199).

Critics have, of course, read *Emily's Quest* as a success, not a failure, and offered spirited defenses of it. Elizabeth Rollins Epperly calls the final novel a "triumph" that "insists on the inseparability of the woman from the writer" (*Fragrance* 183, 182).[7] In a later essay, she argues that the novel's protracted closure is necessary to demonstrate "how even beauty, even for the artist, cannot supply what is human and must be satisfied" so that Emily must learn to "engage with the dailiness of living" ("*Emily's Quest*" 219, 221). Irene Gammel celebrates the Emily trilogy as "a *revisionary* history of her [own] *body-self*," though admittedly one confined to "The Eros of Childhood and Early Adolescence," not of adulthood (100). And Mary Rubio counts an intrusive narrator that "discredit[s] the sanctity of traditional plot and genre conventions" as a specific achievement of the Emily novels (128).

Yet Montgomery's own appraisal, that *Emily's Quest* "is no good," combined with her assessment of Brontë's unwritten novels as afflicted by related failures, suggests a logic of punitive evaluation. Emily's "war / With failure" is also her own. This essay takes Montgomery's self-evaluation seriously and argues that the final Emily novel in fact reflects on its own deficiencies through allusions to and engagement with the "Victorian." Victorian literature and culture are sources of vitality in Montgomery's fiction generally, and specific Victorian modes, such as gothic, energize the Emily novels specifically.[8] But the Victorian historical past and the spokespersons for its values in the Emily novels act to suppress vitality and difference and to support a Trollopian banal narrative conformity. This kind of Victorianism is defined and then, in *Emily's Quest*, redefined under pressure of the marriage plot, and its contradictions come to function as a kind of metacommentary on the marriage plot itself and its failures. The outdated values named "Victorian" signal *how* failure progressively occurs in *Emily's Quest*, with "Victorian" acting, variously, as a set of standards to resist, a marker of nostalgic investment, and finally conventions that are as safe as they are desiccated.[9]

1. THE VICTORIAN PAST

The immediate late-Victorian historical past is represented in the Emily novels as harsh, hypocritical, and repressed. In this, Montgomery resembles other early twentieth-century writers who describe it as a period of stifling conformity and sometimes cruel hypocrisy. In Virginia Woolf's *Orlando* (1928), for instance, the Victorian period is typified by gloom—"All was darkness; all was doubt; all was confusion" (108–9)—a gloom that represents "patriarchal metanarratives" and "outmoded" ideas, according to Jane De Gay (70, 65).[10] Lytton Strachey's *Eminent Victorians* (1918) provides a virtual catalogue of such "outmoded" ideas and, as Edmund Wilson writes, "blast[s] once for all the pretensions of the Victorian age to moral superiority," ensuring that its "legends . . . had been punctured for good" (146, 148). Part of the cultural work of the Emily novels is a similar puncturing of the flattering moral pretenses of the Victorian historical past.

The exemplars of this moralistic creed in *Emily of New Moon* are Emily's aunts and uncles, children of Victorian Canada, who seek to repress her emotions and creativity. Much of the drama of this first novel stems from Emily's refusal to submit to these values and the older generation's resulting anger.[11] On first meeting them, for example, she rebuffs their claim that she is made up of the "scraps and patches!" of her dead relatives (38). Aunt Ruth reprimands her for "answering back"; in *her* childhood, she says, "We were polite and respectful to our elders." When Emily muses, "I don't believe you ever had much fun" and Aunt Ruth replies, "I did not think of fun when I was a little girl," Emily's quiet response, "No, I know," is understood not as submission but as condescending pity for Aunt Ruth's "prim, impeccable childhood" (39). Aunt Ruth is furious. A similar fury is kindled in Aunt Elizabeth when Emily speaks of her love for her dead father and Elizabeth recalls "the ashamed, smothered feeling of relief" when her own father—an "intolerant, autocratic old man"—died and how relatives "behaved impeccably" at his funeral but without "one genuine feeling of regret"; "Elizabeth did not like the memory and was angry with Emily for evoking it" (67–68). Early episodes such as this encapsulate Emily's attachment to genuine emotional expression and resistance to the Victorian generation's empty or hypocritical claims. The older relatives angrily insist that Emily learn to swallow her unhappiness—as they have done.

Emily Climbs intensifies the clash with nineteenth-century values when Emily stays with Aunt Ruth, a woman who replicates a harshness that has now waned at New Moon. In one signal episode, the school puts on a play and Emily, "cast for a part that suited her," becomes "keenly interested" (141). When Aunt Ruth finds out, she is appalled: "Have you no respect for your forefathers? . . . Why, if they knew a descendant of theirs was play-acting they would turn over in their graves!" Emily's retort, "It would be excellent exercise for them," is as irreverent as anything by Strachey (144). Emily acts her part and then, finding the door of Aunt Ruth's house locked, walks home to New Moon. There, Cousin Jimmy is as loving as ever, but he persuades her to return to Aunt Ruth by invoking "the dear, dead ladies of New Moon" looking down on her with "contemptuous pity" (150). These "fore*mothers*" must be appeased, and the pleasures of "play-acting" are never mentioned again. Compare this to *Villette*, for example, where Lucy Snowe also acts in a play. She learns, as she says, that "this new-found faculty might gift me with a world of delight," but it is *she* who decides that she must repress "delight" to ensure survival, *she* who must "put by" "the strength and longing" that dramatic performance offers (210). The differences are clear. Neither Lucy Snowe nor Emily Starr acts in a play again, but where Brontë traces the complex psychological means by which "a world of delight" is foresworn and repression enjoined on the self, Montgomery gives only a slight acknowledgement of the pleasures of acting and attributes prohibition to the older generation.

The values of the Victorian generation are also recalled in the first two Emily novels in the repeated appeals to "Murray traditions" and "Murray pride"—that is, customary practices and values that anchor and determine current choices. Before Emily's father dies, he tells her about these traditions: "One of them is that nothing but candles shall be burned for light at New Moon—and another is that no quarrel must be carried past the grave" (*Moon* 24). This mixture of banal domestic habit and moral imperative continues to characterize Murray tradition. In *Emily Climbs*, Emily learns certain traditional practices—putting "pickles into glass jars in patterns" and "sanding [the kitchen floor] in the beautiful and complicated 'herring-bone pattern'"—and tradition as an impossible standard of behavior: "It is a tradition of New Moon that its women should be equal to any situation and always be graceful and dignified"; "Dignity is a tradition of New Moon" (217, 65, 16, 41).

Yet traditions are increasingly internalized by Emily so that even by the end of the first novel, "she fitted into [New Moon's] atmosphere as a hand into a glove" and learns to love "every 'tradition' of its history" (*Moon* 200,

201). The more traditions cease to be only punitive impositions of the older generations and instead are policed by Emily herself, the more these values work to undermine creativity, difference, and potential *within* Emily. As Cousin Jimmy says aphoristically, "No one can be free who has a thousand ancestors" (*Climbs* 89). Emily is forced to admit that, apart from "a few brief moments" of freedom, "All the rest of our years we are slaves to something—traditions—conventions—ambitions—*relations*" (*Climbs* 223). Thus, tradition, history, and family are understood to constitute a stifling conformity that works against individual freedom.

The clash between liberty and the impositions of the past is consciously reflected on at the end of *Emily Climbs*. Emily affirms a cold reciprocal indifference with regard to Teddy: "If Teddy doesn't want me I won't want him. That is a Murray tradition"; but immediately follows this up with: "I'm only half Murray. There is the Starr half to be considered" (325). Reflecting on what she calls her "divided allegiance," Emily concludes, "On top I am sternly composed and traditional. Underneath that, something that would hurt horribly if I let it is being kept down. And underneath that again is a queer feeling of relief that I still have my freedom" (325). Emily's self-anatomizing matches the novels' representation of the conflict of values. The "composed and traditional" is a Victorian Murray ethos; the "something that would hurt" is the "smothered" Murray admission of the reality of affect, including the "hurt" revealed in "if Teddy doesn't want me . . ."; and the "queer feeling of relief" is the tenacity of her attachment to "freedom" and desire.

It is in *Emily's Quest* that the oppressive narratives and values of the historical past are explicitly named "Victorian." No longer concerning herself with pickles or dignity, but seemingly with plotting out a livable adult life, Emily names the "Victorian" as that which sought and still seeks to limit her. For example, the narrative of tuberculosis leading to early death—used to restrict Emily in the earlier novels—is now named "Victorian." As she recovers from illness, she comments: "I know Aunt Laura thought I was going into consumption. Not I. That would be too Victorian"; instead, "I fought things out and conquered them and I'm a sane, *free* woman once more" (132–33). What is "conquered" is not illness, but an entrapping Victorian narrative inherited from a cultural and familial past. Indeed, this particular "too Victorian" narrative *is* the story of the Brontë family, suggesting an audacious refusal to be "conquered" by what killed her Victorian namesake, Emily Brontë, and, perhaps, another backhanded critique by Montgomery of Charlotte Brontë and her "narrow range."

Nevertheless, over the course of the final novel, Emily's resistance wanes and traditional narratives strengthen. "Victorian" and "tradition" become ways for Montgomery to signal the "limit" her own fiction now reaches. More generally, a historical past that created conditions Emily could act *against*—expressive of creativity, difference, and potential—instead devolves into a conventional "Victorian" narrative and a banal mode of representation. In this banality lies the failure of *Emily's Quest*.

2. REDEFINING THE "VICTORIAN"

Like its predecessors, *Emily's Quest* steadily resists Victorian values—resists them, that is, until the final chapters. Then, in order to achieve the "'inevitable' dénouement," marriage, the "Victorian" is embraced as the solution to otherwise unresolvable difficulties of plot and character. The marriage plot in *Emily's Quest* thus comes to act as a kind of metacommentary, with Emily the *writer* of domestic narratives also *living out* a narrative of true love named "Victorian," using its affordances to construct the required "happy ending." As a writer of domestic fiction about "births, deaths, marriages, scandals— . . . the only really interesting things in the world" (8), Emily reaches a level of professional achievement when her novel is published and some future success seems assured. In the marriage plot—that is, in one of the "only really interesting" subjects of fiction—Emily must marry the "right" man, Teddy Kent. Complications ensue, principally the love triangle of Emily, Ilse, and Teddy—or quadrangle, if one includes the otherwise irrelevant Perry. In order to sort out this comedy of errors and achieve the "correct" marriages, *Emily's Quest* abandons its representation of the "Victorian" as the imposition of stifling conventions and redefines it as the source of solidity and meaning. "Victorian" expectations about marriage thus shape both the writerly and life itself. This embrace of what the novel names "Victorian" takes place despite the energy that the Emily series has invested in demonstrating the stifling effect of the "traditions" of the Victorian historical past. Crucial to this final novel, then, is the definition and redefinition of "Victorian."

In *Emily's Quest*, the name "Victorian" is affixed specifically to the marriage plot and to marriage as a cultural norm. This norm is espoused by the conservative Aunt Laura—"one of the Victorians," who "always cries a bit when any one she knows is . . . married or engaged"—and by the "radical" Dr. Burnley—who "out-Victorians the Victorians" in his relief that Ilse is finally engaged to be married (18, 24, 181). Emily's aunts tell Ilse that she must adopt a "thoughtful and sober" approach to marriage, but Ilse makes "a jest of everything, even her marriage" and rejects their cautions, calling their advice "mid-Victorian screams" (197). Ilse continues to use the "Victorian" label satirically to distance herself from marriage's travails, telling Emily that Teddy probably only proposed marriage to her so she could "catch his heart on the rebound—wasn't that the Victorian phrase?" (200). She follows up with the profanely mocking, "Isn't it charming how things do turn out so beautifully? . . . Isn't it nice to be able to blame everything on God?" (200). Ilse's ironic distancing from Victorian norms is also evident in her statement that she loves *and* hates Perry Miller, since "it's the same thing . . . why can't I get that creature out of my mind! It's too Victorian to say heart. I haven't any heart" (118). Ilse, the cool satirist, the modern thinker, eschews "heart" and "Victorian" convention.

Ilse's upbringing, of course, accounts for this attitude, her father being cast early on as an "infidel" who tells scandalous adult stories at the Murray Christmas dinner and has novels in his bookcase (*New Moon* 189, 230, 225). Emily's New Moon upbringing means she cannot reject her aunts' values entirely, especially those of loving Aunt Laura. But she too maintains an ironic awareness of outdated Victorian marriage conventions. For example, in *Emily's Quest*, Emily comments on Aunt Laura's diction regarding her "love affair—as Aunt Laura Victorianly phrased it" with Rev. James Wallace and then later, after the announcement of her engagement to Dean Priest, comments on her "God bless you, Emily, dear child" with gentle ridicule: "Very mid-Victorian. . . . But I liked it" (42, 75). Emily concedes a certain antique charm in this old-fashioned diction but preserves an ironic awareness of the Victorian values that inform such views. When she speaks ambivalently about Dean Priest, saying that she loves him "—in a way," Aunt Laura replies, "there's only one way of loving"; Emily disagrees: "Oh no, dearest of Victorian aunties. . . . There are a dozen different ways" (67). This rejoinder is much milder than Ilse's mockery of the aunts' marriage advice as "mid-Victorian screams," but Emily too subjects the norms of the "Victorian aunties" to gentle derision.

But all at once, resistance and ironic distancing are abandoned. Closure in *Emily's Quest* requires *true* love, not "a dozen different ways" of loving or loving "—in a way." Under pressure from the approaching marriage of Teddy to Ilse, both Emily and Ilse come to embrace Victorian values. Emily first commits herself to the conventional when she insists—against all evidence—that Teddy and Ilse must be "in love," to which Ilse responds, "Emily, why do you persist in talking as if you thought Teddy and I were madly in love with each other? Is it that Victorian complex of yours?" Emily retorts, "Shut up about things Victorian! . . . You call every nice, simple, natural emotion Victorian. The whole world to-day seems to be steeped in a scorn for things Victorian. . . . But I like sane, decent things—if *that* is Victorian" (*Quest*

212). Emily's commitment to authentic emotional expression vanishes all at once, replaced by the fully imaginary "nice, simple natural emotion"; a "sane, decent . . . Victorian" attitude *requires* that Ilse and Teddy be in love regardless of reality. Ilse follows Emily down the normative "Victorian" path soon after, eschewing knowledge of Teddy's past love life because, she says, "How ugly some things are when you ferret them out! . . . the Victorians were right in covering lots of things up. Ugly things should be hidden" (213). Inconvenient facts, both agree, ought to be repressed. Although both characters have steadily rejected or satirized "Victorian" values, they suddenly accept them—and this acceptance paves the way for a resolution to the marriage plot.

The seeming commitment of the Emily novels to allow some space for complex states of feeling to structure plot and character development is thus relinquished in a few pages. Then, events ensue and the correct marriages are within reach, leaving Emily relieved ("Ilse dear, don't think me hopelessly Victorian if I say I hope you'll be happy 'ever after'") and Ilse grateful ("How blessedly Victorian that sounds!") (220, 227). Ilse is to marry Perry; after a delay, Emily is to marry Teddy. Their new orientations toward the "hopelessly Victorian" and the "blessedly Victorian" are unironic—and fundamentally untrue to the figuration of the values of the Victorian historical past throughout the three novels. Thus, in its ending *Emily's Quest* succumbs to a version of the Victorian that is conventional, uncritical, and "cover[s] lots of things up" in order to achieve the marriages that readers had expected all along.[12] With Victorian values now fully internalized, Emily's new attitudes are less those of a mature adult and more those of an obedient "child grown older."

Yet at times in *Emily's Quest*, a representation of the "basic realities" of adult life—and thus the makings of what Montgomery might have judged a more successful novel—seem tantalizingly close. Plot developments are hinted at and opportunities presented that would have provided escape from the banal and familiar. For example, the offered life in New York would have opened possibilities for Emily as single woman *and* artist, giving her the autonomy that Woolf, in 1929, called "a room of one's own."[13] That she does not do so, is, as MacLulich writes, "a failure on Montgomery's part of both the literary and the social imagination" (466). Or the realities of Emily as a single woman growing older, only hinted at, could have been explored more expansively, something Brontë does in *Villette* and Montgomery herself attempts in *A Tangled Web*. More narrowly, the lasting psychological and social implications of Emily's painful "if Teddy doesn't want me . . ." could have been traced more fully.

This latter narrative actually *is* present in *Emily's Quest*, only transferred to Teddy Kent's mother. Mrs. Kent lives with the corrosive belief that *she* was not wanted, that her husband died hating her and in love with another woman. Finally freed from this long error, Mrs. Kent tells Emily the story of her marriage, a story illustrative of both the strengths and limits of Montgomery's fiction. Mrs. Kent speaks of married life, family hostility, jealousy, pregnancy, loss, and depression, but then stops herself—and stops the narrative too—with the assertion, "I shouldn't talk about such matters to a young girl"; she likewise changes "suddenly from a woman quivering with unveiled feeling to a prim Victorian" (204). With "feeling" veiled, a "prim Victorian" ethos asserts itself, again, as Emily—and readers too—are interpellated as child auditors. Although Emily asserts an adult knowledge of pregnancy and childbirth and Mrs. Kent continues her story—undergoing "another transformation into passionate Aileen Kent again"—this glimpse of adult realities is brief (204).

This episode offers a possible analogy for Montgomery the writer: Montgomery *can* write of adult experience in prose "quivering with unveiled feeling," *can* write in a "passionate" rather than a banal mode. Yet a "prim Victorian" ethos interrupts her narrative again and again, stifling her prose and her representations of adult life. While there are several examples of such stifled expression, Emily's relationship with Teddy Kent is key. In the first two Emily novels, Teddy and Emily are children sharing complex inner worlds, fraught family lives, and complementary drives to creativity. But as adults in *Emily's Quest*, their interactions are rare, brief, and understated. In one of their few meetings, Emily asks herself, "What was there left of the old Teddy in this slim, elegant young man with his sophisticated air and cool, impersonal eyes, and general implication of having put off for ever all childish things—including . . . insignificant little country girls . . . ?" (48). This portrait of the "slim, elegant young man" is resonant with adult sexual longings, longings that are then almost entirely blocked by a self-representation as one of the "childish things" he has rejected. The narrator comments that "in [this] conclusion Emily was horribly unjust to Teddy," but the more important injustice is Emily's to herself and her desires (48). If Teddy has indeed "put off for ever all childish things," surely Emily could as well. But in Montgomery's novels, when adult sexuality is implied, evoked, or intimated, it is usually disavowed. Consider the story of the transgressive sexuality of Beatrice Burnley in *Emily of New Moon*, so transgressive that her very name is unsayable, but this story is in fact false and the recovery of her dead body guarantees that she was always sexually "stainless" (341). Or consider how the initiation of Anne and Gilbert's sexual relations in *Anne's House of Dreams* is side-stepped by a narrative focus on Leslie Moore's marriage to Dick, an asexual "big baby" (209) and, in fact, not Dick Moore at all! The "truth" of both of these stories is a rather boring innocence. Likewise, while the possibilities of an adult life for Emily are intimated by Montgomery, its full contours remain blocked.

3. CREATIVE FAILURES

Victorian values in *Emily's Quest* thus come to function as a means through which the novel signals its own failures and represents its attachment to the familiar and banal. Yet the Emily novels also provide what might be called ironic versions of success, for if adult experience is effectively represented anywhere in the Emily novels, it is to be found—not in sexuality, career, or freedom—but in failure itself. The novels represent instances of failed adult lives that not only work to inoculate readers against the negative associations of failure but also suggest that—however painful it is to live with or as a failure—failure may itself be an unlikely sign of energy and creativity.

Failure in *Emily of New Moon*, *Emily Climbs*, and *Emily's Quest* is different than failure in the Anne novels. In *Anne of Green Gables*, failure is local and inconsequential: for example, will Anne fail geometry? Or in *Anne's House of Dreams*, Anne's "smile that had never yet failed to win confidence and friendliness" fails, briefly, with Leslie Moore (95). But in the Emily novels, failure is a stinging and lasting indictment of character. Failures include Emily's father, who tells her that "from a worldly point of view I've certainly been a failure"; Cousin Jimmy, who is labeled by "Blair Water people . . . a failure and a mental weakling"; and Mr. Carpenter, who declares that "I'm dying—I'm a failure—poor as a rat" (*Moon* 25, 154; *Quest* 30). Each of these characters exhibits the painful, limiting, and enduring effects of living—and in two cases dying—as a failure. Yet each of these "failures" loves Emily and each works to repair the traumas of her early life. If they *succeed* in doing this, are they really failures at all, the novels intimate. Being a failure may thus be transvalued into a version of success. Such a transvaluation is indeed attempted by Emily after Aunt Ruth calls her father "a miserable failure" and Emily replies: "Nobody who was loved as much as he was could be a failure. I don't believe anybody *ever* loved you. So it's *you* that's a failure" (*Moon* 50). A failed life, valued differently, *is* a success.

Alternatively, failure offers ways of being in the world more complex and interesting than success itself. Mr. Carpenter's words, "I'm dying—I'm a failure—poor as a rat. But after all, Emily—I've had a—darned interesting time" (30) suggest his failure has had important compensations, not only for Emily, but also for himself. Indeed, explorations of the meaning of "failure" are common in works by Montgomery's Victorian predecessors; to follow up on only a few of the authors mentioned in this essay, Tommy Traddles is said to be "perfectly good-humored respecting his failure" to learn stenography because "he always did consider himself slow," a remarkably obtuse comment by the condescending David Copperfield (Dickens 512); Hareton Earnshaw in *Wuthering Heights* is called a "dunce" by Catherine before she falls in love with him (E. Brontë 249); and Lucy Snowe meets the questions of the "sneering ... professors" with the response, "as you say, I am an idiot" (C. Brontë 472, 473). As Jack Halberstam argues in *The Queer Art of Failure*, "Under certain circumstances failing, losing, forgetting, unmaking, undoing, unbecoming, not knowing may in fact offer more creative, more cooperative, more surprising ways of being in the world" (2–3). In the Emily novels, perhaps "failures" such as Cousin Jimmy and Mr. Carpenter not only support Emily's creativity but, as characters, also offer Montgomery's fiction imaginative and remarkable models of experience unknown in banal versions of success. While the final Emily novel represents a war with failure and an eventual surrender, the explicit "failures" in the three novels suggest "surprising ways of being in the world" that are anything but banal.

Emily's Quest thus self-consciously reflects on the meaning of failure through an engagement with the values of the Victorian historical past and though the inclusion of failed characters. These representations, combined with Montgomery's critical assessment of *Emily Climbs* and *Emily's Quest* and her critique of Charlotte Brontë, suggest that throughout the 1920s Montgomery was wrestling with the idea of failure. The Emily novels might almost be called studies in failure. At this stage of her career, Montgomery is forced to confront the limits of "writ[ing] of the 'miss,'" the limits of her chosen genre, and the limits of her readership. Yet her career continues and she is able to weigh her work in the balance, knowing both that "my books of children are always good" *and* that *Emily's Quest* "is no good." Although Emily quotes from Carman's "A Song before Sailing," she does not experience the extremity of the poem's speaker whose existential weariness leads to a wish to be blown "beyond the grime / And pestilence of time!" (ll. 5–6). Rather, when Emily—and perhaps Montgomery too—are "Too sick at heart to war / With failure any more," the result is compromise, acceptance of a "narrow range," and foreshortened aspirations. Montgomery may have hoped that generous readers would see that there are worse things than the considered failure of *Emily's Quest*.

NOTES

1. On Montgomery and the Bildungsroman, see, for example, Kathleen Ann Miller and John Seelye. Mary Rubio argues for the expansiveness of "traditional domestic romance," a genre that gives Montgomery "a safe space in which to write [. . . and to] give sharp critical digs to a social system prejudiced against women" (125).

On relevant intertexts, see, for example, Elizabeth Rollins Epperly (*Fragrance*), who argues that the Emily novels should be read in conjunction with *Jane Eyre, Aurora Leigh,* and *The Story of an African Farm*.

2. On children's literature, see Margaret Steffler for an account of the "limitations of such classifications" (88) and Jacqueline Rose for a broader critique, what her subtitle names *The Impossibility of Children's Fiction*.

3. Gillian Thomas makes a similar observation about the Anne novels; as the "progressively unsatisfactory" series continues, Anne matures from "a spirited individualist" into "a rather dreary conformist" (23).

4. On May 26, 1924, Montgomery reports: "This morning I resumed work on my third *Emily* book and this afternoon Lily and I cleaned the horse stable"; six months later, on November 27, 1924, that she is "getting ready to write *Emily III*"; and later still, on June 30, 1926, that "I began work—again—on *Emily III*" (*Journals* 3: 184, 209, 298). She finishes it on October 13, 1926; it was published in September 1927 (*Journals* 3: 310).

5. *The Blue Castle* (1926) is arguably the site of this kind of fresh exploration; I have argued previously that *The Blue Castle* "is the perhaps unlikely site of a kind of resolution to the difficulties of mode and genre that, as of 1924, the still incomplete *Emily* trilogy had raised but left unresolved" ("The Victorian Sickroom" 232).

6. Lefebvre is discussing *Anne of the Island, Rilla of Ingleside, Emily's Quest,* and *Mistress Pat*, novels in which "wedding bells appear to be the 'natural' resolution for her title heroines" (132).

7. Holly Pike's interest in Montgomery's career as a professional writer leads her to read the final Emily novel as one that likewise traces the path of Emily's "success in [a] professional métier," a "progress through rejection, revision, and publication in successively more reputable venues" ("Reading the Book").

The relation of the Künstlerroman to Montgomery's fiction has been much discussed. See, for example, MacLulich, who states that Montgomery "took as a major theme of her work . . . the development of a young female artist," but both Anne and Emily "lose much of their rebelliousness as they grow into womanhood," give up careers, and "meekly agree to marry" (459, 466); Elizabeth Waterston, who writes of *Emily's Quest* that "the artist as a young person seems to have disappeared from the story, just as, long ago, in *Anne of Green Gables*, the story of Anne's literary ambitions veered away into the traditional path of a courtship tale" (141); and Mary Rubio, who provides an analysis of the ways in which the Emily novels allow Montgomery to detail "the impediments to a woman's authorship" (122).

8. On Montgomery and the gothic, see, for example, Kathleen Ann Miller and Lorna Drew.

9. Virginia A. S. Careless offers an anthropological analysis of Montgomery within a "culture" that can be "for ease of identity, labelled 'Victorian'" (150).

10. Rubio provides a comprehensive comparison of Montgomery and Woolf; MacLulich sets Montgomery's fiction within the context of a late nineteenth-century battle between realism and idealism (460); and Lefebvre analyzes Montgomery's relationship to modernism.

11. Steffler perfectly describes this culture: "the oppressive world of society, reflected in Aunt Elizabeth's stuffy bed, the reaction of Miss Brownell to Emily's passionate enthusiasm, the taunting of the schoolchildren, and the critical appraisal of the Murray relatives" (92).

12. It is, admittedly, a challenge to surprise readers when the "correct" marriage is known from the beginning. Jane Austen's handling of the "game of the marriage plot" is exceptionally skillful since, as Andrew Franta writes, readers "consistently experience something like surprise at matches that are well known in advance" (120).

13. See Rubio.

WORKS CITED

Brontë, Charlotte. *Villette*, edited by Kate Lawson, Broadview Press, 2006.
Brontë, Emily. *Wuthering Heights*, edited by Ian Jack, Oxford World's Classics, 1998.
Carman, Bliss. "A Song before Sailing." *Poems*, John Murray, 1904, Representative Poetry Online, https://rpo.library.utoronto.ca/content/song-sailing. Accessed 3 March 2022.
Careless, Virginia A. S. "L. M. Montgomery and Everybody Else: A Look at the Books." *Windows and Words: A Look at Canadian Children's Literature in English*, edited by Aïda Hudson and Susan-Ann Cooper, U of Ottawa P, 2003, pp. 143–74.
De Gay, Jane. "Virginia Woolf's Feminist Historiography in 'Orlando.'" *Critical Survey*, vol. 19, no. 1, Berghahn Books, 2007, pp. 62–72, http://www.jstor.org/stable/41556201.
Dickens, Charles. *David Copperfield*, edited by Nina Burgis, Oxford World's Classics, 1983.
Drew, Lorna. "The Emily Connection: Ann Radcliffe, L. M. Montgomery and 'The Female Gothic.'" *Canadian Children's Literature / Littérature canadienne pour la jeunesse*, vol. 77, Spring 1995, pp. 19–32.
Epperly, Elizabeth Rollins. "*Emily's Quest*: L. M. Montgomery's Green Alternative to Despair and War?" *L. M. Montgomery and War*, edited by Andrea McKenzie, Jane Ledwell, McGill-Queen's UP, 2017, pp. 214–33.
Epperly, Elizabeth Rollins. *The Fragrance of Sweet-Grass: L. M. Montgomery's Heroines and the Pursuit of Romance*. U of Toronto P, 1993.
Franta, Andrew. *Systems Failure: The Uses of Disorder in English Literature*. Johns Hopkins UP, 2019.
Gammel, Irene. "The Eros of Childhood and Early Adolescence in Girl Series: L. M. Montgomery's *Emily* Trilogy." *Windows and Words: A Look at Canadian Children's Literature in English*," edited by Aïda Hudson and Susan-Ann Cooper, U of Ottawa P, 2003, pp. 97–118.
Halberstam, Jack. *The Queer Art of Failure*. Duke UP, 2011.

Lawson, Kate. "The Victorian Sickroom in L. M. Montgomery's *The Blue Castle* and *Emily's Quest*: Sentimental Fiction and the Selling of Dreams." *Lion and the Unicorn*, vol. 31, no. 3, 2007, pp. 232–49.

Lefebvre, Benjamin. "Pigsties and Sunsets: L. M. Montgomery, *A Tangled Web*, and a Modernism of Her Own." *English Studies in Canada*, vol. 31, no. 3, 2005, pp. 123–46. https://doi.org/10.1353/esc.2007.0049.

MacLulich, T. D. "L. M. Montgomery's Portraits of the Artist: Realism, Idealism, and the Domestic Imagination." *ESC: English Studies in Canada*, vol. 11, no. 4, 1985, pp. 459–73. Project Muse, https://doi.org/10.1353/esc.1985.0056.

Miller, D. A. *The Novel and the Police*. U of California P, 1988.

Miller, Kathleen Ann. "Haunted Heroines: The Gothic Imagination and the Female *Bildungsromane* of Jane Austen, Charlotte Brontë, and L. M. Montgomery." *Lion and the Unicorn*, vol. 34, no. 2, 2010, pp. 125–47. Project Muse, https://doi.org/10.1353/uni.0.0502.

Montgomery, L. M. *Anne's House of Dreams*. McClelland and Stewart, 1922.

Montgomery, L. M. *Emily Climbs*. 1925. McClelland and Stewart, 1989.

Montgomery, L. M. *Emily of New Moon*. 1923. McClelland and Stewart, 1989.

Montgomery, L. M. *Emily's Quest*. 1927. McClelland and Stewart, 1989.

Montgomery, L. M. *The Selected Journals of L. M. Montgomery*, edited by Mary Rubio and Elizabeth Waterston, Oxford UP, 1985–2004, 5 vols.

Page, P. K. Afterword to *Emily's Quest*, by L. M. Montgomery, McClelland and Stewart, 1989, pp. 237–42.

Pike, E. Holly. "Reading the Book as Object and Thing in L. M. Montgomery's *Emily* Series." *Journal of L. M. Montgomery Studies*. 15 Dec. 2020. https://doi.org/10.32393/jlmms/2021.0003.

Rose, Jacqueline. *The Case of Peter Pan, or The Impossibility of Children's Fiction*. Palgrave Macmillan, 1992.

Rubio, Mary. "Subverting the Trite: L. M. Montgomery's 'Room of Her Own' (1992)." *The L. M. Montgomery Reader: Volume Two: A Critical Heritage*, edited by Benjamin Lefebvre, U of Toronto U, 2014, pp. 109–48.

Seelye, John. *Jane Eyre's American Daughters: From the Wide, Wide World to Anne of Green Gables*. U of Delaware P, 2005.

Steffler, Margaret. "Brian O'Connal and Emily Byrd Starr: The Inheritors of Wordsworth's 'Gentle Breeze.'" *Windows and Words: A Look at Canadian Children's Literature in English*, edited by Aïda Hudson and Susan-Ann Cooper, U of Ottawa P, 2003, pp. 87–96.

Strachey, Lytton. *Eminent Victorians: Cardinal Manning, Florence Nightingale, Dr. Arnold, General Gordon*. Chatto and Windus, 1921.

Thomas, Gillian. "The Decline of Anne: Matron vs. Child." *Canadian Children's Literature / Littérature canadienne pour la jeunesse*, vol. 1, no. 3, 1975, pp. 37–41.

Waterston, Elizabeth. *Magic Island: The Fictions of L. M. Montgomery*. Oxford UP, 2008.

Wilson, Edmund. "Lytton Strachey." *New Republic* 72, 21 Sept. 1932, pp. 146–48.

Woolf, Virginia. *Orlando: A Biography*, edited by R. Bowlby, Oxford: Oxford UP, 1992.

Chapter 2

EXILE AND INSTRUMENTALITY IN THE EMILY BOOKS

JESSICA WEN HUI LIM

> [...] the light of sense
> Goes out, but with a flash that has revealed
> The invisible world [...]
> [...] whether we be young or old,
> Our destiny, our being's heart and home,
> Is with infinitude, and only there;
> With hope it is, hope that can never die,
> Effort, and expectation, and desire,
> And something evermore about to be.
> (W. WORDSWORTH, *THE PRELUDE* BK. 6, LL. 602–10)

When I was seventeen, I experienced an Emily Byrd Starr–like "flash" while listening to a talk on William Wordsworth and Romanticism featuring the above passage.[1] The "flash" revealing an "invisible world," a glimpse of infinitude—why, this was Emily Starr's "flash" from L. M. Montgomery's Emily books! This was her "inexpressible glimpse of eternity" (Montgomery, *Quest* 119). Wordsworth's fleeting vision of the invisible world, "our being's heart and home," prefigures Montgomery's thin curtain that momentarily parts when Emily "glimpse[s] . . . the enchanting realm beyond" (Montgomery, *New Moon* 8). Wordsworth's desire to reside in that world of "something evermore about to be" impels the same longing as when Emily perceives she is "very, very near to a world of wonderful beauty" (Montgomery, *New Moon* 8). Seized by the triumph of recognition and a sense of the deep connections binding literary texts, I changed my university preferences to enable a major in English literature that afternoon. The "flash" to me, at the time, signaled something of a homecoming.

Ironically, what I perceived as a homecoming—Wordsworth's transcendent "flash" that heralded a glimpse of a home unreached—equally betrays the Wordsworthian speaker's exile. If infinitude alone is where individuals find heart and home, the speaker here and now is displaced, waiting to return. Yet Wordsworth's "home" is "something evermore about to be." The tense indicates something that can never be perfectly realized or fulfilled. Home is an uncertain goal and end. Thus, the Wordsworthian poet must console his displaced self by remembering a time of divine connection and rewriting his mental stance; he cannot look forward teleologically to an ultimate homecoming. This flimsiness of potential homecoming imbues Wordsworthian transcendence with paucity. A more rigorous sense of the extent to which Wordsworth's poetry plumbs poetic exile and explores the limitations of nature's consolatory powers illumines key concerns in L. M. Montgomery's Emily books. Emily Byrd Starr embodies the loneliness of the Wordsworthian poet: she is exiled from her spiritual-creative home, temporarily and unpredictably visited by the creative impulse, and inconsistently consoled by nature. Moreover, as a writer, she is an instrumental receptacle for the creative spirit, conveying messages from a veiled Beauty residing in "infinitude." This vocation inhibits her from committing herself to human relationships, resulting in a kind of social exile. Emily is a dislocated Wordsworthian poet: displaced from the creative realm that she considers home; occasionally disconnected with nature; and alienated from domestic spaces.

EMILY'S WORDSWORTHIAN POETIC EXILE

In Montgomery's Emily books, Emily's sense of home is riven with uncertainty. The first book, *Emily of New Moon*, uses the grounding possessive "of" to connect Emily and New Moon; the later books displace her. *Emily Climbs* charts the beginning of Emily's commitment to follow the Alpine Path to literary greatness. The verb describes an upward movement, suggesting transcendence, but the final book provides no clarity as to how far, or even in which direction, Emily has moved. *Emily's Quest* suggests that Emily has left her rootedness "of" New Moon but has not attained a fixed identity or home. Indeed, the final image of the series has Emily looking at, but remaining outside, a potential future home—the still-named Disappointed House. The Emily books, the titles suggest, are a progressive exploration of exile and un-homing.

Crucially, the "flash" that Emily treasures is inherently isolating and displacing. This is evident in *Emily of New Moon*. At one point when she experiences the "flash" she feels simultaneously homesick and rapturous (328–29). The narrative suggests why Emily may feel this when she experiences the "flash" while being mocked by her Blair Water schoolmates:

> "I can write poetry," said Emily, without in the least meaning to say it. But at that instant she knew she *could* write poetry. And with this queer unreasonable conviction came—the flash! . . . the wonderful moment when soul seemed to cast aside the bonds of flesh and spring upward to the stars. (96)

Emily's declaration is "queer," "unreasonable," and unintended, suggesting an irrational action impelled by something outside her control. In this powerful speech act, Emily is "convicted" of her ability to write, a word with strong religious connotations, especially in Calvinistic discourse. As Emily attends her local Presbyterian church, her actions and statement imply a heterodox version of salvific, spiritual activity. Indeed, the simile describes how Emily's soul "spring[s] . . . to the stars"—a metaphorical realm associated with divinity and the supernatural. This reappropriation of Calvinistic discourse displaces God and religious doctrine with metaphoric creativity. What Emily experiences in this moment is depicted as a spiritual vocation to write, which entails her displacement here on earth. The dichotomy pits "the bonds of flesh" against "the stars" where Emily feels at home, suggesting that (for Emily) embodiment is an imprisoning "bond." However, Emily *is* flesh and blood, and the "flash" is, as its name suggests, temporary. It is also an unpredictable visitor, and its frequency decreases in the later books. These patterns highlight the strain involved in the poetic vocation: Emily cannot invoke the "flash" but must wait for the creative-spiritual realm to initiate creative-spiritual revelations. This process transforms her into a receptacle for the creative impulse and discomforts Emily as she ages.

Montgomery's concern with the fragmented and displaced poet echoes a recurring Wordsworthian topic. Just as Emily's affinity with the "flash" suggests division between her soul and her embodied existence, the Wordsworthian poet is in many ways a fragmented speaker. Susan Wolfson suggests that Wordsworth's interrogative modes convey this self-dislocation, as the poet's brief hesitations that interrupt his philosophical exclamations cast doubt on his ability to transcend earthly disappointment and reexperience past joys and sensations (19, 34). Similarly, Louise Joy's study of *Poems Founded on the Affections* suggests that the Wordsworthian poet depicts personally inaccessible past emotional states for readers to interpret, highlighting the poet's disconnection from his former self (173–202). Laura Quinney, meanwhile, describes Wordsworth as a poet of disappointment, arguing that Wordsworthian consolation is not the same thing as hope and that Wordsworth's poetry betrays an existential disorientation where the speaker finds "time [emptied] of its teleological promise" (8). While Quinney's readings of Wordsworth verge on the overly pessimistic, she insightfully invokes the spatial dimension to suggest that self-knowledge requires a clear teleology. She highlights the lack of teleology in much of Wordsworth's poetry, where the poet uses consolation to reframe his perspectives, without clarifying his sense of the future. Quinney's language of directionality echoes Charles Taylor's descriptions of self-knowledge as being "oriented in moral space" and having "a notion of how we have become, and of where we are going" (28, 47). Wordsworth's "flash" cannot clarify how the speaker is oriented toward this spiritual home, creating an uncertainty that underlies the practicalities of returning to one's spiritual home.

The fragility of Wordsworth's attempts to reclaim a spiritual home are indicated even by triumphant readings of his poetic endeavors. Stephen Gill interprets Wordsworth's literary patterns of revisiting places in his poems, and his literary practice of revisiting poems in different editions, as the creation of a voice that "survive[s] time's depredation" (1). In one sense this is a poetic triumph, but Gill's study also suggests the fragility of return by emphasizing the significance of Wordsworth's "revisitations." If Wordsworth's poems explore the possibilities of reclamation in the face of loss and exile, they also highlight how each revisitation produces a different experience, a different set of emotions, and is necessarily an incomplete reclamation of the past. In other words, creative exile produces the conditions of Wordsworth's poetic endeavors, and cannot secure his return to his creative-spiritual home.

Emily's experience of creative exile largely mirrors that of the Wordsworthian poet: her creative exile enables her to generate literature and poetry, but the consuming nature of this creativity leaves her socially isolated and not-at-home. In elucidating this Wordsworthian inheritance, this essay moves away from Emily studies that focus on the restrictions of patriarchal influence on female self-expressivity (Menzies 60; Rubio 29–30; Epperly 205; McMaster 50–74). This essay more closely parallels some of Kate Lawson's Freudian interpretations, particularly concerning the notion that Emily's "ambiguous sense of the homelike" is the cost Emily bears as a poet (Lawson, "'Disappointed' House" 72). As noted, Montgomery's novel titles progressively "un-home" Emily, and this essay suggests that this is intimately linked with Montgomery's exploration of Emily's Wordsworthian inheritance.

EMILY'S LIMITED WORDSWORTHIAN CONSOLATIONS

Emily's Wordsworthian heritage is sometimes treated as given—Lawson glibly references Emily's "Wordsworthian flash" ("Victorian Sickroom" 73). What Emily's "Wordsworthian flash" consists of is less commonly explored. Margaret Steffler suggests it is like a Wordsworthian "spot in time," an interpretation supported when Emily recalls a previous experience of the "flash" and writes, "I feel again the wonder moment" (Montgomery, *Climbs* 41; Steffler 90). However, the "flash" occurs less frequently as Emily grows older, and it is not the only Wordsworthian inheritance Emily bears in her relationship with nature. Thus far, scholarship on Emily and Wordsworth has overlooked Wordsworth's ambiguous depictions of nature's power. Alicia Pollard, for instance, insightfully argues that Emily experiences "anti-revelation" in her brushes with the impersonal and amoral supernatural but claims this is a Shelleyan, not Wordsworthian, inheritance (paras. 22–32, 34, 39). Wordsworthian scholarship, by contrast, more readily acknowledges the ambiguity of Wordsworthian triumph, suggesting the plausibility of reading Emily's fraught relationship with nature through a Wordsworthian lens.

Emily's intense and typically emotionally fulfilling relationship with nature is marred by episodes of betrayal. This corresponds with Montgomery's association of Wordsworthian poetry with both beauty and dissatisfaction—a pertinent fact, as Emily echoes several of Montgomery's literary reflections, almost verbatim (Montgomery on Tennyson and Keats, *Journal* 2: 235–37; *Climbs* 292–93). In an 1894 journal entry, Montgomery invokes Wordsworth's "Ode: Intimations of Immortality" to bemoan the loss of the "colouring of romance" (*Journal* 1: 241); when she observes that patterns of spring and renewal should bring joy, she quotes Wordsworth's "Ode" to undercut this optimism: "yet I know / Where'er I go / That there hath passed away a glory from the earth" (*Journal* 1: 416). This sense of Wordsworthian loss as disillusionment is a specifically Montgomery-colored interpretation. Wolfson's and Joy's studies emphasize the fragmentation of the Wordsworthian speaker, while Quinney places Wordsworthian disappointment in terms of the teleology of hope: in none of these readings is disillusionment the key feature. By interpreting Wordsworth as a poet of loss or disconsolation, Montgomery aligns herself with a particular school of Wordsworthian criticism and provides her unique framework for understanding Wordsworthian loss as disillusionment.

Disillusionment first requires the illusion, and initially, Emily finds consolation and freedom in nature in *Emily of New Moon*. The later books, however, trouble her communion with nature. In *Emily Climbs*, Emily turns to nature to escape stifling familial obligations, frequenting the Land of Uprightness while boarding with Aunt Ruth. However, one night, her oft-visited Land of Uprightness becomes "eerie—almost sinister . . . strange and aloof" and the sounds become "almost hostile . . . alien and unacquainted" (*Climbs* 281–82). The Freudian insistence on the *unheimlich* of the familiar is something Emily can never explain to herself. She is discomforted to the point where she needs to "exorcise something out of [her] soul" by writing a poem. The language suggests that she has been spiritually contaminated by this hostile environment and can only cleanse herself through poetic creativity. Mr. Carpenter destroys the poem upon reading it, claiming that Emily was possessed by a "streak of diabolism" (288). Mr. Carpenter's suggestion that evil resides in the nature from which Emily draws comfort indicates the ambivalence of nature. Moreover, the fact that Emily can find peace only after writing the poem suggests that Emily's interactions with nature are somewhat transactional: Emily must *produce* something to appease nature and sustain its consolations. In other words, nature is not an unconditional consoler. The idea that nature requires something from Emily transforms her into nature's handmaiden and communicator, indicating nature's power *over* Emily.

Pollard explores up a similar idea when she compares nature's spiritual ambiguity with the psychic forces that discomfort Emily, suggesting that the amoral and impersonal supernatural realms create an "anti-revelation" (para. 28). For all that Emily names natural features like the Wind Woman or the Land of Uprightness, there is something deeply unknowable in nature in the Emily books, freighting her attempts to find consolation in nature with the possibility of defamiliarizing estrangement. Emily's experience in the Land of Uprightness undercuts her seemingly triumphant invocation of Wordsworth in her later years: "Nature never did betray the heart that loved her" (Wordsworth, "Tintern Abbey"; *Quest* 185; cf. Montgomery, *Journal* 2: 190). The exultation is riddled with the apophatic possibility of betrayal, and as we have seen nature betray Emily already, her Wordsworthian allusion summarizes the limitations of nature's consolations.

Emily's uncanny experience with nature is inevitable in a Wordsworthian framework. Alongside Wordsworth's exclamations about the joys of nature lie his awareness of nature's constraints, as in *Home at Grasmere* (later bk. 1 of *The Recluse*):

> such unfettered liberty was his
> [. . .]
> To flit from field to rock, from rock to field
> [. . .]

> [. . .] the bound of this huge concave here
> Must be his home, this valley his world (ll. 37, 39, 44–45)

The political dimensions of Wordsworthian "liberty" are beyond the remit of this essay.[2] Liberty, in any case, is within the "bound" of Grasmere, and the flitting chiasmatic movement between field and rock creates a back-and-forth pattern that highlights the instability of Wordsworth's dwelling. The idea that this concave "must" be his home suggests the possibility that it is *not*. The poet's home and the natural environment are not entirely comfortable bedfellows. Moreover, in *The Excursion* (earlier *Home at Grasmere*), the speaker describes how, while he writes,

> —Beauty—a living Presence of the earth
> [. . .] composed
> From earth's materials—waits upon my steps;
> Pitches her tents before me as I move,
> An hourly neighbour. (ll. 42, 44–47)

By describing Beauty as "a living Presence," Wordsworth recalls Christ's "Presence" in the Christian sacrament of Eucharist, implying that spiritual nurturance occurs when poets allow nature ("earth's materials") to shape the poets' work. This suggests that nature is primally spiritual and creative. Yet Beauty is "composed / From earth's materials." Composition can refer to basic components *and* craft, and the latter concept transforms nature into a vestment. This implies that nature is valuable because of its instrumentality: it enables access to otherwise intangible Beauty. Most ambiguously, Beauty is only conditionally accessible to the poet. She may pitch her tents as "An hourly neighbour," but neighbors, as Robert Frost reminds us in "Mending Wall," are defined as much by the walls between them as by their proximity. Moreover, tents imply impermanence. Our ability to commune with nature, Wordsworth suggests, is vital but conditional, for nature is a form of Beauty, and Beauty chooses when (and if) to manifest itself.

To Emily, too, nature's conditional consolations depend on her willingness to express herself creatively. That Emily can "exorcise" her discomfort in the Land of Uprightness by writing a poem (even if Mr. Carpenter destroys it) suggests that Emily's communes with nature are designed to lead to literary production. Time in nature can unsettle the poet if sought as an end itself because nature should enable literary creativity. This has Wordsworthian resonances; Grasmere is the poet's place of freedom because it is where he writes his poems. Similarly, Blair Water can comfort Emily so long as it helps her generate inspired writings.

In *Emily's Quest*, Miss Royal comments that Emily's novel *The Moral of the Rose* is inflected by a regionalism that justifies Emily's decision to stay in Prince Edward Island and not move to New York. In other words, Emily embodies what Taylor identifies as a post-Schopenhauerian sensibility: she sees nature as a "fermenting source of power" though it is "wild, formless, unreason itself" (445). Correspondingly, nature empowers and consoles Emily when she is open to creative inspiration. While Emily is engaged to Dean and has lost her drive to write, she finds herself "pining for freedom" and goes for a walk. Because she seeks comfort in nature but is not using it as a "fermenting source of power" for self-expression, she finds the walk "inexpressibly dreary and mournful" and is filled with hopelessness (Taylor 445; *Quest* 98). Emily's detachment from nature is deeply Wordsworthian at this narrative moment. If the Wordsworthian speaker of *The Recluse* finds "Beauty" a constant companion while he sings his song and fulfills his creative élan, Emily is unable to access "Beauty" during her walk in *Emily's Quest* because at that point she considers herself an exile from the artistic realm (90). Emily, like the poet in *The Excursion*, is close with nature when she is fulfilling her imaginative literary calling. Sought as an end itself, separate from expressions of literary creativity, nature risks becoming "inexpressibly" bleak—a terrifying prospect for a poet. The books focus, therefore, on the costs of Emily's allegiance to the creative spirit and the implications of embracing an instrumental sense of self as the communicator of beauty in nature.

CREATIVITY AND TEMPORARY POSSESSION

In the Emily books, Montgomery implies that Emily must embrace her instrumentality and her subsequent double exile: as a vessel for the creative spirit, she belongs neither in the creative realm nor in the mundane world. This instrumentality is something Emily both relishes and fears. On one level, Emily delights in being a communicator of ideas from the realm of creative beauty. In *Emily Climbs*, she describes the process of writing a poem: "It didn't seem to me that *I* composed it at all.... *Something Else* were trying to speak through me ... when it is gone the words seem flat and foolish" (10). Similarly, at Shrewsbury, she writes, "Lovely thoughts came flying to meet me.... They came from somewhere" (123). The uncertainty of the source of inspiration—"*Something Else*," "somewhere," emphasizes Emily's passivity: she describes how inspiration tries to speak "through" her, a preposition depicting Emily as the creative spirit's instrument. Emily enjoys these creative encounters—the thoughts are "lovely," and words are "flat and foolish" compared to her visions. However, Emily's discomfort when Cousin Jimmy is temporarily possessed by a poetic urge indicates her fear of being possessed by an external, impersonal source. While introducing Emily to the New Moon gardens, Cousin Jimmy experiences a moment of poetic possession as he speaks of a spell: "a strange sound crept into his voice and an odd look into his eyes" (*New Moon* 82). In Emily's eyes he only becomes "himself again" when he prosaically talks about turnips (82). Emily is unsettled because Jimmy has temporarily become a receptacle for something "strange" and "odd," terms suggesting a momentary dislocation in Emily and Jimmy's generally affectionate and understanding relationship.

Despite Emily's delight in personal visitations by the creative impulse, she is uncomfortable with being an instrument for supernatural forces. She finds her psychic encounters particularly isolating and unsettling. After she miraculously locates little Allan Bradshaw, she "desperately" tries to convince Ilse and Allan's family that she does not have the Second Sight:

> "Perhaps I'll grow out of it," said Emily. . . . ". . . I don't feel *human*. When Dr McIntyre spoke about *something* using me as an instrument I went cold all over. It seemed to me that while *I* was asleep some *other* intelligence must have taken possession of my body." (*Climbs* 236)

Even though this unknown force has saved a young boy's life, Emily is unsettled by her lack of control over herself. Hearing herself described with the language of instrumentality makes her physically cold and invokes such intense disassociation that she doesn't "feel *human*." And yet it is difficult to miss the correspondence between Emily's supernatural gifts and her experience with the "flash" where her soul "spring[s] . . . to the stars"; it is difficult to forget her discomfort with Cousin Jimmy's sudden, strange eloquence. To be an artist, Montgomery implies, is akin to supernatural possession: the poet becomes a receptacle for ideas they cannot own or control. This can be disconcerting and isolating for witnesses—Emily is discomforted by Cousin Jimmy's temporary possession—and for the individual themselves.

Being an isolated receptacle for ideas is not purely bleak in the Emily books, though it comes at a cost: if the poet is an instrument for the creative impulse, their primary allegiance is to imaginative endeavors and not people. This prevents Emily from embedding herself in interpersonal, domestic relationships but enables her to produce literature. The imaginative generativity enabled by the instrumental nature of the poet is explored through Emily's experiences with the Disappointed House. Emily feels a great affinity to the house throughout the series because "It had never been finished . . . then and there she named it the Disappointed House, and many an hour thereafter did she spend finishing that house, furnishing it as it should be furnished" (*New Moon* 77–78). Emily spends her time "finishing" the house by "furnishing as it should be furnished," the alliterative patterns and the chiasmic polyptoton suggesting that the house's emptiness awakes Emily's creative urge.

As a receptacle for Emily's dreams, the house becomes an imaginative generative space (*New Moon* 253). Emily transforms the physical house into a conceptual space of imaginative and imagined life. Yet the house remains uninhabited, unfinished, and geographically isolated on a hill, highlighting a discontinuity between the house's physical temporal reality and its signification in Emily's mind. This discontinuity is reinforced when Emily enters the house with Teddy in *Emily of New Moon*. They light a fire in the grate and imagine purchasing the house, but while they agree on some future visions (eating bacon and marmalade for breakfast every day), they cannot agree on others (Teddy discusses marriage; Emily suggests an alternative way to procure the house) (342). The disagreement between the individuals who dream of inhabiting the house suggests that the Disappointed House may be visited but not lived in. The house thus mirrors Emily's relationship with the "flash": it is a place for temporary visitation and an instrument for imaginative creativity, not a long-term dwelling place.

In fact, Montgomery insists that a poet *must* accept their instrumentality as a receptacle for ideas, or they will suffer. She explores this through Emily and Dean's engagement, an event that alters Emily's interactions with the Disappointed House in *Emily's Quest*. Emily's engagement to Dean is a period when Emily rejects her poetic instrumentality and considers herself an exile from the poetic realm (*Quest* 90). The association between Dean and Emily's muffled creative voice is well-established (Epperly 148; Sardella-Ayres 108–9), and Emily and Dean's engagement reads as Montgomery's criticism of attempts to falsely assert human authority over creatively inspired works. This human interference begins when Dean maliciously lies about the literary merit of Emily's manuscript, *The Seller of Dreams*, a book that has so captured Emily's imagination and emotions that it surpasses the intensity of her romantic love for Teddy (*Climbs* 308–9; *Quest* 54–55). While Emily writes the book, it is life giving and absorbing: she "seemed to live really only when she was writing" and Dean finds her "absent and impersonal" (*Quest* 55). The novel suggests that Emily is most alive when she devotes herself to writing and absents herself, to some extent, from social bonds. When Emily accepts Dean's false assessment of her book as "cobwebs" and "puppets" and destroys her manuscript, it is depicted as a moment of sacrilegious murder (59):

> The flame seized on the loose sheets eagerly, murderously. Emily clasped her hands over her heart and watched it with dilated eyes, remembering the time she had burned her old "account book" rather than let Aunt Elizabeth see it. . . . a heap of crinkled ashes, with here and there an accusing ghost-word coming out whitely on a blackened fragment. . . .
>
> Repentance seized upon her. . . . She had destroyed something incalculably precious to her. What did the mothers of old feel when their children had passed through the fire to Moloch—when the sacrificial impulse and excitement had gone? Emily thought she knew. (61)

Emily's self-inflicted wound transforms her book into an "accusing" ghost; her characters are described later as "reproachful ghosts" and "murdered book-folks" (62). These images of haunting recall the persistence of loss, in which presence can be invoked only through an object's absence. Indeed, in this moment, Emily is haunted by a memory from *Emily of New Moon* where she burned her account book to prevent Aunt Elizabeth from trespassing her private thoughts. In that episode, too, Emily watched her book burn and felt "she had lost something incalculably precious" (*New Moon* 57). The repetition of "incalculably precious" in both episodes suggests that Emily's acts of literary destruction are moments of self-erasure and self-fragmentation.

In *Emily's Quest* the significance of the burning of *The Seller of Dreams* is magnified: Emily likens this literary destruction to Ancient Near Eastern cultic practices of child sacrifice. Emily's creative self-mutilation leads to (and is externalized by) her physical scarring. Blinded by tears, she impales herself on Aunt Laura's scissors. Emily is mentally and literally scarred by her attempts to exert control over a book that was the product of the spirit of inspiration. Later in the book, after Emily has found success with *The Moral of the Rose*, she laments "her unborn *The Seller of Dreams*" (199). The language of incomplete pregnancy and matricide paints Emily as a failed mother. Notably, Emily's child is not a biological infant but a book, suggesting that her primary identity is that of an imaginative creator rather than a romantic heroine and future child-bearer. *Emily's Quest* suggests that when a creator kills their imaginative children, the creator enacts a spiritual Fall (mirrored by Emily's physical fall). This results in further exile, as the writer isolates themselves from communion with the creative impulse, their élan. While this exile is not irrevocable—Emily recovers physically and creatively—Emily's return to the world of creative writing and self-expression requires two unsettling encounters with the Disappointed House that remind her of her imaginative identity and her instrumentality.

Emily's inability to cross the threshold of the Disappointed House with Dean and her intense psychic vision in the house's living room are crucial events that enable Emily to reembrace her identity as an instrumental poet and end her engagement to Dean. When Dean purchases the house for his and Emily's marriage, they furnish it and plan to cross the threshold to "drive out the ghost of things that never happened" (84–85). Yet Emily cannot reconcile the Disappointed House as a site of domestic familial bliss with Dean and as a site of conceptual, imaginative generativity. On the verge of entering, she sees the ashes of the fire she and Teddy kindled as children. Unable to resolve her past association of the house as a primarily imaginative space, and her latent emotions for Teddy, with the prospect of the house as a site of domestic happiness with Dean, Emily leaves. The house thus implicitly repudiates Emily's attempts to transform herself into a romantic figure at the cost of Emily's allegiance to the vocation of writing and cultivating the imagination. Instead, the house reminds Emily of her imaginative affiliations, visually encoded in the ashes of the fire she lit as a child who dreamed about the house's future.

Moreover, the Disappointed House forces Emily to confront her inherent instrumentality when it becomes the site of her most intense psychic vision. Emily's reinduction into the poetic realm is enabled when she has a vision in the living room of the Disappointed House and saves Teddy from sailing on the *Flavian*. Falling asleep in a chair, Emily sees Teddy, although they are in different countries, and leads him away from a ticket booth, preventing him from sailing on the *Flavian*. Awakening from the vision-dream, she sees her reflection: "a dead-white spot that was her face and one solitary taper-light twinkling like an impish star" (102). Emily is the object on whom the taper-light twinkles "like an impish star." This supernatural, celestial simile suggests a force of ambiguous morality, and it reminds Emily of her inherent instrumentality. Following this experience, Emily ends her engagement with Dean and resumes writing. It is almost as if the Disappointed House has prevented Emily's attempts to transform it into a space of domestic generativity with Dean by reminding her, through a deeply disorienting psychic experience, that both Emily and the house have generative capacities that concern the conceptual and supernatural, not the familial and domestic.

Subsequently, for most of *Emily's Quest*, Emily exiles herself from a conventional romantic narrative, suggesting an incompatibility between Emily's creative calling and the conventions of romantic plots. She refuses to contact Teddy even after Aileen Kent admits to tampering with Teddy's letter and suggests that Emily tell him the truth. Instead, Emily allows her life to be shaped by "old accustomed grooves" while "year after year the seasons walked by her door" (257). These descriptions anticipate Gabriel Marcel's definition of despair as a "place of pure repetition" (60). The despair, perhaps, lies in Emily's (or Montgomery's) inability to reconcile the identities of literary generator and romantic heroine/future child-bearer: if the former requires writers' primary allegiance to the creative spirit, the latter requires the heroine to direct her primary allegiance to interpersonal relationships. The tension is never resolved in *Emily's Quest*. Mere pages from the end, Teddy returns, and he and Emily reunite. Few find the ending satisfying (Lawson, "'Disappointed' House" 88; Pollard; Menzies 60; Rubio 29–30; Epperly 196–205).[3] Even Sardella-Ayres's acknowledgement of the triumph of Teddy and Emily's romance focuses on Emily's ability to maintain her creative integrity, transforming the pairing from a celebration of romance into an affirmation of Emily's poetic identity (110–11). Indeed, the final scene forms a tableau capturing the irresolvable tension between Emily's identity as poet and as romantic heroine. While looking at the Disappointed House, Emily receives a letter from Dean containing the deeds to the Disappointed House and requesting her friendship. She haltingly reflects:

> "How very—dear—of Dean. And I am so glad he is not hurt any longer."
> [. . .] Behind her she heard Teddy's eager footsteps coming to *her*. Before her on the dark hill, against the sunset, was the little beloved grey house that was to be disappointed no longer. (266)

Emily is physically suspended between Teddy and the Disappointed House, symbolically unable to claim her romantic ending or transform the Disappointed House into a domestic dwelling. Emily, a master of words, stutters. The double negative of "the house that was to be disappointed no longer" performs linguistic contortions to avoid positive statements about homecoming or fulfillment. Moreover, Dean's letter is a form of haunting that reminds us of Emily's previous failed attempt to turn the Disappointed House into a dwelling space. Prevented at the last minute from entering the house with Dean, who is to say a similar obstacle will not present itself again? To the end, Emily remains outside the uninhabited house. Just as the Disappointed House remains uninhabited but open to temporal possession, so Emily is untethered: a poet whose allegiance to the creative realm renders her innately instrumental and unable to commit fully to romantic unions and domestic relationships on the mundane plane.

Emily embodies the cost of embracing the instrumental sense of self encoded in a Wordsworthian Romantic embrace of "nature as an intrinsic source" where fulfilling one's being requires creative expression (Taylor 385). Emily's élan lies in communicating the results of uncontrollable brushes with supernatural powers, an experience she finds both exhilarating and disconcerting. As a Wordsworthian poet, Emily glimpses and communicates beauty in nature, but she cannot permanently reside in the imaginative realm, and her allegiance to the poetic vision impedes her ability to commit to romantic unions' domestic plotlines. Emily is a vessel for the creative spirit and her children are her books. It is fitting, therefore, that we never see Emily residing in the Disappointed House: it remains a domestically empty but conceptually generative space. If in *The Excursion* Wordsworth presents Beauty as the poetic impulse in an impermanent tent, Montgomery flips the image: Emily, the Wordsworthian poet, must live lightly in a world to which she will never fully belong.

NOTES

1. Will Christie delivered this lecture in 2010 at Presbyterian Ladies' College, Sydney.

2. "Unfettered liberty" recalls William Blake's claim that "Poetry Fetter'd Fetters the Human Race" (*Jerusalem*). In *The Recluse* Wordsworth writes, "such liberty . . . but only for this end," removing the pointedly political Blakean reference.

3. Kirstie Blair and William Thompson claim that Emily's purchase of Lofty John's bush is "a truer ending for the novel than her marriage to Teddy" from an eco-theological approach, revealing an assumption that a "true" ending must be emotionally satisfying (142).

WORKS CITED

Blair, Kirstie, and William V. Thompson. "The Mood of the Golden Age: Paganism, Ecotheology and the Wild Woods in L. M. Montgomery's *Anne* and *Emily* Series." *Literature & Theology*, vol. 30, no. 2, 2016, pp. 131–47.

Blake, William. *Jerusalem, Plate 3* (E 145). www.britishmuseum.org/collection/object/P_1847-0318-93-3.

Epperly, Elizabeth. *The Fragrance of Sweet-Grass: L. M. Montgomery's Heroines and the Pursuit of Romance.* U of Toronto P, 2014.

Frost, Robert. "Mending Wall." *Robert Frost*, edited by Geoffrey Moore, C. N. Potter, 1986.

Gill, Stephen. *Wordsworth's Revisitings*. Oxford UP, 2011.
Joy, Louise. *Eighteenth-Century Literary Affections*. Palgrave Macmillan, 2020.
Lawson, Kate. "The Alien at Home: Hearing Voices in L. M. Montgomery's *Emily Climbs* and F. W. H Myers." *Gothic Studies*, vol. 4, no. 2, 2002, pp. 155–66.
Lawson, Kate. "The 'Disappointed' House: Trance, Loss, and the Uncanny in L. M. Montgomery's *Emily Trilogy*." *Children's Literature*, vol. 29, 2001, pp. 71–90.
Lawson, Kate. "The Victorian Sickroom in L. M. Montgomery's *The Blue Castle* and *Emily's Quest*: Sentimental Fiction and the Selling of Dreams." *Lion and the Unicorn*, vol. 31, no. 3, 2007, pp. 232–49.
Marcel, Gabriel. "Sketch of a Phenomenology and a Metaphysics of Hope." *Homo Viator*, translated by Emma Crawford, Harper, 1962.
Martin, Adrienne M. *How We Hope: A Moral Psychology*. Princeton UP, 2014.
McMaster, Lindsey. "The 'Murray Look': Trauma as Family Legacy in L. M. Montgomery's Emily of New Moon Trilogy." *Canadian Children's Literature / Littérature canadienne pour la jeunesse*, vol. 34, no. 2, 2008, pp. 50–74.
Menzies, Ian. "The Moral of the Rose: L. M. Montgomery's Emily." *Canadian Children's Literature / Littérature canadienne pour la jeunesse*, 65, 1992, pp. 48–61.
Montgomery, L. M. *The Complete Journals: The PEI Years, 1889–1900*, edited by Mary Henley Rubio and Elizabeth Hillman Waterston, Oxford UP, 2012.
Montgomery, L. M. *The Complete Journals, 1901–1911*, edited by Mary Henley Rubio and Elizabeth Hillman Waterston, Oxford UP, 2013.
Montgomery, L. M. *Emily Climbs*. 1925. Virago, 2013.
Montgomery, L. M. *Emily of New Moon*. 1923. Virago, 2013.
Montgomery, L. M. *Emily's Quest*. 1927. Virago, 2013.
Pollard, Alicia. "Wordsworth's Light and Shelley's Shadow: Revelation in L. M. Montgomery's Anne and Emily Series," *Journal of L. M. Montgomery Studies*, 8 March 2021, journaloflmmontgomerystudies.ca/vision/Pollard/Wordsworths-Light-and-Shellys-Shadow.
Quinney, Laura. *The Poetics of Disappointment: Wordsworth to Ashbery*. UP of Virginia, 1999.
Rubio, Mary. "Subverting the Trite: L. M. Montgomery's 'Room of Her Own.'" *Canadian Children's Literature / Littérature canadienne pour la jeunesse*, 65, 1992, pp. 6–39.
Sardella-Ayres, Dawn. "Under the Umbrella: The Author-Heroine's Love Triangle." *Canadian Children's Literature / Littérature canadienne pour la jeunesse*, 105–6, 2007, pp. 100–113.
Steffler, Margaret. "Brian O'Connal and Emily Byrd Starr: The Inheritors of Wordsworth's 'Gentle Breeze.' *Windows and Words: A Look at Canadian Children's Literature in English*, edited by Aïda Hudson and Susan-Ann Cooper, U of Ottawa P, 1999, pp. 87–96.
Taylor, Charles. *Sources of the Self: The Making of the Modern Identity*. Cambridge UP, 1989.
Wiehl, John S. "The Religious and Political Revisions of *The Prelude*." *Romanticism on the Net*, no. 71, 2018, pp. 1–28.
Wolfson, Susan. *The Questioning Presence: Wordsworth, Keats, and the Interrogate Mode in Romantic Poetry*. Cornell UP, 1986.

Wordsworth, Dorothy, and William Wordsworth. *Home at Grasmere: Extracts from the Journal of Dorothy Wordsworth and from the Poems of William Wordsworth*, edited by Colette Clark, Penguin, 2007.

Wordsworth, William. *The Excursion and The Recluse*, edited by Jared Curtis, Humanities-Ebooks, 2014.

Wordsworth, William. *The Prelude: The Four Texts (1798, 1799, 1805, 1850)*, edited by Jonathan Wordsworth, Penguin, 1995.

Chapter 3

EMILY BYRD STARR MEETS BRENÉ BROWN

"Braving the Wilderness" and Achieving "True Belonging"

LESLEY D. CLEMENT

> **True belonging** is the spiritual practice of believing in and belonging to yourself so deeply that you can share your most authentic self with the world and find sacredness in both being a part of something and standing alone in the wilderness.
> —BRENÉ BROWN, *BRAVING THE WILDERNESS: THE QUEST FOR TRUE BELONGING AND THE COURAGE TO STAND ALONE* (40)

In *Braving the Wilderness* (2017) and *Atlas of the Heart* (2021), Brené Brown draws on concepts and grounded theories generated in her previous best-selling books and TED talks and revisits stories she has collected from her qualitative research.[1] In *Braving the Wilderness*, she reconsiders earlier research when examining and narrating her own story, that is, her journey to embrace the words that inspired this book, Maya Angelou's paradoxical statement "You are only free when you realize you belong no place—you belong every place—no place at all."[2] In *Atlas of the Heart*, she reconsiders earlier research to hone the language of emotions and experience that underpins nurturing "meaningful connection" and so enabling journeys "anywhere without the fear of getting lost" (273). Had Brown—as researcher, theorist, and storyteller—known the trilogy featuring L. M. Montgomery's Emily Byrd Starr, she would have understood Emily to be, like herself, among those creators dedicated to the language of affect whose accomplishments reflect their inhabiting a space of "true belonging," a wilderness where inner and outer worlds intersect and often collide.

Emily's defiant declaration at age ten in *Emily of New Moon*, "I am important to myself" (25), and her determined affirmation at age fourteen and again at age seventeen in *Emily Climbs*, "I believe in myself" (86, 373), might indicate that that she has gained entrance to Brown's wilderness at an early age. But her journey to and into the wilderness has just begun. Although she secures a sense of rootedness through "this old cradle of her family" shortly after her Murray relatives take her in (*New Moon* 108), and although she has an instinctive, profound sense of belonging to the winds, sea, hills, and trees throughout her life, it is only after prolonged periods of loneliness and self-reflection, the tenor of *Emily's Quest*, that, at age twenty-three, she begins to understand that "freedom is a matter of the soul" and that those "externals [that] always had a great influence upon her" are not extraneous to and distinct from a liberated soul but rather the threads woven into its fabric (187, 100). And only in the final chapters of this trilogy does Emily, now in her mid- to late twenties, have the courage to "brave" Brown's "wilderness" and achieve, as this chapter's epigraph defines, Brown's sense of "true belonging," that is, "belonging to [her]self so deeply" that she can leave Blair Water and "share [her] most authentic self with the world" (*Braving* 40). Throughout the trilogy, Emily's journey plays out alongside those of Teddy Kent, Ilse Burnley, and Perry Miller, all of whom struggle to find their own entrances to the wilderness. This chapter examines key ideas in Brown's *Braving the Wilderness*, which she has honed in *Atlas of the Heart*—interconnectedness (spirituality and sacredness); shame, humiliation, and fear; authenticity, (im)perfection, and connection; hurt/soul-wounds, vulnerability, and boundaries—to illuminate the challenges that Emily and her three peers undergo as they navigate the social and psychological hurdles of young adulthood, especially in the later chapters of *Emily Climbs* and throughout *Emily's Quest*.

SETTING THE STAGE FOR INTERCONNECTEDNESS: SPIRITUALITY AND SACREDNESS

In *Braving the Wilderness*, Brown refers to "true belonging" as a "spiritual practice" and to the discovery of this paradoxical state of being alone with oneself and being part of something greater than self as "sacred." She continues: "When we reach this place, even momentarily," of aloneness and interconnectedness, "we belong everywhere and nowhere" (40–41). While in a heightened sense we can experience interconnectedness in moments of "**awe** and **wonder** . . . in response to nature, art, music, spiritual experiences, or ideas" when confronted with "the vastness of something that is almost incomprehensible" (*Atlas* 58), it can become part of everyday living and practices. For Emily, this heightened interconnectedness is the "flash" that often inspires her poetic expression and that she experiences much less frequently in *Emily's Quest* as the Wordsworthian "light of common day" dominates (187).[3] Moreover, as Brown writes, interconnectedness demands recognizing, accepting, and ultimately embracing the darkness and danger inherent in the vast, ultimately uncontrollable, "wilderness" of "true belonging" (*Braving* 36). For the four young people featured in the Emily trilogy, the spiritual journey—what Brown describes as one that commits to "the deeply held belief that we are inextricably connected to each other by something greater than ourselves" (*Atlas* 252)—is very much a journey in the tumultuous everyday world infused by the "light of common day" as they attempt to forge a space of "true belonging" at the intersection of their private inner worlds and public social worlds.

WHERE IT ALL BEGAN: SHAME, HUMILIATION, AND FEAR

Brown catapulted to fame in 2010 with her TED talk "The Power of Vulnerability" and *New York Times* best-seller *The Gifts of Imperfection*, drawing on her main area of research: shame resiliency and how that relates to (un)worthiness, fear, and vulnerability. Throughout her many publications, she returns to the key idea that secrecy breeds shame and shame breeds secrecy. "The most dangerous thing to do after a shaming experience is hide or bury our story" (*Gifts* 10). In *Braving the Wilderness*, she discusses how shame-inducing silence permits children "to construct . . . stories that almost always cast them as alone and unworthy of love and belonging" (15). Given Emily's feistiness when she is being humiliated—whether by Ellen Greene, the Murray relatives, Miss Brownell, or Blair Water neighbors (children and adults)—given her refusal to be secretive, and given her propensity to weave stories in which, like the "solitary, intrepid" Christian from *Pilgrim's Progress*, she confronts "all alone the shadows of the Dark Valley" (*New Moon* 3), it might seem that shame—the internalization of humiliation—does not play a large part in Emily's narrative. But despite her resistance to Aunt Laura's and Cousin Jimmy's encouragement to behave in deceptive ways and to Aunt Ruth's tendency to read covert intentions into everything that Emily does, there are several instances when humiliation becomes shame because she remains silent. One is Miss Brownell's mockery of her poetry, a reflection of Emily's innermost being: "To the end of her life Emily never forgot the pain and humiliation," a "shame . . . too deep and intimate"—"Some sacred temple of her being had been desecrated and shamed"—to be exorcized by writing it out in a letter to her dead father (*New Moon* 197, 201). The foundations of the boundaries that will become walls have been laid.

Another secret that becomes a source of silent shame emerges later in life as her childhood friendship with Teddy grows into adult love, which she believes to be unrequited. Granted, mutual misunderstandings are a common plot mechanism of conventional romantic novels and certainly form the basis of the plotting of *Emily's Quest*; however, these misunderstandings have a psychological interest because they result in Emily's faltering belief in herself as worthy of love and belonging and her conviction that she deserves rejection and loneliness. Humiliation occurs, Brown writes, when after being belittled, one feels "unworthy of connection"; once humiliation has been internalized as shame, "the focus is on self.... The result is feeling flawed and unworthy of love, belonging, and connection" (*Atlas* 134–35). As a reaction to the "noiseless tenor of Emily's way" early in *Emily's Quest* (42), she enters a phase of wildness, very different from the wilderness she must brave. She falls "wildly and romantically into the wildest and most romantic kind of love" with the charming Aylmer Vincent only to fall out of love as quickly (44–45). When Aunt Elizabeth accuses Emily of a Starr trait—fickleness—Emily does not defend herself, "suppos[ing] she deserved it all."

Shame fueled by the infamous Murray pride sends her into a downward spiral of believing herself to be so "fundamentally superficial" that "even love with her was like the seeds that fell into the shallow soil in the immortal parable" (46–47). "Shame thrives on secrecy, silence, and judgment," Brown observes (*Atlas* 137). Emily's shame "thrives" for years, beginning with Teddy's next visit to Blair Water. Vowing not to be made "a fool" of again, she ramps up the Murray pride, being "friendly and remote," "gracious and impersonal" (49). When Teddy leaves "with only that soulless, chilly, polite good-bye," Emily again chastises herself for being "a hopeless fool," unworthy of his love, and deserving of his inattention (54). This becomes a recurring motif in subsequent correspondence and encounters with Teddy (118, 124–25, 145, 195–98). Eventually, when Emily learns from Mrs. Kent that Teddy has always loved her, "amid all the whirl of emotions," she is "keenly conscious of only one thing. Bitterness—humiliation—shame ... vanished from her being." She regains her "self-respect" and must now decide which is "a stronger passion"—love or the Murray pride (234–35).

While Teddy may not manifest pride with the same intensity as a Murray, his response to what the narrator declares to be Emily's "unjust" reading of his "cool detachment," his "cool, impersonal eyes" (*Quest* 49), would suggest that he too internalizes the humiliation of being rebuffed and, in turn, feels a certain shame in a covert unrequited love. Like Emily, he builds emotional walls, channeling his feelings into his art, rather than risk being hurt in life. And like Emily, he must ultimately decide between taking action rooted in shame or in love after Ilse jilts him (*Quest* 267).

In contrast are Ilse and Perry, who appear "shameless" and "fearless," respectively. Ilse claims she is "shamelessly happy," anticipating her friend's chastisement of her shameful behavior after she leaves Teddy at the altar for Perry on his (supposed) deathbed (*Quest* 257). Is this an example of what Brown deems the misuse of the word "shameless" to mean "a self-serving or unethical decision," that is, "attribut[ing] unconscionable behavior to a lack of shame" (*Atlas* 140)? From Brown's perspective, Ilse is not shameless but rather suffers from narcissism, "the shame-based fear of being ordinary" that manifests itself as "grandiosity and bluster," a "posturing and selfishness . . . lead[ing] to weaponizing hurt and turning it on other people" (*Atlas* 140), behavior the motherless (and essentially fatherless) Ilse demonstrates from a young age.

In the same scenes from *Emily's Quest* that result in Emily's and Teddy's shame-induced misunderstanding of each other, Ilse and Perry have a parallel encounter, summed up in one sentence: "Perry came to see Ilse, bragged a bit too much over his progress and got so snubbed and manhandled that he did not come again" (52). When Ilse confesses her love of Perry to Emily, she also confesses that she treats him with such disdain because she is infuriated by his "making a fool of himself. I wanted to be proud of him and he always made me ashamed of him" (76). This acknowledgement might seem to illustrate what Brown identifies as "shame resilience," which allows some people to experience "shame without sacrificing their values and authenticity": "recognizing shame and understanding its triggers," "practicing critical awareness," and "owning and sharing [their] story" (*Atlas* 139). It might therefore be argued that Ilse grows behind the scenes after such recognition and awareness. However, her continued nastiness about Perry's Stovepipe Town origins and snide comments about Emily's love interests (for examples, 130–32, 167–68) and her glib and unempathetic comments in the final conversation she has with Emily about her "foreordained" jilting of Teddy and elopement with Perry, actions rooted entirely in impulsive circumstance-driven behavior rather than critical self-reflection (257–60), indicate that, in its more colloquial (albeit perhaps misused) sense, her happiness is truly "shameless" and, as will be seen, reflects qualities impeding entry into the wilderness.

Just as one does not become less shameless by experiencing more shame, so one does not become less fearless by experiencing more fear. As with shame, fear must be confronted, not tamped down. Being fearless is quite different from braving the wilderness, as Perry well illustrates. At the beginning of

Emily Climbs, Emily writes in her journal that "Perry always brags that he is never afraid of anything—doesn't know what fear is. . . . Mr. Carpenter says fear is a vile thing, and is at the bottom of almost every wrong and hatred of the world." Emily then cites Mr. Carpenter's belief that "fear is a confession of weakness," his advice to "remember your Emerson—'always do what you are afraid to do,'" and Dean's response to this advice: "That is a counsel of perfection" (12–13). In being "fearless," Perry does not have the opportunity to find the entrance to the wilderness and develop what Brown calls "grounded confidence"—"the abilities to rumble with vulnerability, stay curious, and practice new skills"—which is a "core learning" in her book *Dare to Lead*: "It's not fear that gets in the way of courage, it's armor. . . . As we learn to recognize and remove our armor, we replace it with grounded confidence" (*Atlas* 254).

In the opening pages of *Emily's Quest*, the narrator makes a distinction between Emily and Teddy as seekers open to "the delight and allurement and despair and anguish of the rainbow quest" and Perry "with his eyes fixed firmly on several glittering legal goals" (6–8), followed by a conversation between Emily and Teddy in which they again cite Emerson while discussing belief in themselves and the need to address their fears during their journeys, not simply in hindsight (9). In their quest for their rainbows, fear will always be along for the ride. From Brown's perspective, they will need to recognize that fear must be "understood and respected, perhaps even befriended" to benefit from it (*Atlas* 13). Rita Bode argues in "Vulnerable Situations: Boys and Boyhood in the *Emily* Novels" that "Perry's self-confidence and determination act as buffers to the discrimination that his circumstances engender. He remains focused on his goals. . . . Montgomery suggests in Perry's resilience a defiance against the hostile pre-judgments directed at him" (83–84). Because his goals are different from those of the artists Emily and Teddy, Montgomery does not afford him the same narrative to discover and enter the wilderness and navigate vulnerable situations by himself being vulnerable enough to explore side roads during his journey. For Brown, Perry would not exemplify courage because vulnerability, "the birthplace of innovation, creativity, and change," is "our most accurate measurement of courage" ("Listening to Shame").[4]

DISCOVERING THE WILDERNESS: AUTHENTICITY, (IM)PERFECTION, AND CONNECTION

In his 1841 *Essays*, Ralph Waldo Emerson counsels "always do what you're afraid to do" (as referenced above) in the context of heroism in everyday practice ("Heroism"). His counsel is rooted in an earlier discussion of "self-reliance": "Nothing is at last sacred but the integrity of your own mind" ("Self-Reliance"). Recent variations on concepts of self-reliance, integrity, and *Hamlet*'s "to thine own self be true" (Shakespeare 1.3.78) have been couched in the language of "authenticity" or the "authentic self." But how can authenticity be reconciled with "fitting in," or as Richard Chase observes discussing themes that engrossed Emerson and other American writers—"solipsism, hypnotic self-regard, imprisonment within the self"—how does one navigate between "death—spiritual, emotional, physical . . . the price of self-reliance when it is pushed to the point of solipsism" and "the ability to share with others the common vicissitudes of the human situation" (58, 57)?

As researcher, theorist, and storyteller, Brown returns to these age-old ideas of and concerns about authenticity as the major distinction between "fitting in" and "belonging." In *Braving the Wilderness*, she narrates her own personal journey from the toxic life of "settling for fitting in" "everywhere and nowhere" (the title of her first chapter) to the authentic life of "true belonging" of Angelou's "no place" and "every place" (13, 5), but only in writing *Atlas of the Heart* does she discover a "symmetry" of ideas in the messiness of life's data she has been collecting and studying for years:

Authenticity is a requirement for belonging, and fitting in is a threat.
Authenticity is a requirement for connection, and perfectionism (a type of fitting in) is a threat. (172)

Throughout the Emily trilogy, the two most seemingly unconventional of the four young friends—Perry and Ilse—are the two who fail to complete the journey and enter the wilderness of "true belonging" because they lack the qualities needed to navigate shame and travel solo and so opt for conventional narratives. In the passages cited above from *Emily's Quest* that describe Emily and Teddy as seekers of rainbows—a journey with many paths—Perry's chosen path is described as narrow; hence his journey is fixed (7). Young Emily may talk of artistic endeavors—hers and Teddy's—in terms of fame and fortune (*New Moon* 45, 116, 120, 151, 350–51, 370, 408–9), but when at seventeen, she turns down Janet Royal's offer to pave the way to "success and fame" in New York City's stimulating literary world, she does so with the understanding that to retain an authentic self, an authentic voice, she must remain in Blair Water (*Climbs* 351).

As *Emily's Quest* begins, she has "settled down very determinedly and happily to her pursuit of fame and fortune—and of something that was neither. For writing . . . was not primarily a matter of worldly lucre or laurel crown. It was something she *had* to do" (2), as she has known from a young age intuitively but now through experience. Her aspirations are a reflection of her authentic self. Although Perry's aspirations may also reflect his authentic self, his path is necessarily limited. "Even Ilse thinks that Perry has by far the better chance of bringing home the bacon," says Teddy (9–10), an assessment that reveals as much about Ilse as it does Perry. Ilse may be a "madcap" in her impulsive behavior and "gorgeous violations of accepted canons of taste" (50), but as Emily will learn, a life of gaiety is not the wilderness and can impede the self-reflection necessary for authenticity and real growth. Ilse's declaration that Emily will "be surprised to see what a dutiful wife" to Perry she will become (260) suggests either she is willing to forego completely who she is to fit in or she has always been conventional at heart. Lacking critical self-awareness, she will never understand and actualize her authentic self. Like Perry, who can switch his politics "just for the sake of getting into partnership" with a law firm (and shift the target of his love to gain a wife), Ilse does not mind being "too Victorian" when it serves her own heedless self-interest (131).

When Emily turns down Miss Royal's offer, the narrator suggests that (among several possible reasons) Emily fears her Murray ancestors would "turn over in their graves at the whisper that one of their descendants could never succeed without the help and 'pull' of a stranger" (*Climbs* 351). A major element of the Murray pride is this sense of self-reliance and that they "were an independent folk" (*Quest* 39). In the transformative "At the Sign of the Haystack" chapter of *Emily Climbs*, Emily experiences a rapturous moment of being "sufficient unto herself, needing not love nor comradeship nor any human emotion to round out her felicity." At that moment, Emily experiences life's "flawless beauty," questioning whether she is a "worthy"—pure or perfect—enough conduit to carry the vision "back to the everyday world of sordid market-place and clamorous street." When she emerges from "this rapt mood," she "find[s] herself at the bottom of the haystack" and exclaims, "I think I'm all in one piece still" (205–6). Emily is learning that the external is interwoven into her inner self and that this intersection of inner and outer is the true place of belonging. She can maintain her integrity—her authentic self—and not become so solipsistic that the outer world—celestial, natural, or human—does not matter. She does not reach "the point of solipsism" that Chase defines as a deathlike (or even dead) state "where the world has no existence apart from the all-sufficient self" (57).

Because the Murrays pride themselves on being self-reliant, their pride, rooted in a fear of being open and vulnerable, repeatedly wins out, especially in decisions when connection and love should lead. To the "Murray pride,"

Emily adds the "Starr reserve" (*Quest* 209), and the combination threatens to turn her into the "Ice-maiden." In the most absurd scene of lovemaking in *Emily's Quest*, an enraged author whose "sorrowful and artistic" ending has been "barbarously mutilated" by a "happy ending" under Emily's editorial pen, suddenly turns to aggressive wooing, only to be spurned by his aghast object of attention. "Ice-maiden! Chill vestal! Cold as your northern snows," he says in farewell (158–60). As ridiculous as Emily (and the reader) may find this scene, Teddy has also witnessed her ice-maidenness, which he aspires to capture in his art (44). As I argue elsewhere, Teddy's true inspiration in his Emily paintings is the flawed "Joan of Arc—with a face all spirit" (*Climbs* 91) and not the unattainable, "ultimately destructive Ice Maiden" ("Visual Culture").[5] The scene near the end of *Emily's Quest* when the wounded Mrs. Kent confesses that she has burned a love letter to Emily from her son closes with Mrs. Kent declaring that "pride is a stronger passion with you than love" (235). However, Emily is now ready to enter the wilderness and embrace "true belonging" because the shame of thinking herself not loved or lovable—indeed of being "of no importance to anybody" (222)—has "vanished." "The wound will heal now," Emily predicts (235).

ENTERING THE WILDERNESS: HURT/SOUL-WOUNDS, VULNERABILITY, AND BOUNDARIES

To enter the wilderness—"breaking down the walls ... and living from our wild heart rather than our weary hurt" (Brown, *Braving* 37)—both Emily and Teddy learn to apply to their own lives, contrary to what Mr. Carpenter espouses, that fear is not a "weakness" but an opportunity to share in the imperfection of the human condition and the vulnerability—"the emotion that we experience during times of uncertainty, risk, and emotional exposure"—that fear makes possible (Brown, *Atlas* 13).

As Teddy begins to gain independence from his mother and she fears losing him to his art and/or another woman, Emily pities her for the "strange barrier between her and her kind" and for her "sick soul": "Mrs. Kent got some kind of terrible soul-wound some time, and it has never healed" (*Climbs* 247). The reclusive Mrs. Kent has become so greedy of her son's love and attention that she relishes the hurt Emily suffers from Teddy's perceived rejection. Brown sketches her own journey from attempting to fit in by "seek[ing] relief" from "constant pain" through "inflicting it on others" to discovering "the courage to own the pain" (*Braving* 14). Like Ilse, who does not "own the pain" of her father's neglect of her, Mrs. Kent also projects unacknowledged pain onto others. As Emily and Teddy enter the wilderness, leaving Ilse and Perry to continue their own journeys without acquiring the understanding of self required not to fit in but rather to brave this place of "true belonging," their challenges are how to embrace vulnerability as a strength and not a weakness, establish boundaries without their becoming walls, and experience hurt as a marker of "our shared humanity" (Brown, *Atlas* 118) and so find healing from their wounds.

"True belonging and self-worth are not goods; we don't negotiate their value with the world. The truth about who we are lives in our hearts" (Brown, *Braving* 158). When *Emily Climbs* closes, both the narrator and seventeen-year-old Emily consider "true belonging" and "meaningful connection" (Brown, *Atlas* 271–73), as embodied by Emily's love for Teddy, in terms of exchangeable loss and gain: "Emily was never really to belong to herself again" (314). Emily views her "sense of belonging" to Teddy as a "fetter of terrible delight that had so suddenly and inexplicably made her a prisoner—her, who hated bonds" in contrast to the wilderness beyond, "unfathomable spaces of white storm" (315). But Emily is aware that her emotions are nuanced, that denying a connection with Teddy is denying her authentic self and that there is "something that would hurt horribly if . . . kept down" (376).

The consequence of this burial—this denial—of her authentic and vulnerable self is that she enters a prolonged period of extreme loneliness, the dominant mood and theme of *Emily's Quest*, as has been seen. While she can sometimes be content with this quiet life—"alone but not lonely" (178)—Emily's boundaries become walls. Sequestering herself within the walls of New Moon, she undergoes "hours when sheer loneliness wrings the stamina out of [her]," lamenting "the loneliness of unshared thought" (148, 150). Ultimately, she is faced with the alternatives that Chase remarks: a deathlike reclusivity or acceptance of the precarious emotional fabric of the human condition. Even after experiencing such "great weariness" that "death seem[s] a friend" and believing that she has "spilled [her] cup of life's wine" and life has no more to give her "thirsty" soul, Emily continues for several years "measur[ing] her strength with pain and again conquer[ing]" it (208–9). The first of several meetings with Mrs. Kent gives her the opportunity to confess her unrequited love for Teddy and share her authentic self: her love is "so much a part of herself that it had a divine right to truth. And was there not, too, a secret relief in feeling that here at least was one person with whom she could be herself—before whom she need not pretend or hide?" (220).

Several years later, Emily's openness and vulnerability lead to reciprocal openness and vulnerability from Mrs. Kent: "The tortured soul was—at last—off the rack" (230). Always underpinning the conventional romantic plot twists throughout these final chapters of *Emily's Quest* are psychological observations about Emily's emotional growth and her understanding that freedom is achieved not by isolation and alienation from meaningful connection and interconnectedness but only by risking rejection and hurt and allowing Teddy into her place of belonging: "Teddy has always belonged to me and I to him. Heart, soul, and body," Emily says to her family at the end of *Emily's Quest* in the face of accusations of being "indecent," "sly," and second-best, that is, of taking "Ilse's leavings" (268). "There are always boundaries. Even in the wilderness," Brown captions a section of *Braving the Wilderness*. "Maintaining the courage to stand alone when necessary in the midst of family or community or angry strangers feels like an untamed wilderness" (70).

EPILOGUE: "THE WORLD WAS ALL BEFORE THEM" (MILTON, *PARADISE LOST* 12.646)

One hundred years separate the writing and publication of the Emily trilogy and Brené Brown's research and influential books, podcasts, lectures, and training seminars, in which she is always the storyteller: "I am a storyteller. I'm a qualitative researcher. I collect stories; that's what I do. And maybe stories are just data with a soul.... I'm a research-storyteller" ("Power"). The crucial steps that the adult Emily and Teddy take to avoid a similar fate as Ilse's, Perry's, and Mrs. Kent's are seminal ideas not only for Brown but also for current popular-culture movements that profile storytelling and scripting one's own narratives, from the plethora of self-love and mindfulness books (different from the earlier craze of self-help manuals)[6] to Louise Penny's hugely popular Three Pines mystery novels and Netflix's award-winning *Queer Eye*. Unlike the final decades of the twentieth and first decade of the twenty-first centuries when, as Will Storr argues in *Selfie*, "the self-esteem craze arrived" into a "manic phase of individualism" (183), these recent cultural products deploy individual personalized stories as opportunities to revisit perennial considerations of shame and fear, imperfection and authenticity, hurt and vulnerability, boundaries and connection, as integral to understanding and attaining interconnectedness.[7]

Storr cites a 2010 study titled "Fitting In or Standing Out" that argues how beginning in 1983 "a sharp increase in noncommon names that would only become more pronounced in the 1990s and 2000s" demonstrates parents "seeking unique names because they wanted their child to 'stand out and be a star'" (183). The star power of Montgomery's characters, as with many participants Brown has interviewed for her research, is different because the "stars" recognize and embrace being part of a galaxy. When in the final scene Emily Starr and Teddy Kent stand separate yet together at the intersection of private disappointments and dreams and public life and service, their boundaries are no longer walls but a place of their shared humanity. With echoes of Estella (another "star") and Pip's reunion in the garden in Charles Dickens's (revised) ending of *Great Expectations*, which in turn echoes John Milton's description of a fallen Eve and Adam leaving the garden at the end of *Paradise Lost*, Emily and Teddy join other literary representations of those who have entered the wilderness by valuing their "perfectly imperfect"[8] humanity after regaining their self-respect and learning to love themselves and commit to their love of one another. "The wilderness demands this level of self-love and self-respect," observes Brown in response to Angelou's "I belong to myself" (*Braving* 150).

NOTES

1. In addition to the books and talks in the bibliography, Brown (Huffington Foundation Endowed Chair, University of Houston) has published, among others, *I Thought It Was Just Me (but It Isn't): Making the Journey from "What Will People Think?" to "I Am Enough"* (2007), *Daring Greatly: How the Courage to Be Vulnerable Transforms the Way We Live, Love, Parent, and Lead* (2012), and *Rising Strong: How the Ability to Reset Transforms the Way We Live, Love, Parent, and Lead* (2015).

2. Brown, *Braving* 5, 163. Brown quotes from Bill Moyers's "A Conversation with Maya Angelou," which aired on November 21, 1973, and is now archived in the Bill Moyers Journal Original Series. https://billmoyers.com/content/conversation-maya-angelou/.

3. One of the fullest discussions of Emily's flash is found in Brenton Dickieson's comparison of C. S. Lewis's *Sehnsucht* and Emily's flash. Focusing on the flash as a "dialectical, evasive, mercurial, almost fantastic experience of oneness with Eternal Beauty," for both Emily and Montgomery, Dickieson argues that it is "an integrated view of the literary, the vocational, the natural, and the spiritual," especially by "provid[ing] deep sight for everyday life in the vocation of a writer" (153). For more on this point, see Jessica Lim's chapter in this collection.

4. It is interesting to note that when Brown mentions "innovation, creativity, and change," it is with reference to the topics for which she has received the most requests to talk from the business sector. Much more could be said about entrepreneurial Perry and current leadership practices in the context of Brown's "grounded confidence" as discussed in *Atlas of the Heart* (254–66), a fuller discussion than she originally developed in *Dare to Lead*, particularly when considered in the light of Bode's argument that Perry's

fearlessness situates him among "literary models of the self-made boys of the dime novels, especially the rags-to-riches boy heroes that Horatio Alger created, starting with Ragged Dick in 1868" (81).

5. For Montgomery, "the real tragedy of Joan, and of Mankind," as conveyed through her "second martyrdom" in the epilogue of George Bernard Shaw's play, is summed up in a letter to the editor preserved in Montgomery's *Black Scrapbook*: "Our saints ... must be kept on pedestals and in stain-glass windows, to be worshipped but not be met with." For a contextualization of this clipping, its application to the "isolating lionization" that Montgomery herself experienced as a celebrated writer, and her identification with Joan, see Clement, "Toronto's Cultural Scene" 254–60 (quotations from 256).

6. Brown distinguishes her own work from self-help manuals with their "quick and dirty 'how-to' list for happiness" because her research is focused on analyzing what interferes with "liv[ing] a joyful, connected, and meaningful life" (*Gifts* 35). The celebritization and "neoliberal" agenda of self-help manuals have been criticized for holding the individual rather than social, political, and economic institutions accountable—even to blame—for problems and solving those problems, including Heidi Marie Rimke's "Governing Citizens through Self-Help Literature" and "Self-Help, Therapeutic Industries, and Neoliberalism." While Rimke mentions Brown, who has reached "self-help guru status" because she is "supported and promoted by corporate powerhouses" ("Self-Help" 46), others take a more considered, less antagonistic approach to how Brown, as a "public intellectual," produces data different from the self-help trend, noting the importance of reaching a wide audience that information technology, social media, and storytelling afford (Ream et al.) and the value that Brown's social work background and qualitative research and bibliotherapy in general have (Haslam).

7. These considerations distinguish the emphases of Brown, Penny, and *Queer Eye* from the proliferation of quick-fix self-help manuals, one of the outcomes of the "self-esteem" movement of the 1980s and 1990s that greatly influenced pedagogical policies and practices (as argued by Storr in *Selfie*, chapters 5 and 6). Reviews repeatedly note these themes in Penny's (to date) eighteen Three Pines novels as well as in the spy thriller she coauthored with Hillary Rodham Clinton, *State of Terror* (2021). In the same fashion as the five *Queer Eye* hosts' insistence that they can expect their "heroes" to be vulnerable and grow only if they themselves are candid about their own stories of addiction, family tensions, body-shaming, bullying, homophobia, racism, and so on, Penny has been open about details of her life such as past struggles with alcohol and with grief when her husband died of dementia and about how she "own[s] [her] insecurities" through reflecting them in the recurring character of Clara ("Annotated Three Pines").

8. The phrase "perfectly imperfect," a buzzword in current popular culture, is used in the promotional material for Brown's *Gifts of Imperfection*. While this idea runs throughout all her books, she discusses it most fully in the chapter "Cultivating Self-Compassion: Letting Go of Perfectionism," in which she cites a line from Leonard Cohen's song "Anthem": "There is a crack in everything. That's how the light gets in" (*Gifts* 61). Cohen's metaphor is central to the themes of Penny's Three Pine series and even becomes the title of the ninth book, *How the Light Gets In* (2013).

WORKS CITED

Bode, Rita. "Vulnerable Situations: Boys and Boyhood in the *Emily* Books." *Children and Childhoods in L. M. Montgomery: Continuing Conversations*, edited by Rita Bode, Lesley D. Clement, E. Holly Pike, and Margaret Steffler, McGill-Queen's UP, 2022, pp. 68–90.

Brown, Brené. *Atlas of the Heart: Mapping Meaningful Connection and the Language of Human Experience*. Random House, 2021.

Brown, Brené. *Braving the Wilderness: The Quest for True Belonging and the Courage to Stand Alone*. Vermilion, 2017.

Brown, Brené. *Dare to Lead: Brave Work. Tough Conversations. Whole Hearts*. Random House, 2018.

Brown, Brené. *The Gifts of Imperfection: Let Go of Who You Think You're Supposed to Be and Embrace Who You Are*. Hazelden, 2010.

Brown, Brené. "Listening to Shame." TED, March 2012. https://www.ted.com/talks/brene_brown_listening_to_shame?language=en.

Brown, Brené. "The Power of Vulnerability." TEDxHouston. 2010. https://www.ted.com/talks/brene_brown_the_power_of_vulnerability?language=en.

Chase, Richard. "The Meaning of Moby-Dick." *Melville: A Collection of Critical Essays*, edited by Richard Chase, Prentice-Hall, 1962, pp. 56–61.

Clement, Lesley D. "Toronto's Cultural Scene: Tonic or Toxin for a Sagged Soul?" *L. M. Montgomery's Rainbow Valleys: The Ontario Years, 1911–1942*, edited by Rita Bode and Lesley D. Clement, McGill-Queen's UP, 2015, pp. 238–60.

Clement, Lesley D. "Visual Culture, Storytelling, and Becoming Emily: An Illustrated Essay." *Journal of L. M. Montgomery Studies*, 2020. https://journaloflmmontgomerystudies.ca/vision-forum/becoming-emily-illustrated-essay.

Dickieson, Brenton. "C. S. Lewis's *Sehnsucht* and L. M. Montgomery's *Flash*: Vocation and the Numinous." *The Faithful Imagination: Papers from the 2018 Frances White Ewbank Colloquium on C. S. Lewis & Friends, Taylor University*, edited by Joe Ricke and Ashley Chu, Winged Lion Press, 2019, pp. 144–65.

Emerson, Ralph Waldo. "Heroism." *Essays, First Series*, 1841. https://www.gutenberg.org/files/2944/2944-h/2944-h.htm#link2H_4_0008.

Emerson, Ralph Waldo. "Self-Reliance." *Essays, First Series*, 1841. https://www.gutenberg.org/files/2944/2944-h/2944-h.htm#link2H_4_0002.

Haslam, Nick. "The Rise of Pop-Psychology: Can It Make Your Life Better, or Is It All Snake-Oil?" *The Conversation*, 3 May 2021. https://theconversation.com/the-rise-of-pop-psychology-can-it-make-your-life-better-or-is-it-all-snake-oil-158709.

Milton, John. *Paradise Lost*. *John Milton: Complete Poems and Major Prose*, edited by Merritt Y. Hughes, Odyssey, 1957, pp. 207–469.

Montgomery, L. M. *Emily Climbs*. 1925. Tundra, 2014.

Montgomery, L. M. *Emily of New Moon*. 1923. Tundra, 2014.

Montgomery, L. M. *Emily's Quest*. 1927. Tundra, 2014.

Penny, Louise. "The Annotated Three Pines—*A Trick of the Light*." St. Martin's Press, 2022. https://www.gamacheseries.com/the-annotated-three-pines-a-trick-of-the-light/.

Ream, Todd C., et al. "The Promise and Peril of the Public Intellectual." *Higher Education: Handbook of Theory and Research*, edited by Michael B. Paulsen and Laura W. Perna, vol. 34, 2019, pp. 241–90.

Rimke, Heidi Marie. "Governing Citizens through Self-Help Literature." *Cultural Studies*, vol. 14, no. 1, 2000, pp. 61–78.

Rimke, Heidi Marie. "Self-Help, Therapeutic Industries, and Neoliberalism." *The Routledge International Handbook of Global Therapeutic Cultures*, edited by Daniel Nehring et al., Routledge, 2020, pp. 37–50.

Shakespeare, William. *Hamlet*. *The Complete Works of William Shakespeare*, edited by David Bevington, updated 4th edition, Longman, 1997, pp. 1060–116.

Storr, Will. *Selfie: How We Became So Self-Obsessed and What It's Doing to Us*. Abrams, 2019.

Part Two

Emily's Things

Chapter 4

EVERYDAY OBJECTS

Material Culture in the Emily Trilogy

ALLISON McBAIN HUDSON

> Our lives are characterised by innumerable encounters with objects.
> —IAN WOODWARD

A flickering candle. A gingham sunbonnet. Diamond-patterned wallpaper. These are the sorts of physical details in fiction that readers often skim over, barely noticing, and that scholars dismiss as inconsequential or, at best, symbolic. But what if we focus our attention on these objects—the everyday things with which the characters constantly interact—and attend to their potential significance as material things? L. M. Montgomery's Emily trilogy is an ideal fictional world in which to conduct a study of objects in novels, rich as it is in such details. Montgomery's portrayal of the orphaned Emily Starr as a young woman and budding writer is brimming with commonplace but significant objects, and an examination of these objects through the lens of material culture studies reveals their various roles in this narrative and the potential for a new way of looking at children's literature in general. Rather than being symbolic or metaphorical, the objects in the Emily trilogy have functions *as objects* that are well worth examining, including (but not limited to) connecting characters, creating atmosphere, and most importantly, developing the protagonist's career.

Material culture studies as a means of studying literature is a relatively new and growing field. Most often used by archaeologists and anthropologists, material culture studies is, in the simplest terms, the study of physical, usually man-made, objects. It is the discipline used to examine cultures, past or present, through the objects they make and use. Recently, material culture has also been used as a lens through which we can examine literature, under the premise that fictional objects reveal as much about the characters and their culture within the narrative as their real-world counterparts reveal about the people and cultures who use them. Anthropologist Daniel Miller describes material culture studies as "an academic discipline whose specific area of study [is] artefacts, the object world created by humanity" and states that it is "becoming recognized as a vital contribution to half a dozen established disciplines, from archaeology to design" (2)—including literature. Miller goes on to say that "a more profound appreciation of things will lead to a more profound appreciation of persons" (6), and I believe that a more profound appreciation of the objects in such novels as Montgomery's will lead to a more profound appreciation of her characters—their development, relationships, and societies. In fact, Woodward goes so far as to say that "even the most commonplace object has the capacity to symbolise the deepest human anxieties and aspirations . . . people require objects to understand and perform aspects of selfhood, and to navigate the terrain of culture more broadly" (vi). As we shall see, the everyday objects with which Montgomery's Emily interacts indeed enable her to "perform acts of selfhood"—that is, to develop her individual identity as both a young woman and a writer.

A recent focus on the material in literary theory, in contrast to the postmodern emphasis on the discursive, has great potential for the study of children's literature in particular, as such literature is often rich in objects. Scholarship in this field is growing, with such works as Laura Oulanne's *Materiality in Modernist Short Fiction: Lived Things* (2021) demonstrating a focus on material objects in short stories and Jane Suzanne Carroll's *British Children's Literature and Material Culture: Commodities and Consumption 1850–1914* (2021) specifically focusing on children's literature. Carroll points out that "reading fictional objects does not always come easily . . . we have to practice giving our attention to objects in literary texts, to take note of their properties and qualities, to recognize their value among other elements of a narrative" (12). This practice can reveal much about a novel that might otherwise be overlooked, particularly in Montgomery's novels, which are full of everyday objects that she often describes in illuminating detail. Carroll states that

> fictional objects perform various functions: they can appear in texts as narrative devices, as metaphors or as external signs of a character's inner qualities. Descriptions of objects, especially richly ekphrastic descriptions, may lend a sensual, haptic quality to a narrative, or provide a sense of verisimilitude. . . . Narratives may also call the reader's

attention to a particular object . . . : this may be an object of exceptional material or symbolic value. (12)

In terms of Montgomery's Emily, material culture fulfils many of these roles and others, particularly regarding the protagonist's development as a young woman and as a writer. Montgomery is well known for her descriptions of the natural world, but in the Emily trilogy in particular, she describes even everyday household objects in a richly detailed way that helps the reader picture them clearly. Natural things abound in the trilogy, of course, but *Emily of New Moon*, of all Montgomery's novels, is the most grounded in everyday domestic objects, perhaps because of its close relationship to Montgomery's own development as a writer and young woman as described in her journals. Mary Rubio, for example, points out that the series is semi-autobiographical ("Subverting the Trite" 8). A close examination of certain physical objects in this trilogy, particularly as they relate to the development of the protagonist, provides a fresh new perspective on Montgomery's fiction and on children's literature in general.

CANDLES

One of the most prolific and significant objects in the trilogy despite their small size, candles are mentioned eighty-eight times. They are such common and quotidian items (in fiction of the preelectrification era) that they are easy to overlook, and Montgomery seems to mention them in passing as an item so common that they barely need description or explanation, but they have an important role in Emily's life, and their physical presence is worth noting.

In Emily's context of the early twentieth century, candles were still a common source of light, and they are a normal part of everyday life at New Moon. Mikkel Bille and Tim Flohr Sørensen speak of light in social terms, pointing out that "it is argued that light may be used as a tool for exercising social intimacy and inclusion, of shaping moral spaces and hospitality, and orchestrating movement, while working as a metaphor as well as a material agent in these social negotiations" (263)—and these "social negotiations" are also present in fiction. Although more modern lamps are becoming available, Aunt Elizabeth refuses to use any light but candles at New Moon (*New Moon* 16), and Emily eventually grows to appreciate this tradition, sensing the "social intimacy" and "hospitality" of their light. In keeping with her habit of personifying objects, Emily says that "you can be—friends—with candles.

I believe I like the candles best after all" (281). Emily's appreciation for them provides a rare moment of connection with Aunt Elizabeth, who responds, "You have some sense in you" (281).

Candles also provide atmosphere for Emily on her first night at New Moon, when she enjoys "the friendly gleams and flickers from the jolly hardwood fire in the open stove that mellowed the ghostly candlelight with something warm and rosy-golden" (54). Later, she and Perry enjoy working on school lessons by candlelight in the kitchen; she writes, "The light is very dim. It keeps us snuffing it [trimming the wick] all the time. It is great fun to snuff candles" (153). Then, when Emily is at high school, she describes a first-years' meeting at which the gas for the lights had been cut off and a box of candles is necessary. She writes that "we had such fun improvising candle holders that we got off to a good start, and somehow the candle-light was so much more friendly and inspiring than gas. We all seemed to be able to think of wittier things to say" (*Climbs* 160). These are minor incidents, but Montgomery weaves them into the narrative in such a seamless, natural manner that candles are portrayed as an essential element of Emily's life.

Candles are a very practical aspect of Emily's development as a writer, being her only source of light after sundown. Montgomery mentions Emily writing by candlelight many times throughout the trilogy. At the beginning of *Emily Climbs*, for example, Emily sits in her own room, "coiled on the ottoman before the fire, writing, by the light of two tall, white candles—which were the only approved means of illumination at New Moon" (1). Later in the same chapter, Emily thinks of an idea for a story and gets up to write it down, using a "half-burned candle, secreted there for just such an emergency" (14); the candlelight along with the freedom of her own room enable her to write a story that was "the best she had ever written." This use of an object is an ideal example of Woodward's "acts of selfhood"—Emily's use of a candle here enables her growth as a writer and as a somewhat rebellious individual. After her return from high school, Emily writes, "I think Aunt Elizabeth means to let me have a kerosene lamp to write by" (*Climbs* 324), hinting that Aunt Elizabeth at last accepts Emily's writing and is even willing to support her career by providing a better and more modern source of light.

Significantly, it is a candle on the mantelpiece that catches Emily's attention on her visit to the Disappointed House when she has a vision of Teddy and realizes that she loves him. Montgomery mentions the candle and its flame "like a tiny, impish star" (*Quest* 88) both before and after Emily's vision, bracketing the gothic intrusion with a flame that could be interpreted as a symbol of Emily's love for Teddy. Interestingly, despite the constant presence of candles throughout the rest of the trilogy, candles are only mentioned as decorations (and not lit) in the Disappointed House once during the period following Emily's injury when she does not write; the first lit candle she mentions is the one Emily notices above. Candles, then, could be seen as synonymous with both Emily's writing ambition and her relationship with fellow artist Teddy. The near-constant presence of candles in the trilogy echoes the near-constant presence of ambition and creativity in Emily's life, underscoring their significance to the narrative and to her development.

BOOKS

Although a book is primarily a means of conveying information, various forms of books are often present in Montgomery's fiction as objects with other purposes. E. Holly Pike points out that books "as material objects independent of consideration of their designed function . . . transmit and store meaning in other ways in the Emily novels, as fetishes, taboos, and archives" (2). Pike recognizes the various roles of books in the trilogy when she states that "Emily's sensory response to books is a response to the book as a thing—it is independent of the textual content—but it nevertheless constitutes an experience of books as conveyors of meaning or experience" (2). A look at the books in Emily's life demonstrates these purposes.

Journals

There are many examples of books as objects in this trilogy, the most significant being Emily's blank books. Emily's "account book" (*New Moon* 6) provides an early means of practicing the craft of writing as well as a channel for healing and emotional growth. When she is shamed by the Murrays after listening to their conversation about which of them should adopt Emily, for example, she "forgot about the Murrays although she was writing about them—she forgot her humiliation—although she was describing what had happened" (41). Montgomery focuses on the fact that "in the writing, pain and humiliation had passed away" (42), pointing to the importance of writing for Emily's well-being. The account book's significance to Emily is particularly clear later, when she snatches it away from Aunt Elizabeth and burns it rather than let anyone else read it (47). The fact that the account book is a physical object is significant: rather than simply thinking her thoughts, Emily can write them down, making them both more "real" (tangible and physical) and more permanent (less forgettable). Ironically, this physicality also creates vulnerability—to unsafe eyes such as Aunt Elizabeth's, and to Emily's own hasty decision to burn it.

After this loss, Emily longs for some way to write down her thoughts, but paper, according to Cousin Jimmy, "is scarce at New Moon. Elizabeth has some pet economies and writing paper of any kind is one of them" (*New Moon* 67). Aunt Elizabeth's tyranny is subverted by Aunt Laura, however, when the latter finds "a big, flat bundle of dusty paper—paper of a deep pink color in oddly long and narrow sheets" that she plans to burn (92). Emily is desperate to have these "letter bills" because "they have such lovely blank backs for writing on," and Aunt Laura lets her have them and warns her not to let Aunt Elizabeth see them (92). This paper renews Emily's ability to write, in the form of letters to her father. The physical act of writing to him "seemed to bring him so near" (94), an example of an object facilitating connection—but, again, the material presence of the letters leaves them vulnerable to discovery. Indeed, Aunt Elizabeth finds these letters later, and as Kate Lawson points out, "Emily's connection to a fantasy version of her father is broken late in the first novel when Aunt Elizabeth reads Emily's 'letters' to him and thus destroys her sense of closeness to him" ("'Disappointed' House" 75). This becomes a positive development for Emily with Aunt Elizabeth, however, because it initiates a crisis that ends in a healthier relationship. In fact, Emily discovers that "Aunt Elizabeth really had an affection for her; and it was wonderful what a difference this made" (*New Moon* 315).

Another important step in Emily's personal and career development is the birthday gift of a blank book from Cousin Jimmy (179). These blank books continue to provide writing material, and he sometimes gives them to her because he senses her need—"when the notion occurred to him that Emily probably wanted another 'blank book,' that blank book materialised straightaway" (*Climbs* 2)—and sometimes to mark milestones in her career (*Quest* 15). The books, like the account book and letter bills, provide a way for Emily to materialize her thoughts, lending them permanence and giving Emily the ability to look back on her writing and learn from it—an important opportunity for growth in her writing ability, and providing another good example of Woodward's "acts of selfhood." As gifts from Cousin Jimmy, the blank books also signify the supportive, empathetic relationship he has with Emily, which is as encouraging and helpful for Emily as the books themselves.

Emily keeps these books private but sometimes allows her teacher, Mr. Carpenter, and her friend Dean Priest to read what she has written, leading to both constructive and destructive criticism. During their initial friendship, Dean is "a companion who could fully sympathize" (*New Moon*

272), and Emily is happy to show him the things she has written because he "read them gravely, and, exactly as Father had done, made little criticisms that did not hurt her because she knew they were just" (273). Later, however, Dean reads her first novel and lies to her about its worth because of his jealousy, and his unjust criticism leads to devastating consequences, as will be discussed later. Mr. Carpenter, on the other hand, is a healthy critic (truthful and just), and allowing him access to the Jimmy-books only leads to the development of her skills. He is somewhat harsh, not shying away from telling Emily about the work that needs improvement, and when he reads her work, she describes it is a "very terrible experience" (331). Mr. Carpenter is equally encouraging, however, exclaiming, "By gad, it's literature—*literature*—and you're only thirteen" (337). Montgomery dedicates several pages to Mr. Carpenter's specific criticism of Emily's poems and character sketches (when Emily mistakenly gives him her Jimmy-book that contains descriptions of local people, including himself). The significance of these books to the development of Emily's burgeoning career is unmistakable, and Mr. Carpenter's criticism and encouragement lead Emily to decide to write a diary, which replaces the letters to her father and represents the next step in the development of her craft.

Another important aspect of the Jimmy-books for Emily, that of a "vent," is revealed at the beginning of the second novel. Montgomery writes,

> Sometimes Emily felt that if it were not for her diary she would have flown into little bits by reason of consuming her own smoke. The fat, black "Jimmy-book" seemed to her like a personal friend and a safe confidant for certain matters which burned for expression and yet were too combustible to be trusted to the ears of any living being. (*Climbs* 2)

The process of writing out her feelings in physical form gives Emily a way to externalize emotions such as frustration, grief, anger, and joy in a safe, private manner. There is always, of course, the danger of the diary being destroyed or seen because it is physical, but this danger is outweighed by the benefits to Emily. Enclosing her emotions in this (mostly) safe way is a healthy and essential practice, echoed by Montgomery herself in her own journal entry of February 11, 1910: "I could not live without my journal now. Temperaments such as mine *must* have some outlet, else they become morbid and poisoned by 'consuming their own smoke.' And the only *safe* outlet is in some such record as this" (*Selected Journals II* 1). Helen Buss points out, regarding certain journal entries about Montgomery's romantic relationships, that it is not only her temperament that requires this vent: "A 'writing out' indeed occurs in these six entries, not just the writing out of emotions to relieve the pressure of her powerless place in patriarchy, but also her writing herself out of an imprisoning ideology by which femaleness and creative writing are mutually exclusive categories" (90). Emily, of course, struggles with the patriarchy as represented by such characters as Aunt Elizabeth and Dean Priest, who attempt to block Emily's attempts at writing in various ways.[1]

Emily uses her journal to "write out" negative experiences, such as overhearing two women discuss her shortcomings while she hides in a closet, and feel "clean" again, as writing enables her to take "a less distorted view of it and summoned philosophy to her aid" (*Climbs* 69). Having done so, Emily says, "Now that I've written it all out I feel differently about it" (76). Simply thinking about what happened would not suffice, and the physical existence of the blank book enables Emily to use the experience, both at that time and any time in the future, to learn about herself and grow. She also uses her Jimmy-book to console herself after her rival Evelyn Blake had a poem published and writes that she "got so much fun out of it that I didn't feel sore and humiliated any more" (110).

Montgomery also uses the fictional blank books as a narrative device. Several chapters of this novel contain "extracts" from this diary and often demonstrate the growth that Emily experiences, both personally and in her writing. For example, she writes that Mr. Carpenter has told her to stop using so many italics (3), and she continues to note her tendency to use them for emphasis and finally comments when she seems to have learned to do without them (161). (Additionally, the italics would not exist except as a function of Emily's physical writing, so this is an apt example of the significance of writing as a physical act.) Montgomery interjects as Emily's "biographer" and mentions the value of the journal as a means of portraying "a proper understanding of her personality and environment" that "gives a better interpretation of her and of her imaginative and introspective mind" than a biographer could (15). Emily uses her journal to muse about her skill and ambition (10), discuss her strengths and weaknesses, chronicle her writing successes and failings (such as her poems being accepted or rejected by publishers), and express herself, and as such, her Jimmy-books are one of the most significant objects in the trilogy in terms of both personal and professional growth.

One particular chapter of *Emily Climbs* often refers to the blank books in which Emily writes and forms a significant step forward in her character development: the incident in which she is locked in the church at night with Mr. Morrison and "passed from childhood to girlhood" (37). First, Emily mentally describes the people around her during the evening church service and finds a bit of paper to write down an idea for a story (40), and plans to write her descriptions in her Jimmy-book the next day (42). Then, Emily must go back to retrieve the paper on which she had been writing, leading to her being left behind and locked in. During the terror of being trapped with a "madman" hunting for her in the darkness, she manages to think, "What a chapter for her diary—or her Jimmy-book—and beyond it, for that novel she would write some day!" (48). She even falls asleep afterward thinking of writing about the incident in her diary (59). The trauma of this experience, along with the sweetness of her time with Teddy at the end of it, is a major milestone in Emily's young life, and it is enabled entirely by physical objects.

Later, Emily uses the journal to summarize what she has learned during her years at high school (323), and the Jimmy-books continue to mark steps in her career: at the beginning of the third novel, Emily writes that "every time I pass a new milestone on the Alpine path Cousin Jimmy celebrates by giving me a new Jimmy-book" (*Quest* 15). She then finds "a pile of old Jimmy-books" and rediscovers her idea for a novel, *A Seller of Dreams*, and decides to write it out (47). The physical presence of Emily's past ideas enables her to remember and develop these ideas into a potentially successful novel—although, as we will see, the manuscript's physicality makes it vulnerable to destruction.

Novels

Emily, who has been raised by her father to believe that books should be freely available, is surprised when Aunt Elizabeth rebukes her for looking in the New Moon bookcase (*New Moon* 54). Emily is then allowed to read some of the books, such as "'a history of the reformation in France' and 'a little fat book deskribing [*sic*] the months in England'" (99), but wonders how she will learn to write novels because Aunt Elizabeth will not let her read them. Emily then tries to read the books in the bookcase at Dr. Burnley's house, but when the puritanical Aunt Elizabeth finds out, she tells him to keep his bookcase locked and says to Emily, "You know that I have forbidden you to read novels, Emily Starr. They are wicked books and have ruined many souls" (*New Moon* 224). Montgomery even mentions specific novels that Emily had managed to read before this: Ann Radcliffe's *The Mysteries of Udolpho* (1794) and *The Romance of the Forest* (1791), which had the effect of making her feel "like one of the heroines in a Gothic romance, wandering at midnight through a subterranean dungeon, with some unholy guide" at her great-aunt Nancy's strange house (*New Moon* 238).

Such experiences with books as forbidden objects, despite Aunt Elizabeth's religious strictness, help to shape Emily's tastes and writing style. In fact, the forbidden nature of the books can be seen to represent Aunt Elizabeth's (rather Victorian) attempt at preserving Emily's innocence; as G. A. Woods notes,

> Montgomery seems to indicate that everything will be fine as long as the patriarchal structure is preserved. Moreover, there is a strong hint that there would have been no traumatic experience had Emily not somehow transgressed the norms of female behaviour within the patriarchy. This transgression has very much to do with the heroine's own identity as a developing writer ... there is a sense of prohibition (on the part of Aunt Elizabeth, alias the 'phallic mother' and representative of the patriarchal order) associated with inscribing one's own feelings in one's own discourse. (148)

Emily subverts Aunt Elizabeth's authority, and therefore the patriarchy, by borrowing books from Dean (*Climbs* 29) and by reading Washington Irving's *Tales of the Alhambra* (1832) with him. One of the books that Dean lends Emily is, he claims, a mistake, and Emily recognizes it as unsuitable, "just like a pig-sty"; Montgomery is clearly hinting here at a novel with sexual content that threatens Emily's naivete. Despite Aunt Elizabeth's attempts to guard her innocence, reading this book makes Emily feel "as if my hands were soiled somehow and I couldn't wash them clean" (30). Although Emily regrets reading it, this novel undoubtedly affects her personal growth (robbing her of some childhood innocence) and, by extension, her development as a writer.

Aunt Elizabeth finally gives Emily her father's books on her fourteenth birthday, which contributes to her education and provides a connection to him that she had been lacking (32). She later writes that while reading these books, she feels "beautifully near to Father ... as if I might suddenly look over my shoulder and see him. And so often I come across his pencilled notes on the margin and they seem like a message from him" (220)—pointing to marginalia as another physical aspect of books, one that fosters connection.

Books and magazines help Emily during her visits to the "Booke Shoppe" in Shrewsbury, "where the aroma of books and new magazines was as the savour of sweet incense in her nostrils" (115). This is one of several examples of Emily responding to books in a multisensory manner; the mention of the aroma demonstrates her regard for them as objects with qualities and purposes other than that for which they were originally designed. As previously mentioned, Pike suggests the idea that books have a fetish value to both Emily and Montgomery, which she defines as "a function outside of or beyond their object status" (3). Books for Emily perform both their intended function, the transmission of writing, and secondary functions for which they were not originally designed. Emily looks at the items that she cannot afford to buy "to learn what kind of stuff they published," using them for career advancement. A magazine then becomes a repository for Emily's first published poem, which was "the first sweet bubble on the cup of success" (*Climbs* 131), a major milestone. These experiences reflect Montgomery's own, as evidenced by her journal entry (*Selected Journals I* 260), and she writes of the experience of seeing her poem in physical form: "The moment we see our first darling brain child arrayed in black type is never to be forgotten" (261).

The book as a physical object is, of course, vulnerable to destruction, and Emily's first novel, *A Seller of Dreams*, is the prime example of this vulnerability. When Emily asks Dean for his opinion of this novel after it has been rejected by publishers, he lies and tells her it is "only cobwebs" (51) because he is jealous of the time her writing career takes from her attention to him. Emily is distraught and burns the sole manuscript, but later, Dean tells her the truth, saying that "it is a good piece of work—very good.... It is out of the ordinary both in conception and development" (97). Emily, having just broken her engagement to Dean, feels that at last "the balance hung level between them" (97), so the book, even when destroyed, represents Emily's freedom and confidence in her ability to write—and another of Woodward's "acts of selfhood." This episode echoes the one in which Emily burns her "account book," which she misses "next to her father" (*New Moon* 89); she strongly regrets burning her novel ("But oh, for her unborn *Seller of Dreams!*" *Quest* 170). These examples of destruction are traumatic for Emily but also enable her development, both personal and professional, even if only by making her realize the value of her own work.

Significantly, Emily manages to save some of her poems from being burned when her unsympathetic teacher, Miss Brownell, tries to punish her by throwing them in the school stove (*New Moon* 166). As she matures, however, she chooses to burn much of her old writing: "This sort of thing was happening frequently now. Every time she read her little hoard of manuscripts over she found some of which the fairy gold had unaccountably turned to withered leaves, fit only for the burning. Emily burned them,—but it hurt her a little. Outgrowing things we love is never a pleasant process" (303). This evidence of painful but healthy creative growth is one of the most obvious and significant aspects of the trilogy, and it is made possible by the physical presence of Emily's writing and of the fire that burns it. Near the end of the first novel, Emily is mature enough to decide what is worth keeping:

"much of her 'old stuff' she burned.... But the little pile of manuscripts in the mantel cupboard of the lookout was growing steadily larger" (315).

Later, she writes another, though very different, novel, *The Moral of the Rose*, to amuse Aunt Elizabeth while she recovers from a broken leg (*Quest* 145), and its publication marks another big step in her career: "It was a proud, wonderful, thrilling moment. The crest of the Alpine Path at last?" (170). It also creates great excitement for her family at New Moon, with Cousin Jimmy saying that he liked it more every time he read it and Aunt Elizabeth saying, "I never could have believed that a pack of lies could sound as much like the real truth as that book does" (182). This novel's main function in the narrative is to signify Emily's career success, but its physical form also acts as a marker of pride in Emily as a Murray to outsiders: Aunt Elizabeth leaves the book "on the parlour table" when she sees visitors arriving and is annoyed when they fail to notice it (171).

ROOMS

As physically defined spaces within houses, rooms are particularly important for Emily. Most of her time is spent at New Moon, but there are also spaces within other houses, including Aunt Ruth's house in Shrewsbury and the "Disappointed House," that provide significant opportunities for growth and self-determination.

When she first arrives at New Moon, Emily has to sleep in Aunt Elizabeth's bedroom, so she has no private space. She discovers the garret and uses it for writing and storing her work away from prying eyes; Montgomery describes this space as "the quiet corner of the dormer window, where shadows always moved about, softly and swingingly, and beautiful mosaics patterned the bare floor" (*New Moon* 93). She hides her letters to her father in "an old, worn-out sofa in a far corner" because it was "a lovely hiding-place for secret documents" (94). Once Emily has lived at New Moon for a while, however, Aunt Elizabeth decides to give Emily the "lookout" room, which had belonged to Emily's mother. She immediately begins to use this room to write in: "her own dear lookout was the best place for that" (316), and this is the most significant aspect of the room. Montgomery begins to fully develop the space as Emily's haven at the beginning of the second novel, when she describes Emily as being "as perfectly happy as any human being is ever permitted to be" (*Climbs* 1) and states that she is writing in her diary, a "dominant factor in her young, vivid life" (2). She enjoys the freedom of being able to get out of bed to write a story (14), and this freedom is particularly important as her need to write is neither encouraged nor understood by her aunts. Lawson writes that "her aunts disapprove of her writing. A room of her own becomes important to Emily not just because she needs to write but because being allotted her mother's room acknowledges her identity as a Murray" ("Victorian" 155).

Rebecca Thompson points out that "of all the spaces in New Moon, the lookout room is the most freeing and the most influential.... By having a room of her own and material objects that connect her to her matriarchal line, Emily is able to write and create and, eventually, earn money, which allows her to be even more independent" (159). The lookout room is clearly vital to Emily's creativity, and when Dean unfairly criticizes Emily's first novel, she burns it in the lookout room's fireplace, flees in despair, and is badly injured—for months unable to climb the stairs to access her own room and writing space, even losing the ambition to write. Scholars have pointed out the significance of this inability to access her writing space; Thompson, for example, states that "when she falls under the patriarchal control of Dean, Emily also loses the matriarchal haven and protection of her room. It is not until she rejects Dean ... that both the lookout and her writing come back into focus" (160). She goes on to point out that "after breaking free from Dean, the lookout again offers Emily the space to channel her energies into writing" (161), which leads to her writing another novel, her first published one.

Aunt Ruth's House

After enjoying the freedom and beauty of her own room at New Moon, Emily encounters a very different sort of room when she arrives at Aunt Ruth's house, where she boards during her three years at high school. Montgomery describes the house as "a very ugly house" (*Climbs* 94) and Emily's bedroom as "such an ugly one" that she "hated at sight," with ugly furnishings and decoration and a door that does not shut tight, resulting in a lack of privacy (96). Emily is as homesick for New Moon as she was for her father's house on her first night in New Moon, and again, her only saving grace is the view outside the window. Emily later writes that she will "never like Aunt Ruth's house. It has a disagreeable personality" (101)—reflecting Aunt Ruth herself. She goes on to say that her room "hasn't improved on acquaintance" and that she feels "like a little fly under a microscope" under Aunt Ruth's constant scrutiny and criticism (103). Despite, or perhaps because of, these challenges created by the physical aspects of the house, Emily grows in skill and character, writing after three years that she is "oddly sorry to leave this little room I've never liked and that has never liked me" (324). She discusses the things she has learned that will help her career, including using fewer italics, learning to smile over a rejection slip, and gaining "a bit of bitter, worldly wisdom" (323).

Montgomery significantly does not name Aunt Ruth's house; as a negative domestic space, she may have felt that it does not deserve a name as so many of her positive houses (Green Gables, Silver Bush, New Moon) do. As a physical object, the house creates as much difficulty for Emily as its owner and is therefore aptly called only "Aunt Ruth's house."

The Disappointed House

When Emily first arrives at New Moon, she is fascinated by a nearby unfinished building that she calls the "Disappointed House." This house holds both personal and career significance for Emily throughout the trilogy. She writes, "When I grow up and write a great novel and make lots of money, I will buy the Disappointed House and finish it" (*New Moon* 213). The physical existence of this house provides Emily with a target toward which she can direct her ambition; Thompson writes that "in one of her first concrete statements of ambition, Emily claims the house" (162). Years later, when Emily is engaged to Dean and he buys the house for them, his "oppression of her creative spirit is echoed by Dean's attempted control of the physical space of the Disappointed House as he condescendingly allots Emily a mere 'corner between the windows' for her writing desk" (163). Through one of Montgomery's gothic intrusions, the Disappointed House becomes an important link between Emily and Teddy, and the vision she experiences that saves Teddy's life makes her realize how deep their connection is and that she cannot possibly marry Dean. Later, when she is finally engaged to Teddy, Dean gives her the deed to the Disappointed House and its contents. Thompson points out that Emily becomes "a landowner, a house owner, and a successful author, who has ... chosen to be joined with a fellow artist who has always encouraged her artistic pursuits" (168). She states that the "eventual and complete appropriation of the Disappointed House tips the argument toward her artistic freedom" (162).[2]

An important object within the Disappointed House is its fireplace. Not long after her discovery of the house, Emily writes that she and Teddy broke into it, lit a fire in the fireplace, and talked, deciding to buy the house when they are older and live there. Significantly, Emily says that "Teddy will paint pictures and I will write poetry" (*New Moon* 288), foreshadowing their future marriage as artistic equals and the possibility that Emily will be able to continue her career. This fireplace continues to symbolize Emily and Teddy's troubled relationship; she mentions the fire and their plans in her diary several years later, after Teddy has gone away to art school, lamenting that "Teddy has forgotten all about that childish nonsense" (*Quest* 17). Then, when Dean buys the Disappointed House for himself and Emily, they visit it and Emily is upset by the sight of the ashes of the old fire, telling Dean that "the ghosts of things that never happened are worse than the ghosts of things that did" (74). They later light a new fire, which could symbolize Emily's new start with Dean, but Emily cannot help thinking of Teddy while they sit there. Dean, due to his possessive and jealous nature, does not allow Emily to grow as an artist in the same way that Teddy would, so it is fitting that Emily thinks of Teddy at the fireplace.

The physical domestic spaces in which Emily lives and writes are therefore a significant agent in Emily's development. Thompson points out that "Emily's growth is reflected in the rooms and houses with which she comes in contact, and they ultimately help her to mature as both an artist and a woman" (169). Emily's very identity is shaped by these rooms as they enable her to develop her craft and, indeed, her personality.

CONCLUSION

A close reading of Montgomery's work, particularly her Emily trilogy, reveals the major roles that she assigns to everyday objects. Items that aid in Emily's personal and career development, including books, rooms, and candles but many more besides, are discussed in vivid detail and are vital to the trilogy for far more than symbolic reasons. This trilogy provides an ideal example of the significance of material culture studies to children's literature, and Montgomery's many uses for physical objects in her narrative point to a fresh perspective on the genre. If, like Woodward states, "our lives are characterized by innumerable encounters with objects" (vi), characters such as Emily are equally defined by the objects they encounter and with which they interact, and these objects enable them to perform "acts of selfhood," becoming the individuals that their authors wish them to be.

NOTES

1. See Kate Lawson's article "Adolescence and the Trauma of Maternal Inheritance in L. M. Montgomery's *Emily of New Moon*," *Canadian Children's Literature / Littérature canadienne pour la jeunesse*, no. 94, 1999, for a thorough discussion of female patriarchal figures such as Aunt Elizabeth.

2. For more on this point, please see Jessica Wen Hui Lim's chapter in this collection.

WORKS CITED

Bille, Mikkel, and Tim Flohr Sørensen. "An Anthropology of Luminosity: The Agency of Light." *Journal of Material Culture*, vol. 12, no. 3, 2007, pp. 263–84.

Buss, Helen M. "Decoding L. M. Montgomery's Journals/Encoding a Critical Practice for Women's Private Literature." *Essays on Canadian Writing*, no. 54, Winter 1994, pp. 80–100.

Carroll, Jane Suzanne. "Introduction." *British Children's Literature and Material Culture: Commodities and Consumption 1850–1914.* Bloomsbury Academic, 2021, pp. 1–19.

Lawson, Kate. "The 'Disappointed' House: Trance, Loss, and the Uncanny in L. M. Montgomery's Emily Trilogy." *Children's Literature*, vol. 29, 2001, pp. 71–90.

Lawson, Kate. "The Victorian Sickroom in L. M. Montgomery's *The Blue Castle* and *Emily's Quest*: Sentimental Fiction and the Selling of Dreams." *Lion and the Unicorn*, vol. 31, no. 3, 2007, p. 232–49.

Miller, Daniel. *Stuff.* Cambridge: Polity Press, 2010.

Montgomery, L. M. *Emily Climbs.* 1925. Bantam Books, 1983.

Montgomery, L. M. *Emily of New Moon.* 1923. Bantam Books, 1983.

Montgomery, L. M. *Emily's Quest.* 1927. Bantam Books, 1983.

Pike, E. Holly. "Reading the Book as Object and Thing in L. M. Montgomery's Emily Series." *Journal of L. M. Montgomery Studies: L. M. Montgomery & Reading*, December 2020, pp. 103–20.

Rubio, Mary. "Subverting the Trite: L. M. Montgomery's 'Room of Her Own.'" *Canadian Children's Literature / Littérature canadienne pour la jeunesse*, no. 65, 1992, pp. 6–39.

Rubio, Mary, and Elizabeth Waterston, eds. *The Selected Journals of L. M. Montgomery, Volume I: 1889–1910.* Oxford UP, 1985.

Rubio, Mary, and Elizabeth Waterston, eds. *The Selected Journals of L. M. Montgomery, Volume II: 1910–1921.* Oxford UP, 1987.

Thompson, Rebecca J. "'That House Belongs to Me': The Appropriation of Patriarchal Space in L. M. Montgomery's *Emily* Trilogy." *L. M. Montgomery and Gender*, edited by E. Holly Pike, and Laura M. Robinson. McGill-Queens UP, 2021, pp. 152–72.

Woods, G. A. "The (W)rite of Passage: From Childhood to Womanhood in Lucy Maud Montgomery's Emily Novels." *Gender and Narrativity*, edited by Barry Rutland. McGill-Queens UP, 1997, pp. 147–58.

Woodward, Ian. *Understanding Material Culture.* SAGE, 2007, p. vi.

Chapter 5

"SOMETHING INCALCULABLY PRECIOUS"

Diary Writing in *Emily of New Moon*

LINDSEY McMASTER

L. M. Montgomery's very first diary began when she was nine and "sewed four sheets of foolscap into a book and covered it with red paper. On the cover I wrote 'Maud Montgomery's Diry'" (*Selected Journals I* 281). Sadly, this little red volume no longer exists: "When I was about fourteen I burned all the 'note book' diaries I had kept—something I shall always regret having done. They were quaint little documents, as I remember them—quaint and naive and painfully truthful and sincere, whether I wrote of my own doings or of others. Poor little diaries, long ago ashes" (*Selected Journals I* 375). Though her thirty-six-year-old self looks back with regret for this painful loss, fourteen-year-old Maud was unrepentant on the day she burned it, saying the old diary "was so silly I was ashamed of it"; instead, she takes a renewed command as author, with the assured statement, "I am going to begin a new kind of diary" (*Selected Journals I* 1).

Emily of New Moon is structured between a twinned pair of conflicts over diaries threatened with fire. In the first dispute, throwing her "account books" on the fire is the only way Emily can save them from being read by Aunt Elizabeth, even though "she felt as if she had lost something incalculably precious" (57). But in the second confrontation, despite a bitter quarrel, the victory goes the other way, leaving Emily "mistress of the field," her writing carefully stowed in her room where it won't be disturbed again (377). Emily's life writing evolves through the course of the novel, moving steadily toward the center of two dramatic showdowns: the struggle of wills between Emily and Elizabeth, and the putting to rights of the collectively held misjudgment of Ilse's mother. Assuming command of her life writing was essential for the young Montgomery as it is essential for Emily; it is a quest for self-determination that confirms a newfound agency in her social world.

EMILY OF NEW MOON AS LIFE WRITING

For readers who give in to the irresistible urge to see Emily as Montgomery's fictive doppelgänger, *Emily of New Moon* provides clues to Montgomery's earliest beginnings as a writer, when she wrote the diary with the red cover and made use of discarded "letter bills" from a post office, exactly as Emily does (*Complete Journals I* 459). Diary and life writing in *Emily of New Moon* deserves our sustained attention as representing Montgomery's thinking on the nature of diary writing—a formative passion and practice in Montgomery's life and a generative interventionist medium, allowing for a degree of disruptive political commentary. Emily experiments with many kinds of diary writing as the novel unfolds;[1] of special interest in this chapter is the diary's potential as a space for social critique, at first privately for Emily alone, but ultimately with broader effect through Emily's solution of the years-long mystery surrounding Beatrice Burnley's death, which works to extinguish deep-seated misogyny in her community. Insofar as Emily's diary functions as a kind of detective's notebook, the efficacy of diary writing in the quest for social justice is prominent in the novel's representation of life writing. In essence, Emily's use of fictional strategies, realist observations, and detective work within the private parameters of her life writing contribute to a burgeoning and gradually emboldened social critique.

Montgomery's lifelong devotion to her own journaling confirms her deep involvement with the diary form, one she uses to creatively complicate the polyphonic narrative of *Emily of New Moon*. We know that in the years prior to composing the novel she recopied her early journals into larger uniform volumes, an ideal way to reflect on the nature and significance of childhood life writing. Though the Emily novels are a clear example of the Künstlerroman, charting Emily's development as a young artist climbing the "Alpine Path" of the writer, I read Emily's life writing as more than just a step on her vocational journey toward artistic success. It is also an exploration of the child writer's quest to achieve a sociopolitical agency, a fitting narrative given the book's creation story where Montgomery used her own childhood writings to produce a book that champions a girl's authorial voice.

In her 1981 address to Amnesty International, Margaret Atwood suggested that writers have a responsibility to use their gifts "not as a shelter from the world's realities but as a platform from which to speak" (396). Early in the novel, Emily finds shelter in the secrecy of her diary, but as she develops, her life writing matures into a platform for the working out of problems both personal and social. The last line of the novel asserts Emily's calling to become not just an author but specifically a public diarist: "I am going to write a diary, that it may be published when I die" (410). In life writing's many forms, Emily uses her impulse for social critique to traverse the continuum of public and private.

As Marlene Kadar points out, when we consider life writing, "we usually think immediately of autobiography, letters, diaries, and anthropological life narratives, genres in which the conventional expectation is that the author does not want to pretend he/she is absent from the text" (12): the author is front and center as the diarist. In fictional modes, by comparison, the author is not immanently present as the experiencing "I" of the text, so we don't think of fiction as life writing. But Kadar suggests that we may have placed those dividing lines too hastily. "Add to these original life-writing genres the fictionalized equivalents," she suggests, "including self-reflexive metafiction, and life writing becomes both the 'original genre' and a critical comment on it, and therefore the self-in-the-writing" (12).

As readers we know that Emily's life experiences and happy ending were not Montgomery's own, but when we read the journals we cannot help but see formative moments—like their mother's funeral, or the use of "letter bills" for their earliest writings—being shared between author and heroine, indicating a provisional suspension of fixed generic rules in Montgomery's body of work. "*New Moon*," she said when the novel was published, "is in some respects but not all my own old home and 'Emily's' inner life was my own, though outwardly most of the events and incidents were fictitious" (*Selected Journals III* 147). Life writing, says Kadar, "is best viewed as a continuum that spreads unevenly and in combined forms from the so-called least fictive narration to the most fictive" (10). Read this way, *Emily of New Moon* is one example of Montgomery's own life writing, her themes of empowerment through authorship exhibiting her use of life writing to engage a public world and readership. Emily similarly bends the barriers between life writing and fiction, realism and fantasy—with her more experimental modes triggered by feeling attacked, as I explore below.

EMILY THE DIARIST

Emily's earliest life writing is driven by close attention to the real world, an urge to "describe," and an incipient impulse to reject abuses of power that, as a child, she experiences all too regularly. Not all authors start out by recording their real-world environment. Jane Austen's notebooks from when she was eleven or twelve contain fiction and drama, crafted to be read aloud to family and friends and containing shared jokes for that audience. Virginia Woolf and her siblings collaborated on a humor-filled magazine containing jokes, riddles, advice, letters, poems, fiction, essays, and more.² But Emily's earliest writings reflect the real world. When her father is still alive, her attention gravitates to the benign world of nature. Struck by the "pinky-green lake of sky with a new moon in it," she feels a visceral need to transcribe the moment: "She must go home and write down a description of it in the yellow account book. . . . It would hurt her with its beauty until she wrote it down" (7–8). Her affinity for life writing also surfaces in the life story of her cat, "Mike's Biograffy" (8), which naturally engenders the sequel, "a biograffy of Saucy Sal" (122). Attention to the human world emerges with the arrival of the Murray clan: "In the back of her mind a design was forming of writing all about it in the old account book. It would be interesting. She could describe them all—she knew she could" (34). Quickly though, writing about the Murrays engenders something more than simple "description." After the excruciating family conclave where she is dragged from under the table, the act of writing becomes a salve for the hurts they inflict: "She forgot the Murrays although she was writing about them—she forgot her humiliation—although she was describing what had happened" (50).

Curiously though, when she records these and similar events, fact begins to morph into fiction. In the same entry describing the Murray conclave, for instance, "she had wound up by a pathetic description of her own deathbed, with the Murrays standing around imploring her forgiveness" (50). Charged by a strong sense of ill treatment, Emily uses writing to remodel reality, compelling her tormenters to regret their actions. The idea of the funeral had occurred to Emily earlier that day, when the Murrays claimed she would die young from consumption:

> "It would serve you all right if I *did* die and you suffered terrible remorse for it all the rest of your lives," Emily thought. Then in the pause that happened to follow, she dramatically pictured out her funeral, selected her pall-bearers, and tried to choose the hymn verse that she wanted engraved on her tombstone. (46)

Writing aesthetically pleasing death scenes to assuage an excess of anguish becomes a pattern for Emily, who later writes "a deskription of myself being drowned on a letter-bill" after being called a "little hussy" by Aunt Elizabeth (118). She also pens "an account of her death by poison, of Lofty John being tried for her murder and condemned to death, and of his being hanged on a gibbet as lofty as himself, Emily being present at the dreadful scene, in spite of the fact that she was dead by his act" (170). And she composes a letter about Miss Brownell's cruel mockery of her writing so that "if I die of consumption Aunt Elizabeth will find it and know the rites of it and mourn that she was so unjust to me" (214). This life writing with a vengeance underscores Montgomery's special interest in how writing can provide an emotional release while also clearly expressing a wished-for social justice of the kind systemically denied to children, especially girls. But to attain these outcomes, a few generic laws about fiction and nonfiction must be broken.

IMPROVISATIONAL FORMS

In the context of her work "Decoding L. M. Montgomery's Journals," Helen Buss describes the special qualities of the diary format:

> It is a revisionary, improvisational form in which a writer can practise her full range of literary conventions in manners not encouraged by public formats, and an "unconscious" can be constructed that the text shares, at least partially, with the writer, who can find in the private text a tenable, if secret, place to begin the subversion of her enslavement in ideology. L. M. Montgomery had great need of such a place. (11)

Montgomery imagines for Emily a subversive compulsion to break through generic norms that would restrict life writing to nonfiction, imbuing her with "revisionary, improvisational" methods—not to mention the text's further enthusiasm for Emily to write about gruesome deaths, executions, and funerals, subjects not likely to be deemed appropriate for a young girl's journal.

Indeed, where a conventional diary accepts an absence of narrative resolution—insofar as each day takes up the narrative again without knowing where events will lead—Emily bursts through this barrier, writing right through the fiction/nonfiction divide to a fully narrative closure: the tragic death scene peopled with repentant mourners. Her audacious disregard of generic norms arises specifically at traumatizing moments in her contretemps with the brutal tendencies of the outside world. With her dramatic funeral trope, Emily formulates a literary convention, in Buss's words, "not encouraged by public formats" and tailor made to "begin the subversion of her enslavement" (11).

Unshackling herself from the judgments and expectations of her social world (not to mention literary conventions) via elaborate death scenes is a writing activity best kept secret for Emily. The privacy of a diary is an enabling feature for the putative author, but such privacy can also be limiting, for the social critique contained therein cannot effect social reform if it remains locked in permanent secrecy. Emily's powers of social critique developed through life writing must ultimately traverse the continuum of public/private, a key journey that unfolds gradually.

If Emily's letters are a *crie de ceour*, a place for the grieving child to pour out her internal anguish, they are at the same time an outward-looking account of a world beset by unfairnesses large and small. Mary Henley Rubio confirms that "Montgomery said her diaries were 'grumble' books serving a specific function: expressing the unhappiness that she was conditioned as a woman to suppress" (58). The outward reason for unhappiness, after all, is often an exterior world systemically oppressive to women and girls. Attuning the feminism of *Emily of New Moon* to a 1920s popular audience, Montgomery deploys various means of indirection, Emily's diary being one of them. Consider this passage from Emily's early letters describing Ilse's father, Dr. Allan Burnley:

> He has big yellow eyes like Ilse and a loud voice and Rhoda says when he gets mad you can hear him yelling all over Blair Water. There is some mistery about Ilse's mother which I cannot fathum. Dr. Burnley and Ilse live alone. Rhoda says Dr. Burnley says he will have no devils of women in that house. That speech is wikked but striking. Old Mrs. Simms goes over and cooks dinner and supper for them and then vamooses and they get their own breakfast. The doctor sweeps out the house now and then and Ilse never does anything but run wild. The doctor never smiles so Rhoda says. (116)

As a writer whose raw material stems from close observation of reality, Emily senses potential in the "wikked but striking" features of the Burnley home, recording her impressions in a tone more curious than critical. But a matter-of-fact summary might be "Ilse's father is well-known for his angry outbursts and habitual derogatory comments about women, an attitude consistent in his home life where he neglects his only daughter, barely keeps the home habitable, and never smiles." Blair Water may be content to hush up the mystery of Ilse's missing parent and to ignore Dr. Burnley's festering rage, but Emily's diary begins to pay attention to social ills too long overlooked. All told, the home lives of children in Blair Water—Ilse, Teddy, Perry, and Emily—provide a seemingly endless supply of troubled homes, damaged guardians, and desolate semi-orphans. Outside the family, the children similarly meet with little empathy. Schoolteacher Miss Brownell gets this miniportrait:

> She is too sarkastik and she likes to make you rediklus. Then she laughs at you in a disagreable, snorting way. But I forgave her for slapping me and I took a boquet to her to school next day to make up. She receeved it very coldly and let it fade on her desk. In a story she would have wepped on my neck. I don't know whether it is any use forgiving people or not. (117)

While the children ultimately prevail and mend their fractured communities, an implicit critique remains of a society in which neglect and abuse are commonplace. Emily's letters filter these matters through a child's sense of puzzlement and unfairness, but they expose systemic wrongs and position diary writing as a wellspring of oppositional awareness.

THE DIARY AS DETECTIVE'S NOTEBOOK

Diaries make especially compulsive reading when you perceive things the diarist herself was unconscious of at the time of composition. "I suspect that people who like to read diaries—as I do," says Lynne Vallone, "are secretly voyeurs at heart, eavesdroppers and perhaps gossips who enjoy being 'in the know'" (166). Such moments encourage a form of "detective reading" for those paying close attention. In Montgomery's journals for example, when sixteen-year-old Maud is living in Saskatchewan in 1891, she is baffled by a series of overly frequent evening visits from her teacher, Mr. Mustard: "Whatever did he want to come here again to-night for, when he was here only Friday?" (*Complete Journals I* 60). And a month later, "Mr. Mustard was furious with me to-day because he caught me exchanging notes with Will. What *does* make him act so?" (61). She eventually realizes his intentions, a good deal later than we do (at least assuming we recall Mr. Phillips and Prissy Andrews in *Anne of Green Gables*). In a fictional diary, of course, the author can implement this kind of dramatic irony by design, and Montgomery does so with the mystery of Beatrice Burnley's unsolved disappearance.

In Blair Water, no one will talk about what happened to Ilse's mother, Beatrice. In gossip behind closed doors, her disappearance the same night her cousin went to sea has left her branded an adulteress. Given the community's eager embrace of this fallacy despite scanty evidence, the well-known fact that Dr. Burnley "hates women" (103) because of it, and the community's tolerance of his angry outbursts and child neglect, Beatrice Burnley's story is indicative of the community's unexamined misogyny, a social ill and miscarriage of justice Emily stands against from start to finish. Her ultimate victory imbues the novel with a pronounced feminist ethos.

Early on, the hush surrounding the matter draws Emily's attention—and ours if we want to solve the mystery. Her very first diary entry on the letter bills makes note of the "mistery" of Ilse's mother that she "cannot fathum" (116). Indeed, many twists and turns make solving the mystery a labyrinthine task—including a bull guarding the key location, and an unmentionable bull at that. "I said Ilse and I were afraid to go through Mr. James Lee's pasture where the old well was because he had a cross bull there," says Emily in her diary; "Aunt Elizabeth gave me an awful skolding and told me I was never to use *that word* again" (154). Thus banned from open discourse, James Lee's English bull takes up residence in the unconscious: "Emily sometimes had fearful dreams of being chased by him and being unable to move. And one sharp November day these dreams came true" (179). Despite her terror, Emily visits the bull's field to see the old Lee well, a site supposedly haunted by the ghost of Thomas Lee, murdered by his brother when they had just dug the well. Unsayable words, untimely death, disused wells, and prophetic dreams are all breadcrumbs Montgomery lays down as evidence for Emily and the attentive reader to sort through. Although new information is slow to surface, Emily's unconscious makes steady progress, as recorded in her diary:

> I do wish I could find out what Ilse's mother did. It worrys me after I go to bed. I lie awake for ever so long thinking about it. Ilse has no idea. Once she asked her father and he told her (in a *voice of thunder*) never to mention *that woman* to him again. And there is something else that worrys me too. I keep thinking of Silas Lee who killed his brother at the old well. How dreadful the poor man must have felt. (209–10)

In seemingly unplanned clusters of daily thoughts, mention of Ilse's mother is consistently (though seemingly haphazardly) paired with references to the Lee well—the site where Beatrice, as we learn much later, lost her life. More repression takes place as Emily gets closer to the solution: upon finally hearing the false report of Beatrice's alleged adultery and child abandonment, Emily finds herself unable to commit the story to words: "I have found out all about the mistery of Ilse's mother. It is so terrible I can't write it down even to you," she says; "I did not think there could be such terrible things in the world" (307). Yet unlike the rest of her community, who not only believe but, in Aunt Nancy's case, enjoy rehearsing the sordid tale, Emily rejects it: "I *know* Ilse's mother *couldn't* have done anything like that" (307). Unable to commit more to paper, Emily returns to it in her mind at key moments. Her cliffside fall spurs a telling comparison: "She would just disappear from the world as Ilse's mother had disappeared" (317). And without the diary as an outlet, her sleuthing migrates over to her fiction (though characteristically, fiction derived from real-world description): "The Ghost in the Well" is the final manuscript she wrestles with the day she succumbs to measles and the fever dream that shows Beatrice walking eagerly home, only to fall to her death on the one night the well was left uncovered.

Emily's vision of Beatrice is attributed to her "second sight," a power that will reemerge at key moments in the other novels. In *Emily Climbs*, her diary is the key to solving another mystery—this time a lifesaving one—when she wakes up to find a drawing evidently done in her sleep that miraculously reveals the location of a missing child. Moments like this that weave Emily's half-formed perceptions into her life writing and then imbue them with clairvoyance suggest the two abilities, writing and second sight, are a conjoined gift—essentially that writing is her superpower.[3]

Crucially, unravelling the mystery of Beatrice Burnley's death sets under way the needed push for social justice in Blair Water, where the false narrative of Beatrice's infidelity has for too long fueled misogyny in the community and neglect in the Burnley home. Emily's fever-driven directive to Elizabeth to search the well is the final and public result of months of conscious and unconscious detective work, and it confirms the importance of Emily's life writing in negotiating the public/private continuum of social critique. Despite resistance from Aunt Laura, who fears social disapproval, Elizabeth acts on Emily's directive, finally replacing Blair Water's gossip and conjecture with the facts that clear Beatrice's name. Together with Emily, the reader's own unraveling of the mystery effectively puts them through the steps of parsing the private and public of Emily's written world, her diary and fiction forming the lens for the reader's revisioning of Beatrice and her memory. With the truth made public, Dr. Burnley commits to a new version of fatherhood, Ilse finds herself properly cherished, and Emily is honored and credited for bringing it about. If Emily's life writing plays even a small role in this larger transformation, it is an important message about the revolutionary potential of the written word—even when penned in a girl's diary in the privacy of a garret window seat.

DIARY WRITERS AND NIGHTMARE READERS

The working through of the mystery takes place in the midst of Emily's triumphs and defeats as the adoptee of the Murray family. Emily's diary triggers the novel's dramatic showdown with Aunt Elizabeth, who is forced to see herself through the child's eyes when she discovers Emily's hidden stash of letters in the garret and reads their unflattering depiction of her. The ensuing conflict narrowly rescues the letters from the fire and leads to the novel's ultimate redistribution of power, placing Emily and Elizabeth on equal footing: "Elizabeth Murray had learned an important lesson—that there was not one law of fairness for children and another for grown-ups. She continued to be as autocratic as ever—but she did not do or say to Emily anything she would not have done or said to Laura had occasion called for it" (381).

Elizabeth finding Emily's letters invites further consideration of the intended reader for diaries. Scholarship by Lynn Z. Bloom and Elizabeth Podnieks among others has productively unraveled the diary's bifurcated mode of address: on the one hand, diaries pose as the most private of personal documents; on the other hand, as crafted textual products, diaries ultimately anticipate a reader and a public. Emily's early diaries at New Moon are intensely private and personal; as she matures, however, she adopts increasingly outward-looking practices, suggesting a burgeoning appetite for a wider readership. "Contrary to popular perception," says Bloom, "not all diaries are written—ultimately or exclusively—for private consumption" (23). There is a contrast, she explains, between the truly private diary and the private diary as public document, the latter being more common than we usually think, especially when the diarist is a career writer. Bloom's distinction between truly private diaries and diaries as public documents is helpful because it maps out the different intended readers a diary may have, where even a seemingly "private" diary may ultimately be intended for a public readership.

But I would add that diaries are unique documents in having not only a complex *intended* readership but also what we might call a nightmare reader: the one person who absolutely must not read it—Aunt Elizabeth being the prime example in Emily's case. Earlier in the novel, when Emily is forced to burn her account book, she thinks "she would never dare to write *anything* again, if Aunt Elizabeth must see everything" (57). Elizabeth opposes Emily's writing in all its forms, and crucially with respect to diaries, she absolutely rejects the notion of privacy: "Aunt Elizabeth thought she had a right to know everything that this pensioner on her bounty did, said, or thought. She read the letters and she found out what Emily thought of her" (374). Her verdict: "They are disgraceful letters—and must be destroyed" (376). Emily's response is testimony to the primacy of the diary in her quest for selfhood: "I'd sooner burn myself" (376).

The nightmare reader poses a real threat to the diarist and the survival of her writing. A similar confrontation unfolded in real life when famed diarist Samuel Pepys discovered that his wife Elizabeth's diary held passages about "the retiredness of her life and how unpleasant it was" (Pepys qtd. in Podnieks 49). As Podnieks describes the conflict, "Enraged by certain passages about their marriage which his wife read aloud to him, Pepys took it upon himself to destroy her diary. He recorded this brutal act within his own diary (unaware of the irony implicit in the fact that he, unlike his wife, still had a diary to turn to)" (48). Pausing on the idea of the nightmare reader is important because diary writers must often contend with this figure, a reader who takes personal offense to the text and embodies the world's hostility toward art and self-expression. It is especially threatening to writers in positions of subordination or dependence, like a wife in the seventeenth century or a child in the nineteenth. Diaries have always held a special place for women writers, whose admittance to more public literary forms has been fettered. In Mary McDonald-Rissanen's words, "the unpublished diary cumulatively reveals through its textual and thematic features the profound process involved in women finding their voice" (7). The nightmare reader epitomizes the barriers to this essential process. Emily's survival as a writer depends on her ability to confront and recover from nightmare readers—and all they represent about a society unsympathetic to women artists.[4]

THE WRITER'S RESPONSIBILITY

In the wake of the confrontation with Elizabeth, Emily's diary, written all along in the form of letters to her father, is saved from annihilation. Emily matures as a writer, but not without heavy losses. She commits to a set of revisions, not realizing what the effects will be:

> "I'll go over them all and put a star by anything I said about you and then I'll add an explanatory footnote saying that I was mistaken."
> Emily spent her spare time for several days putting in her "explanatory footnotes," and then her conscience had rest. But when she again tried to write a letter to her father she found that it no longer meant anything to her. The sense of reality—nearness—of close communion had gone. Perhaps she had been outgrowing it gradually, as childhood began to merge into girlhood—perhaps the bitter scene with Aunt

> Elizabeth had only shaken into dust something out of which the spirit had already departed. But, whatever the explanation, it was not possible to write such letters any more. She missed them terribly but she could not go back to them. A certain door of life was shut behind her and could not be reopened. (379–80)

When penned in secret, Emily's letters kept open a delicate strand of communication with her father, but imagining a public readership brings that connection all at once to an end. "Diaries that are public documents" says Bloom, "are sufficiently developed to be self-contained. Unlike truly private diaries, they form coherent, free-standing texts that are more or less self-explanatory if the entries are read in toto" (30). To illustrate, Bloom examines a passage of Anne Frank's diary both in its original form and after Frank revised it with postwar publication in mind. The second version is amended with brief introductions for named persons and aesthetic touches like changing "quiet as mice" to "quiet as baby mice" (30). Emily's shift toward self-conscious, public-oriented processes begins gradually, even earlier than the revisions for Aunt Elizabeth. Her first entries are endearing because of errors like how "aristokratik" her family is, considering they have a "sun dyal" (114), and in a purely private diary, spelling wouldn't matter. But gradually, the author's instinct for self-correction takes hold: "Do you notice how my spelling is improved?" she asks about two-thirds of the way through the novel; "I have thought of such a good plan. I write my letter first and then I look up all the words I'm not sure of and correct them" (254–55). As Cecily Devereux points out, "It is not simply the act of, or the intention for, publication that shifts the diary into the public sphere: it is the act of writing itself" (245). Emily's "explanatory footnotes" soften her criticism of Elizabeth—not silencing it, but intentionally guiding the anticipated reader's interpretation, forming the more "coherent, free-standing text" Bloom describes as the public diary. What began as a secret, spontaneous outpouring to a lost parent develops into the self-conscious, public-oriented practice of an author who not only corrects and edits but ultimately feels responsible to her readers.

Standing up to Elizabeth and rescuing the diary from oblivion proves Emily's readiness to take her life writing to the public stage, a critical step if she is to exert social critique more effectively. Emily mourns the loss of the letters to her father she can no longer continue, just as Montgomery mourned the loss of the early diaries she threw on the fire; the accountability that comes with asserting a public voice is a burden Emily hadn't counted on. But it is necessary if Emily is to become, like Montgomery, an author who takes her social responsibility deeply to heart.

With the letters at an end and a new kind of diary about to take their place, Emily also takes a major step toward public recognition by sharing a careful selection of her best poems and stories with Mr. Carpenter, but she mistakenly hands over her nonfiction sketches from real life, including a "mercilessly lucid" portrait of Mr. Carpenter himself. It is this descriptive life writing that wins him over: "By gad, it's literature—*literature*—and you're only thirteen.... Thirty years from now I will have a claim to distinction in the fact that Emily Byrd Starr was once a pupil of mine" (408–9). Life writing, specifically in critical mode, carries the day.

In the case of *Anne of Green Gables*, Devereux shows how "Montgomery herself compellingly linked her novel to her own experience" (253). Montgomery's intentional self-crafting in her journals invites readers to see her heroines through her own life story: "Metaphor of self aptly describes the ways in which Montgomery represented herself in all her writing through carefully established continuities and connections," says Devereux (254). By reading the journals and fiction as a conjoined body of work, we may read *Emily of New Moon* as representing Montgomery's reflective thinking on the nature of diary writing—its impetus, benefits, and creative possibilities for both novice and seasoned writers, but also its efficacy for a heroine with the will and agency to influence her society for the better.

Montgomery intended her journals to be published one day, and that fact has only increased the fascination both scholars and everyday readers have in her life and works. "When reading a diary," says Vallone, "you become a partner in the relationship that develops between writer and page, and this special relationship exists whether you are the only audience, or one of many" (166). In *Emily of New Moon*, Montgomery charts the earliest steps of the future author, from the most private expression of daily hurts and triumphs to the self-conscious assurance of an author with her public in mind. At the very heart of this journey is the diary, its generative capacity for social observation, investigation, and critique forming the essential building blocks for a writer engaged with her world and committed to its betterment.

NOTES

1. Emily's letters to her father adhere to a form of diary writing as defined by Harriet Blodgett in *Centuries of Female Days: Englishwomen's Private Diaries*: "The diary's essential property as a form, however, is not its choice of subject matter, but rather its more or less dailiness. Entries about whatever interests the diarist are made periodically, at dated intervals, by a writer living chiefly at the moment and expressing her immediate self rather than, as in autobiography or memoirs, remembering the self that once she was

or creating the self she would like to have been" (21). Blodgett also points out that some diarists address their entries to lost loved ones; for instance, "for the lonely Mary Shelley her diary replaces her late husband as confidant. She sees herself for at least part of her widow's diary as addressing him" (85).

2. Descriptive accounts of the juvenilia of Jane Austen and Virginia Woolf may be found in "Jane Austen's Juvenilia" by Kathryn Sutherland for the British Library, and "Hyde Park Gate News" by Gill Lowe for *Literature Compass*.

3. For more on this point, please see Jessica Wen Hui Lim's chapter in this collection.

4. Dean Priest is another example of the nightmare reader, albeit of Emily's fiction not diary, in *Emily's Quest*. Especially sinister because he is posing as a connoisseur, Dean disparages Emily's first novel so brutally as to cause her almost-fatal fall down the stairs and the near death of her career—all motivated by a narcissistic desire to concentrate all of Emily's attention on himself. The damage is so severe that Emily cannot write even in her diary for over a year.

WORKS CITED

Atwood, Margaret. "Amnesty International: An Address." *Second Words: Selected Critical Prose 1960–1982*. Anansi Press, 1982.

Blodgett, Harriet. *Centuries of Female Days: Englishwomen's Private Diaries*. Rutgers UP, 1988.

Bloom, Lynn Z. "'I Write for Myself and Strangers': Private Diaries as Public Documents." *Inscribing the Daily: Critical Essays on Women's Diaries*, edited by Suzanne L. Bunkers and Cynthia A. Huff, U of Massachusetts P, 1995, pp. 23–37.

Buss, Helen M. "Decoding L. M. Montgomery's Journals/Encoding a Critical Practice for Women's Private Literature." *Essays on Canadian Writing*, no. 54, 1994, pp. 80–100.

Devereux, Cecily. "'See My Journal for the Full Story': Fictions of Truth in *Anne of Green Gables* and L. M. Montgomery's Journals." *The Intimate Life of L. M. Montgomery*, edited by Irene Gammel, U of Toronto P, 2005, pp. 241–57.

Kadar, Marlene. "Coming to Terms: Life Writing—from Genre to Critical Practice." *Essays on Life Writing: From Genre to Critical Practice*, edited by Marlene Kadar, U of Toronto P, 1992, pp. 3–16.

Lowe, Gill. "Hyde Park Gate News." *Literature Compass*, vol. 4, no. 1, Jan. 2007, pp. 243–51.

McDonald-Rissanen, Mary. *In the Interval of the Wave: Prince Edward Island Women's Nineteenth- and Early Twentieth-Century Life Writing*. McGill-Queen's UP, 2013.

Montgomery, L. M. *The Alpine Path: The Story of My Career*. 1917. A Celebration of Women Writers, edited by Mary Mark Ockerbloom, UPenn Digital Library, 2021, digital. library.upenn.edu/women/montgomery/alpine/alpine.html.

Montgomery, L. M. *The Complete Journals of L. M. Montgomery: The PEI Years, 1889–1900*, edited by Mary Henley Rubio and Elizabeth Hillman Waterston, Oxford UP, 2012.

Montgomery, L. M. *Emily Climbs*. 1925. Tundra Books, 2014.

Montgomery, L. M. *Emily of New Moon*. 1923. Tundra Books, 2014.

Montgomery, L. M. *Emily's Quest*. 1927. Tundra Books, 2014.

Montgomery, L. M. *The Selected Journals of L. M. Montgomery, Volume 1: 1889–1910*, edited by Mary Rubio and Elizabeth Waterston, Oxford UP, 1985.

Montgomery, L. M. *The Selected Journals of L. M. Montgomery, Volume 3: 1921–1929*, edited by Mary Rubio and Elizabeth Waterston, Oxford UP, 1992.

Podnieks, Elizabeth. *Daily Modernism: The Literary Diaries of Virginia Woolf, Antonia White, Elizabeth Smart, and Anaïs Nin*. McGill-Queen's UP, 2000.

Rubio, Mary. "'A Dusting Off': An Anecdotal Account of Editing the L. M. Montgomery Journals." *Working in Women's Archives: Researching Women's Private Literature and Archival Documents*, edited by Helen M. Buss and Marlene Kadar, Wilfrid Laurier UP, 2001, pp. 51–78.

Sutherland, Kathryn. "Jane Austen's Juvenilia." *British Library*, 15 May 2014, https://www.bl.uk/romantics-and-victorians/articles/jane-austens-juvenilia.

Vallone, Lynne. "Suzanne L. Bunkers and Cynthia A. Huff, Editors, *Inscribing the Daily: Critical Essays on Women's Diaries*." Review. *Nineteenth-Century Prose*, vol. 25, no. 2, 1998, p. 166–68.

Part Three

Gender

Chapter 6

THE JAPANESE RECEPTION OF THE EMILY TRILOGY THROUGH TRANSLATION

YOSHIKO AKAMATSU

INTRODUCTION

Since its publication in 1923, L. M. Montgomery's *Emily of New Moon*, with its strong-willed protagonist who strives to be a writer, has been a source of encouragement to career-oriented women readers throughout the world. Elizabeth Epperly points out that two of Montgomery's works, her 1917 autobiographical *Everybody's World* (published as *The Alpine Path* in 1975) and the transcribing of her own diaries from her younger days, influenced the author's writing of the book (Epperly 145–46). Montgomery has claimed that the protagonist, Emily Byrd Starr, reflected her own struggles to be a writer, and the Emily trilogy is another biography of a woman writer who finds success. In Japan, Hanako Muraoka, the first Japanese translator of *Anne of Green Gables*, titled *Akage no An* (*Red-Haired Anne*, 1952), introduced an unabridged *Emily of New Moon* to Japanese readers seven years after the publication of *Red-Haired Anne*. Muraoka also translated its sequels, and her translation of the last Emily book, *Emily's Quest*, was her final work as a translator. Since then, the Emily trilogy has been warmly received by Japanese readers, especially Japanese women with aspirations of success. The popularity of the Emily books, however, has not matched that of the Anne books. Analyzing Muraoka's imprint on L. M. Montgomery's Emily trilogy, this chapter will consider the contribution that Muraoka made as a translator, what the translation meant for her, how Japanese readers have embraced the trilogy differently from the Anne books, and how Muraoka's altered title for *Emily of New Moon* embodies one of the problems of translation.

THE INFLUENCE OF THE EMILY TRILOGY
ON JAPANESE WOMEN READERS

In *Everybody's Favourites: Canadians Talk about Books That Changed Their Lives* (1997), edited by Canadian journalist, literary critic, and author Arlene Perly Rae, seven famous Canadians, Alice Munro, Kit Pearson, Budge Wilson, Val Ross, Goldie Semple, Ann Shortell, and Jane Urquhart, name the Emily books as having had the strongest influence on their lives (91–102). For instance, Pearson says that from the trilogy "I learned all about my future career before I started it" (95). These writers found a deeper kinship with Emily than with Anne. In fact, the Anne books were not mentioned as often as the Emily books.

In Japan, Hanako Muraoka's unabridged Japanese translation of the Emily trilogy has had a great impact on Japanese women readers. One example is popular artist Sachiko Takayanagi (1941–), who wrote about her own shock upon hearing of Muraoka's death (in 1968) in her book *Akage no An no "Fukushin no Tomo" Nōto* (*Red-Haired Anne's "Bosom Friends'" Notebook*) in 1992. Grieving over Muraoka's death, she expressed her concern over whether Muraoka had finished translating *Emily's Quest* before her death, then expressed her gratitude that she had done so. Drawing her artistic inspiration from Muraoka's translation of Montgomery's books, Takayanagi published a book of essays called *Akage no An Nōto* (*Red-Haired Anne's Notebook*) in 1991, visualizing the worlds of Anne, Pat, and Emily. Takayanagi especially loves to draw images from the Emily books, such as the Wind Woman (*Emily of New Moon*), the Land of Uprightness (*Emily Climbs*), and Emily's sublunary walk (*Emily's Quest*) (Takayanagi 42–45, 22–23, 101). She repeatedly credits Muraoka's translations as having inspired her art and writing.

Well-known independent scholar of potpourri and essayist Akiko Kumai (1940–) says that she owes her study of fragrance to Muraoka. Her interest in aroma arose from Muraoka's choice of the unusual word *zakkō* to mean potpourri in the short story "Aunt Olivia's Beau" in *Chronicles of Avonlea*, which Muraoka translated in Japanese as *An no Tomodachi* (*Anne's Friends*). When Muraoka's translation of this book was published in Japan in 1956, most people had never heard of potpourri, and Kumai decided to make a study of it. She eventually ended up introducing potpourri to Japan through her books on the subject. In her essay "Hanako, Anne and Shakespeare," she first gives thanks to Muraoka's translation of the Anne books, because it led to her own calling as a writer, but later, she claims that it was Muraoka's translation of the Emily trilogy that inspired her even more profoundly than the Anne books (Kumai 22–23). In a conversation between Kumai and novelist Kaho Nashiki

(1959–), included in a book of essays edited by Eri Muraoka, it is revealed that Nashiki herself is also a great fan of the Emily books, admiring Emily's sense of pride both as a child and as a woman (Kumai and Nashiki 33).

Another example is editor Mari Hayakawa, who first encountered Montgomery through Muraoka's translation of *Emily's Quest*. She wrote of how much the book taught her, and one of the greatest things was the significance of reading. For her, the highlight of the book was the episode of the letter Emily wrote "from herself at fourteen to herself at twenty-four" (*Quest*, 189–91), and Hayakawa wrote to her future self as a "bosom friend," just as Emily had done. Hayakawa declares that she was led to her present profession as an editor by Muraoka's Emily trilogy (Hayakawa 29).

Following Emily's lead like Hayakawa, I too as a fourteen-year-old girl wrote to myself at twenty-four, and writing of this experience in an essay won me a literary prize and encouraged my aspiration to be a scholar.[1] I also began to grow in my garden some of the same flowers that Emily grows in *Emily Climbs* and *Emily's Quest*, with such charming names as "Baby's Breath" and "Love-in-a-Mist" (*Climbs* 297), instilling in me a deep and continuing love of gardening.

These are but a few examples of how Montgomery's Emily trilogy has led Japanese women with a passion for reading and writing to find fulfillment in careers that they love, and all of them encountered Emily through Muraoka's translations. They share the same enthusiasm with women all over the world who have found a role model in Montgomery's fledgling writer.

HANAKO MURAOKA'S CONTRIBUTION

As previously mentioned, Montgomery's *Emily of New Moon* was first translated into Japanese by Hanako Muraoka (1893–1968) in 1959, thirty-six years after the publication of the original book. It was published in two volumes under the titles *Kaze no naka no Emiri* (*Emily in the Wind*) and *Ame ni Utau Emiri* (*Emily Who Reads to the Rain*) by Akimoto Shobo publishers. The book covers of both were very modern for the times and have no connection to the protagonist's appearance as described in the original book, but they give Japanese people the impression that this is the story of a modern, foreign young woman. On the front cover of *Kaze no naka no Emiri*, a young lady with brown hair leans against a tree, while on the back cover, as the caption explains, stands a house between pine trees representing New Moon farm (see figures 1a and 1b). On the front cover of *Ame ni Utau Emiri*, a young woman in a green dress with white lace gloves stands in front of a white car with an open door, while a lotus pond represents Blair Water Pond on the back cover (see figures 2a and 2b). In the translator's commentary in the first book, Muraoka explains: "I named the book *Emily in the Wind* to emphasize Emily's freedom and naturalness so like the wind" (177). However, in the second book's commentary, there is no mention of why she named it *Emily Who Reads to the Rain*. It remains a mystery why such a title was given to the second volume of *Emily of New Moon* in 1959. As Emily in the original book names the wind blowing around her "Wind Woman" (Montgomery, *New Moon* 1, 6), Japanese readers can understand that the protagonist is connected to wind, but no connection is made between Emily and rain in the original book. Perhaps the latter's name came from the Japanese combined word, *Fu-u* (wind and rain), a natural phenomenon. At any rate, the pair of titles emphasizes Emily's strong ties to nature.

In 1964, when Muraoka changed publishers to Shinchosha, the two companion books were reincorporated into one volume and newly renamed *Kawaii Emiri* (*Dear Emily*, or *Sweet Emily*), which remains its (controversial) title to this day.[2] In her commentary, Muraoka simply says that she has changed the title because the literal Japanese translation of the original English did not sound attractive (545). Muraoka's granddaughters Mie (translator) and Eri (writer) told me that Hanako left no notes on the background of her titles, and it is still a topic of speculation. In the same commentary, Muraoka mentions that L. M. Montgomery's biographer wrote that the

Figures 1a and 1b. *Kaze no naka no Emiri* (front cover and back cover depicting New Moon farm among pine trees) (1959)

Figures 2a and 2b. *Ame ni Utau Emiri* (front cover and back cover depicting Blair Water Pond, full of lotuses) (1959)

author's characteristics were reflected more in Emily than in Anne (498). Perhaps Muraoka hoped to highlight the attractiveness of Emily, who is less talkative and amiable than Anne, by calling her "*kawaii*." Emily's personality is not always understood by those around her, and she is accused of being "deep and sly" by her aunt Ruth in *Emily Climbs* (118, 278). The closer readers get to Emily, however, the more they come to love her. This may have been Muraoka's intention and the reason she gave the book such a title. As Japanese scholar Hiroharu Ayame argues, when the translator and her or his publisher create a different title from the original, it reflects both the values of the age as well as a commercial strategy to make it more appealing to its potential readers (180). Muraoka and her publisher's strategies are likely no exception.

Muraoka went on to publish translations of the two sequels in 1967 and 1969. The former was a literal translation of the original title, *Emiri wa Noboru* (*Emily Climbs*), and the latter was a close translation, *Emiri no Motomerumono* (*What Emily Seeks*). *Emiri wa Noboru* includes Muraoka's commentary in which she says that Emily, who has a passion for writing, seems to share Montgomery's heartbeat (496). The latter translation was Muraoka's final work as a translator as she died unexpectedly before seeing its publication.[3]

The book covers of the Emily trilogy by Shinchosha had portraits of a young girl surrounded by flowers and were illustrated by Yoshimasa Murakami (1922–2022), a well-known artist whose work was often featured in magazines for girls (see figures 3, 4, and 5). Muraoka's title choice of *Dear*

Figure 3. *Kawaii Emiri* (1964)

Emily for the first book, her translation of the whole trilogy, and Murakami's book covers left a lasting impression on readers for long years.

After Muraoka's death, two translators made new unabridged translations of *Emily of New Moon*. In 2002, Nobuo Kandori (1931–2007) published his translation in three volumes as soft cover pocket books for children with the publisher Kaiseisha. His version is simply titled *Emiri* (*Emily*). The book covers were drawn by Takayanagi (mentioned previously), and her illustrations faithfully depict scenes from the original books (see figures 6, 7, and 8). In the translator's commentary, Kandori says that he believes this book is an autobiographical supplement to the author's own autobiography, *The Alpine Path* (258).

Figure 4. *Emiri wa Noboru* (1967)

Figure 5. *Emiri no Motomerumono* (1969)

In 2006, Naoko Ikematsu published a new translation with the title *Shingetsu Noen no Emiri* (literally *Emily of New Moon Farm*) with the publisher Shinozaki Shorin. Ikematsu's translation seems to be intended for adult readers because she includes advanced *kanji* expressions (Chinese characters) in her book that would be too difficult for most children to understand. The book cover is the same as those in the Montgomery Books series by the same publisher, which uses a photographic portrait of the author (see figure 9). Ikematsu's afterword explains that Emily is like the author, who strongly wanted to be a writer, and that the author and Japanese readers share the similar belief that nature can be a reflection of one's feelings (476).

Figure 6. *Emiri I*

Figure 7. *Emiri II*

Unfortunately, neither Kandori nor Ikematsu translated the sequels, and Ikematsu's translation went out of print in 2021, meaning that only Muraoka's translation of the full Emily trilogy remains available to Japanese readers. Both Kandori's and Ikematsu's translations make use of some of Muraoka's Japanese translated words, such as the names of Emily's close friend Ilse, translated as *Iruze*, and the Disappointed House as *Shitsubō no Ie* (House of Disappointment). Muraoka's mark on the Emily trilogy extends not only to Japanese readers but also to Japanese translators of subsequent generations, which is why the animated version of the Emily trilogy (2007) was mainly based on Muraoka's translations.

Figure 8. *Emiri III*

New Montgomery Books

30

新月農園のエミリー

L.M. モンゴメリ作

池松　直子訳

篠崎書林

Figure 9. *Shingetsu Noen no Emiri*

THE MEANING OF THE EMILY TRILOGY FOR MURAOKA

Eri Muraoka, Hanako Muraoka's granddaughter, writes in her book *Anne's Cradle*, "Hanako felt a special affinity for Montgomery" (249). One of the reasons was because "Hanako had studied English under Canadian [missionary] women of Montgomery's generation and had been raised within the Canadian culture and customs of that era" (249). Montgomery also had a strong sense of familial duty and valued family ties as Hanako had. Montgomery cared for her aged grandmother who had raised her, and after marrying the reverend Ewen Macdonald, she worked hard as the wife of a minister and mother of two children while "writing and advocat[ing] for better status for women" (249). Because Hanako came from a broken home, as a result of poverty, she valued and treasured her married life and own family, fully understanding Montgomery's struggle of balancing "being a writer and the demands and responsibilities of life" (249). Muraoka wanted to introduce Japan to wholesome books that could be enjoyed by the whole family, and she believed Montgomery's Anne and Emily books were worthy of being translated and shared. In two of her essays, Hanako Muraoka wrote of an eleven-year-old girl who wanted to be a writer, which she was herself ("*Shoujo no Me*" [Girls' Perspective] 161–62), and on the original book's power, which sparked her interest in translation ("*Kotoba no Inshō*" [The Impressions of Words] 112–13). Both essays show that Muraoka recognized herself in the eleven-year-old protagonist in *Emily of New Moon* and that the appeal of Montgomery's novels comes from the author's gift of language rather than any achievement of the translator.

In 2008, the centennial year of the publication of *Anne of Green Gables*, Mie and Eri Muraoka, granddaughters of Hanako, reprinted the Emily trilogy under their grandmother's name, revising a certain inconsistency in the Japanese translation of the trilogy. The original translations had mistakenly identified Emily's aunts as *oba* (叔母), which would mean that they were Emily's mother's younger sisters, though Emily's mother was the youngest of the Murray sisters. The word needed to be replaced with a different version of *oba* (伯母). The book covers, by young artist Ai Noda, were also redesigned to represent the contents more faithfully (see figures 10, 11, and 12). Avid Montgomery readers as well as Hanako Muraoka's fans roundly welcomed the revisions.

Hanako Muraoka was not only a translator but also a writer, interpreter, and cultural icon who made a huge impact on Japanese readers. As mentioned, Muraoka died just before the publication of the third Emily book,

Figure 10. *Kawaii Emiri* (2008)

Emiri no Motomerumono, and therefore did not write the commentary that accompanies it. The commentary dated January 8, 1969, was written by Michio Namekawa, Muraoka's friend as well as a well-known scholar of children's literature. In the commentary to *Emiri no Motomerumono*, Namekawa draws a comparison between the deaths of Muraoka and Montgomery.

Namekawa writes that in the same month that Muraoka sent her manuscript to Shinchosha publishers, she died suddenly of cerebral thrombosis on October 25, 1968 (330, 336). He also notes that Montgomery died suddenly (of coronary thrombosis) at her home in Toronto on April 24, 1969, after submitting to her publishers her final book, *Further Chronicles of Avonlea* [sic].[4] He

Figure 11. *Emiri wa Noboru* (2008)

Figure 12. *Emiri no Motomerumono* (2008)

emphasizes that in addition to their sudden, unexpected deaths, both writer and translator had just completed and submitted their final works shortly before their deaths (330–31).[5]

In September 2008, the centennial year of the publication of *Anne of Green Gables*, Kate Macdonald Butler, one of Montgomery's granddaughters, claimed that her grandmother "took her own life at the age of 67 through a drug overdose" after suffering from depression ("Heartbreaking Truth"). Mary Rubio, a Montgomery scholar who wrote the author's biography, however, finds no evidence to support the claim of suicide (Rubio 45–62). The truth remains unknown. Although the causes of the deaths of Muraoka and Montgomery were different, both succeeded in completing their final works before they died.

JAPANESE SOCIETY AT THE TIME OF THE FIRST EMILY TRANSLATION

Muraoka's Emily books are printed by Shinchosha as *bunko* (pocket-sized) books and have never been out of print since their original publication in 1964. The 1960s was a time of great economic growth in Japan, and more and more Japanese women were entering the workforce for the first time. Japan, as a peaceful nation, regained its place on the world stage, and Japanese people traveled abroad in great numbers. In 1967, after recovering from cataract surgery, Hanako Muraoka herself experienced her first trip abroad, visiting her daughter Midori's home in America. Midori's husband was a visiting scholar at the University of California, Davis. Dressed in kimono, Muraoka enjoyed sightseeing and communicating in English with people. During her time in California, she began translating *Emily's Quest*. She "could concentrate [on the translation] more easily [than at home in Japan], and the work proceeded much faster than she had expected" (E. Muraoka, *Anne's Cradle* 245). She planned to visit Prince Edward Island with her daughter Midori, but over concerns for Midori's pregnancy, Hanako decided to postpone their visit to the island for another time. She returned to Japan in early September and finished the translation with a sense of fulfillment (E. Muraoka, *Anne's Cradle* 246). Unfortunately, however, Muraoka's sudden death in 1968 prevented her from ever stepping foot on the island.

Like Muraoka, more and more Japanese women went to work in the 1960s. For them, Emily Byrd Starr with her strong will to be a writer would have been a better role model than Anne Shirley Blythe was as a housewife. The Japanese women who encountered Emily through Muraoka's translation found the encouragement to pursue their careers. Muraoka must have been conscious of the different societal values in place at the time of her translation of the Anne books (early 1950s) compared to those of the time she worked on the Emily trilogy (late 1950s through the 1960s).

DISSATISFACTION WITH MURAOKA'S JAPANESE TITLE

Kandori and Ikematsu titled their translations differently from Muraoka's original. In fact, Muraoka's choice of *Kawaii Emiri* (*Dear Emily* or *Sweet Emily*) did not sit well with readers or scholars, including me. The subjective title indicates the name-giver's feelings about the heroine. Muraoka's Japanese title of *Anne of Green Gables*, *Red-Haired Anne*, has been accepted and continuously used by almost all Japanese translators because of its objective view of the protagonist. Why, then, has the title *Kawaii Emiri* caused such discontent among readers? It is because of the adjective "*kawaii*." The word *kawaii* came to be overused in Japanese popular culture in the 1980s.

Scholar Sharon Kinsella wrote on the domination of *kawaii* style in her article "Cuties in Japan." She writes "kawaii or 'cute' essentially means childlike; it celebrates sweet, adorable, innocent, pure, simple, genuine, gentle, vulnerable, weak, and inexperienced social behaviour and physical appearances" (220). She admits that "kawaii is a derivation of a term whose principle meaning was 'shy' or 'embarrassed' and secondary meanings were 'pathetic,' 'vulnerable,' 'darling,' 'loveable' and 'small'" and "the modern sense of the word kawaii still has some nuances of pitiful" (221–22). Muraoka's use of the word surely comes from its principle meaning. Unfortunately, however, this word became synonymous with a subculture that was "cute and popular" in the 1980s. "Cute culture has provided an escape exit into childhood memories" and is "most visible in comics, animation and computer games" (Kinsella 252). According to film and literature scholar Inuhiko Yomota, "*kawaii*" reigns over the twenty-first-century's consumer society as a new aesthetic (13–15; my translation). Those who harbor negative feelings toward such popular culture would have misgivings about Muraoka's Japanese title, *Kawaii Emiri*. Muraoka could not have imagined such "cute culture" would become both popular and problematic in later years. Unfortunately, it still may leave a negative impression on some people who come across the Japanese title in bookstores. As time goes by, if a new translator were to give a new Japanese title to *Emily of New Moon*, it would likely be warmly welcomed.

ADAPTATIONS OF THE EMILY TRILOGY IN JAPAN[6]

The Emily trilogy has been adapted as a musical play as well as a television drama in Canada.[7] In Japan, it was made into an animated series in 2007, thanks to the creativity of a new generation of artists/writers. For six months in 2007, from April 7 to September 29, the animated program *Kaze no Shoujo Emiri* (*Emily, Girl of the Wind*) was broadcast on Japanese television, coproduced by the Japan Broadcasting Corporation and the animation company TMS Entertainment, the latter of which promoted it internationality (see figure 13). The world of *anime* (animation) is booming in Japan and is now recognized as a legitimate art form popular among both children and adults. In 2006, I was invited to the Emily anime team as literary adviser, reading scripts written by a team of five writers and offering advice. The scripts mainly relied on Muraoka's translation because it was decided that the anime would cover the whole trilogy in twenty-six episodes. I revised errors in Muraoka's translation and answered cultural questions as the team worked to depict rural life on Prince Edward Island, but I was not asked to be involved in the actual visualization of the scenes. According to the website *Emiri no Sekai* (The World of Emily), the female director of animation, Harume Kosaka, wanted to represent the simple life, clear air, and beauty of the island to appeal to present-day people of all generations, but especially to girls and women.

The subtitle for *Kaze no Shoujo Emiri* is "Another Story of Youth." Besides showing that the anime will follow the growth of the protagonist, Emily, as well as her close friends Ilse, Teddy, and Perry, all of whom have career-centered ambitions, the word "another" is in reference to the Anne anime from 1997. The wildly popular fifty-episode animation is almost entirely faithful to the original text, and is considered a masterpiece on which world-renowned artists Hayao Miyazaki and Isao Takahata worked. The creators of the Emily anime wanted to produce an animation with more modern techniques than were used in the Anne anime, hoping to appeal to a new and younger generation. Emily and her friends are career-oriented children longing to fulfill their own dreams and do meaningful work in the future, though their characters are not as deeply drawn as they are in the original text. Ilse's wish to be an elocutionist comes about when she happens to recite some of Emily's poems and entertains those listening. Teddy's gift of drawing is portrayed effectively, but the way by which he gets a chance to study abroad is an added fiction. Perry first appears as the hired boy at New Moon farm when Emily is brought there, and his illiteracy is emphasized as being a result of his impoverished background, but his love for Emily becomes his motivation to learn to read and eventually become a politician.

Spring often symbolizes youth in literature, and the Emily anime utilizes this season very effectively. In the original text, Emily's father, Douglas Starr, tells her when he is on his deathbed: "I want you to be brave.... The universe is full of love—and spring comes everywhere" (*New Moon* 20). In the anime,

Figure 13. *Kaze no Shojo Emiri* ©NHK/TME (2007)

script writer Mitsuru Shimada adds the lines: "You mustn't be afraid of losing me. You will go on to open many doors into tomorrow." Emily's father's words are echoed throughout the series, and finally when Emily succeeds as a writer, she realizes her father's words have come true.

As the title *Emily, Girl of the Wind* emphasizes, Emily is described as a person sensitive to the wind. The anime creators depict Emily's ability to see invisible beings. For instance, her imagined character, Wind Woman, is portrayed by the artists as a transparent goddess with a flower garland on her head; in fact, they give her the role of narrator of the anime. Wind and inspiration often go together, and Emily catches her own inspiration to write poems and novels from the wind. The animators also cleverly visualize the cold deathly wind blowing on Emily's teacher and mentor Mr. Carpenter's last day. Wind plays a larger and more symbolic role in the anime than it does in the original text of the Emily trilogy.

Because of the wind, nature and life on Prince Edward Island appear to be more vividly in motion. The beauty of the island's landscape is presented more effectively in the Emily anime of 2007 than in the Anne anime of 1997. Sometimes scenes are exaggerated, reflecting the inner feelings of Emily. The animators employed modern techniques of animation to show natural phenomena, such as the movement and sparkle of the sea. As Emily is a born and bred Islander, unlike the outsider Anne Shirley, she doesn't show as much surprise or delight with the natural beauty of the island, but instead, the animators have worked to dazzle the audience with it.

While her three friends venture out from Prince Edward Island, Emily chooses to stay as she struggles to be a writer. The animators depict how she faces the hardships of daily life and eventually attains success: gaining both fame as a writer and happiness in marriage. One of the adaptations created by the Japanese team was that manuscripts of Emily's novel are circulated among the local people and that this leads to the publication of her first book. The anime team emphasizes Emily's identity as a Canadian woman writer by having her remain faithful to her island.

THE ROLE OF TRANSLATORS

Translators in the twentieth century were usually behind-the-scenes supporters whose backgrounds were not reported on to the public. Hanako Muraoka was an exception, as she engaged in various activities such as essay writing and introducing good books to the public, both of which led to her being widely known and embraced as a translator. As proof of her acclaim, a new edition of her original translation of *Anne of Green Gables* was most recently published in 2022.[8] Translators in the twenty-first century are expected not only to do their work of translation but also to provide commentary and anecdotes about their process. In other words, in this century of technology, they are expected to do what Muraoka did long before this computer age.

Scholar Yoko Hasegawa mentions six skills of the translator that are "essential for effective translation performance." I believe the sixth point, which she identifies as the "ability to evaluate and discuss translations objectively," is the most difficult (22). She writes of the essence of translation:

> For many, translation is like puzzle-solving fun, and the creativity involved provides deep satisfaction.... Moreover, translation involves continuous encounters with problems caused by linguistic and cultural differences, and each instance of decision-making enables the translator to penetrate deeper into another culture, as well as into the complexities of human cognitive and expressive faculties. This adventure can be an inspiration to the language learner. (3–4)

As Hasegawa suggests, translators can be called adventurers, and their adventures seem to vary according to the age and circumstances of the present-day societies for which they are translating at the time.

CONCLUSION

Hanako Muraoka translated L. M. Montgomery's Emily trilogy, consulting dictionaries and working to reflect the culture she had learned about when she studied under her Canadian missionary teachers at Toyo Eiwa Girls' School. Her translations relied on what her imagination gleaned from her educational background. She understood the universal difficulties that a girl hoping to become a writer would face. There were no internet searches in her day and few opportunities to go abroad. She strove to express unfamiliar words and concepts in ways that would be familiar to her Japanese readers. The back covers of *Kaze no naka no Emiri* and *Ame ni Utau Emiri* bore no resemblance to the actual landscapes of Prince Edward Island, but they certainly helped the Japanese readers of 1959 imagine those distant places. Muraoka was a pioneer translator who worked to introduce unfamiliar literary works written in English to Japanese people. Today's readers can easily search and see what life is like on PEI, supplementing what Muraoka hoped to express in words. Readers of the twenty-first century should recognize the admirable efforts made by the early translators and publishers.

Through Hanako Muraoka's translations, Japanese readers have come to love and embrace L. M. Montgomery's Emily trilogy, which is a Canadian would-be writer's coming-of-age story. The Emily anime, based mainly on Muraoka's translations, conveys the universal appeal of the woman artist and the peculiarity of its time and setting to resonate with a modern-day, non-Canadian viewer. Literary works adapted into popular culture have new value, even for child readers discovering a character for the first time. If an original text is worthy, its adaptation can be worthy. L. M. Montgomery's *Emily of New Moon* (1923) will be picked up and reread in celebration of the centenary of its publication, and present-day Japanese people will surely understand Emily's struggles well, beyond the boundaries of time and nationality. New translations and adaptations can help to keep beloved books alive in the hearts of people living in this technological twenty-first century.

NOTES

1. On January 24, 2020, American writer Ann Napolitano published an essay in the *New York Times* titled "'Dear Me': A Novelist Writes to Her Future Self" about how a fourteen-year-old Napolitano wrote a letter to her future twenty-four-year-old self, inspired by fourteen-year-old Emily's endeavor in *Emily of New Moon*. Like Hayakawa and I, Napolitano was impressed with the same episode, and like Emily, Napolitano fulfilled "two goals for her life: to be a mother, and to be a writer."

2. Discussed later in this chapter.

3. Discussed later in this chapter.

4. Namekawa wrote that Montgomery submitted the manuscript of *Further Chronicles of Avonlea* to her publisher, but the name of the work was evidently a mistake. It was the manuscript of *The Blythes Are Quoted*. A part of this work was posthumously published under the title *Road to Yesterday* in 1974, but later it was published in its original form and with its original name in 2009.

5. Rubio and Waterston wrote that the "primary cause" of death on her death certificate was "Coronary Thrombosis" (*Selected Journals* Vol. 5, 399).

6. This section includes the same content found in my article "The Problems and Possibilities Inherent in Adaptation: *Emily of New Moon* and *Emily, Girl of the Wind.*"

7. Stinson directed *Emily of New Moon: A Children's Musical* in 1998 in Prince Edward Island, but it remains unpublished. https://lmmontgomery.ca//islandora/object/lmmi:4819; Ouzounian and Norman directed *Emily*, a musical based on *Emily of New Moon*, *Emily Climbs*, and *Emily's Quest* in 2000; *Emily of New Moon* was a television series that originally aired in 1998–1999 and in 2002–2003 on CBC. This information comes from Lefebvre's website, L. M. Montgomery Online. https://lmmonline.org/emily-of-new-moon-1998/.

8. See Akamatsu, "*Anne* in Twenty-First Century Japan."

WORKS CITED

Akamatsu, Yoshiko. "*Anne* in Twenty-First Century Japan." *The Anne of Green Gables Manuscript*. The Confederation Centre of the Arts, 2023. https://annemanuscript.ca/stories/anne-in-japan/.

Akamatsu, Yoshiko. "*L. M. Mongomeri no Emiri-sanbusaku to Muraoka Hanako*" ("L. M. Montgomery's Emily Trilogy and Hanako Muraoka"). *Akage no An kara Kurokami no Emiri e* (*From Red-Haired Anne to Black-Haired Emily: Reading of Fiction by L. M. Montgomery*). Ochanomizu Shobo, 2022, pp. 167–75.

Akamatsu, Yoshiko. "The Problems and Possibilities Inherent in Adaptation: *Emily of New Moon* and *Emily, Girl of the Wind.*" *Children and Childhoods in L. M. Montgomery: Continuing Conversations*, edited by Rita Bode, Lesley D. Clement, E. Holly Pike, and Margaret Steffler, McGill-Queen's UP, 2022, pp. 223–41.

Ayame, Hiroharu. "*Ibunka-ron no Kansei: Honyaku nituite no Genriteki Kosatsu kara*" ("The Pitfall in Cross-Cultural Theories: A Consideration of Translation in Principle"). *Rinriteki de Seijiteki na Hihyou e: Nihon Kindai Bunngaku no Hihanteki Kenkyu* (*Ethical and Political Criticism: A Critical Study of Japanese Modern Literature*). Koseisha, 2004, pp. 179–99.

Butler, Kate Macdonald. "The Heartbreaking Truth about Anne's Creator." *Globe and Mail*, 20 Sept. 2008.

Emiri no Sekai (*The World of Emily*). Special Talk: Act 1–3 by Kenji Saitoh, Hideaki Miyamoto, and Harume Kosaka. NHK/NEP/TMS, 2007. http://www.vap.co.jp/emily/commentary.html.

Epperly, Elizabeth Rollins. *The Fragrance of Sweet-Grass: L. M. Montgomery's Heroines and the Pursuit of Romance*. U of Toronto P, 1992.
Hasegawa, Yoko. *The Routlege Course in Japanese Translation*. Routledge, 2012.
Hayakawa, Mari. "*Shiawaseyo, Kaetteoide / Yorokobiyo, Ikikaette / Genki ni Hanete Oddotte-goran*" ("Happiness, Come Back, and Gladness, Be Reborn, Leap Lively / and Dance"). *Muraoka Hanako*, edited by Eri Muraoka, pp. 28–34.
Ikematsu, Naoko. Afterword. *Shingetsu Noen no Emiri* (*Emily of New Moon*), translated by Ikematsu, pp. 476–77.
Ikematsu, Naoko, translator. *Shingetsu Noen no Emiri (Emily of New Moon)*. By L. M. Montgomery. Shinozaki Shorin, 2006.
Kandori, Nobuo. Commentary. *Emiri* (*Emily*), 3, translated by Kandori, pp. 257–60.
Kandori, Nobuo, translator. *Emiri* (*Emily*). (*Emily of New Moon*). 3 vols. By L. M. Montgomery. Kaiseisha, 2002.
Kaze no Shoujo Emiri (*Emily, Girl of the Wind*). NHK and TMS Entertainment, 2007. http://www6.nhk.or.jp/anime/program/detail.html?i=emily.
Kinsella, Sharon. "Cuties in Japan." *Women, Media, and Consumption in Japan*, edited by Lise Skov and Brian Moeran, U of Hawaii P, 1995, pp. 220–54.
Kumai, Akiko. "*Hanako, An, Sheikusupia*" ("Hanako, Anne and Shakespeare"). *Muraoka Hanako*, edited by Eri Muraoka, pp. 21–27.
Kumai, Akiko, and Kaho Nashiki. "*Taidan: Mongomeri to Muraoka Hanako ga Kureta mono*" ("A Conversation about What Montgomery and Muraoka Gave Us"). *Muraoka Hanako to Akage no An no Sekai* (*The World of Hanako Muraoka and Red-Haired Anne*), edited by Eri Muraoka, pp. 21–36.
Lefebvre, Benjamin. *L. M. Montgomery Online*. https://lmmonline.org/screen/directors/.
L. M. Montgomery Institute. "Montgomery, L. M., and Hank Stinson. 'Emily of New Moon Musical Debuts in Prince Edward Island.'" *Avonlea Traditions Chronicle*, no. 23–24, Spring 1998, https://lmmontgomery.ca//islandora/object/lmmi:4819.
Montgomery, L. M. *Emily Climbs*. 1925. Tundra 2014.
Montgomery, L. M. *Emily of New Moon*. 1923. Tundra, 2014.
Montgomery, L. M. *Emily's Quest*. 1927. Tundra, 2014.
Muraoka, Eri. *Anne's Cradle: The Life and Works of Hanako Muraoka, Japanese Translator of Anne of Green Gables*. Translated by Cathy Hirano, Nimbus Publishing, 2021.
Muraoka, Eri. *An no Yurikago: Muraoka Hanako no Shogai*. 2008. Magazinehouse; Shinchosha, 2011.
Muraoka, Eri, editor. *Muraoka Hanako*. Kawade Shobo Shinsha, 2014.
Muraoka, Eri. *Muraoka Hanako to Akage no An no Sekai*. Kawade Shobo Shinsha, 2013.
Muraoka, Hanako, translator. *Ame ni Utau Emiri*. By L. M. Montgomery. Akimoto Shobo, 1959.
Muraoka, Hanako. Commentary. *Emiri wa Noboru*, rev. ed., translated by Muraoka, pp. 495–97.
Muraoka, Hanako, translator. *Emiri no Motomerumono* (*Emily's Quest*). By L. M. Montgomery. 1969. Shinchosha, 2008.
Muraoka, Hanako, translator. *Emiri wa Noboru* (*Emily Climbs*). By L. M. Montgomery. 1967. Shinchosha, 2007.
Muraoka, Hanako. Commentary. *Kawaii Emiri*, rev. ed., translated by Muraoka, pp. 545–47.

Muraoka, Hanako, translator. *Kawaii Emiri* (*Emily of New Moon*). By L. M. Montgomery. 1964. Shinchosha, 2008.

Muraoka, Hanako. Commentary. *Kaze no naka no Emiri*, translated by Muraoka, pp. 177–78.

Muraoka, Hanako, translator. *Kaze no naka no Emiri*. By L. M. Montgomery. Akimoto Shobo, 1959.

Muraoka, Hanako. "*Kotoba no Inshō* (*The Impressions of Words*)." *Muraoka Hanako*, edited by Eri Muraoka, pp. 112–13.

Muraoka, Hanako. "*Shoujo no Me* (Girls' Perspective)." *Ikiru to iukoto* (*What Is to Live*). Asunaro Shobo, 1969, pp. 161–62.

Namekawa, Michio. Commentary. *Emiri no Motomerumono*, rev. ed., translated by Hanako Muraoka. Shinchosha, 2008, pp. 330–37.

Napolitano, Ann. "'Dear Me': A Novelist Writes to Her Future Self," *New York Times*, 24 Jan. 2020. https://www.nytimes.com/2020/01/24/books/review/emily-of-new-moon-montgomery-letters-ann-napolitano.html/.

Ouzounian, Richard, and Marek Norman, screenwriters. *Emily, a Musical*. By L. M. Montgomery. McArthur and Company, 2000.

Rae, Arlene Perly, editor. *Everybody's Favourites: Canadians Talk about Books That Changed Their Lives*. Viking Penguin, 1997.

Rubio, Mary Henley. "Uncertainties Surrounding the Death of L. M. Montgomery." *Anne around the World: L. M. Montgomery and Her Classic*. Edited by Jane Ledwell and Jean Mitchell, McGill-Queen's UP, 2013, pp. 45–62.

Rubio, Mary, and Elizabeth Waterston. "Notes 1939–42" to *The Selected Journals of L. M. Montgomery, vol. 5: 1935–1942*. Oxford UP, 2004, p. 399.

Takayanagi, Sachiko. *Akage no An Nōto* (*Red-Haired Anne's Notebook*). Daiwa Shuppan, 1991.

Takayanagi, Sachiko. *Akage no An no "Fukushin no Tomo" Nōto* (*Red-Haired Anne's "Bosom Friends'" Notebook*). Daiwa Shuppan, 1992.

Yomota, Inuhiko. *Kawaii-ron* (*Analyzing "Kawaii."*) Chikuma Shobo, 2006.

Chapter 7

CLAIMING AND RECLAIMING THE MATERNAL

Mothering and Mothers in the Emily Books

RITA BODE

Early in *Emily of New Moon*, Douglas Starr asks his daughter, "Emily, do you remember your mother?" Reflecting her future vocation, Emily responds poetically: "Just a little—here and there—like lovely bits of dreams" (15). But her memory of one incident stands out clearly. "I remember the funeral, Father," she tells him. "I remember it *distinctly*" (18). Emily's words echo her creator's own memory of maternal loss. In her April 8, 1898, journal entry, L. M. Montgomery recounts remembering "perfectly" her experience of gazing on the "coffined face" of her own dead mother (*Complete Journals 1889–1900* 390). Attempts to forge bonds with the missing mother whom she knew for only twenty-two months of her life appear throughout Montgomery's journals. Hearing her mother's second cousin and girlhood friend speak of the unknown mother "as a beautiful, spiritual, poetical girl full of fine emotions and noble impulses" brings great joy to the thirty-year-old daughter in the knowledge that if her mother "had lived I would have found in her all that I could wish in a mother" (*Complete Journals 1901–1911* [2 Jan. 1905] 117). She expresses self-confidence that she and her mother would have been "*chums*—we would have understood each other," she concludes (*Complete Journals 1918–1921* [25 June 1918] 26). These entries reflect maternal scholar Andrea O'Reilly's theories of the mother-daughter relationship in which she challenges the dominant narrative of Anglo-American culture that demands a daughter "distance and differentiate herself from the mother if she is to assume an autonomous identity as an adult" (92). O'Reilly rejects "the pathologizing of mother-daughter identification and intimacy" (95) into a restrictive dependency. Adopting a feminist turn in her analyses of mother-daughter relationality, she privileges connection over separation in a daughter's growth toward independent selfhood.

Montgomery's bittersweet longings for the absent mother emerge as a lifelong process of mourning, seeking, and imagining that also informs her fiction.[1] For the fictional Emily, the young protagonist most like herself, absent mothers intensify the need for the mother-connection as they do for Montgomery. Through their eponymous young protagonist, the Emily books effectively record the growth and development of the young girl into the young woman and artist—a Künstlerroman that has inspired many female readers who have themselves aspired to artistic achievement—but they also tell the story of missing mothers and their place in the lives of motherless daughters. Montgomery positions this absent mother as a complicated presence: Emily's motherless state calls out for other adults to step into the responsible maternal role providing Montgomery with an opportunity to explore motherhood's means and methods across a range of variables and to identify and privilege maternal principles. She does not hold back: she suggestively disputes essentialist views of the maternal in privileging Cousin Jimmy's fulfillment of a maternal role for Emily and dismantles any facile understandings of Aunt Elizabeth's harsh substitute mothering. At the same time, however, Montgomery retains a sharp focus on Emily's actual mother. Despite the mother's death, the mother-daughter relationship is central to Emily's growth and development as she discovers and recovers the lost mother. The recovery requires Emily to negotiate a maternal legacy fraught with familial negations and societal misjudgments. Emily's attempts to reclaim the lost mother restore the maternal reputation and the mother's rightful familial place, allowing a matrilineage in which the mother-daughter connection flourishes, with Emily recognized as a worthy Murray daughter of a valued mother.

The absence/presence of the maternal in the Emily books has received limited critical attention, appearing mostly as a means of developing other of the series' preoccupations and interpretations. Kate Lawson effectively traces Emily's development into sexual maturity through "a sexually rebellious maternal lineage which," she argues, "counteracts the repressive matriarchal power of aunts and family" (22). Building on Lawson, Lindsey McMaster addresses the patriarchal legacies of trauma that characters like Archibald Murray perpetrate on their families, while Joe Sutliff Sanders's study of the "classic orphan girl story" explores how Emily redirects the pattern of disciplining girls toward the mother substitute, Aunt Elizabeth, who "is in sore need of discipline" herself (120). While Lawson provides an overview of the other maternal figures in the series, the focus on mothers in all three is mostly on Aunt Elizabeth, rightly seeing her, in Sanders' words, as "central to the narrative" (128). This critical attention that Aunt Elizabeth's commanding character demands, however, tends to obscure Montgomery's attempts to create a maternal context that examines mothering more broadly from among both the living and dead characters.

Emily of New Moon's opening pages invoke the missing mother both obliquely—the details of Emily's home life and domestic activities make no mention of her—and directly—Emily's image in the glass gives back "her dead mother's smile" (5). Montgomery presents no shortage of maternal substitutes who might assume the maternal place, albeit mostly inadequately. Grunting, opinionated Ellen Greene, the Starr housekeeper at the opening of the novel, means well, but her self-righteous, conforming ways contrast sharply the nurturing traits of care-giving characters like Susan Baker and Judy Plum in other Montgomery works. The Murray aunts fare little better. Montgomery's journal entry of January 2, 1905, coolly assesses the potential of her own aunts to fulfill the maternal role, concluding that if her mother had lived and been like her own "Aunt Emily, or even like Aunt Annie, . . . that would have been for me a worse tragedy than her death" (*Complete Journals 1901–1911* 117). Although in "writing herself out" (*Climbs* 1), Montgomery shows a greater sympathetic understanding for her fictional aunts than the real ones, she nonetheless limits their maternal potential. Aunt Laura's maternal practice is kind, but in the shadow of Aunt Elizabeth's rule, it becomes necessarily stealthy and uneven. Montgomery allows Aunt Elizabeth herself to undergo a slow and hard-won transformation toward greater understanding of what lies outside her knowledge and experience, but even so, Aunt Elizabeth remains far removed from fulfilling for Emily "all that [she] could wish in a mother" (*Complete Journals 1901–1911* [2 Jan. 1905] 117). With the mother's centrality looming large in the Emily series, Montgomery shows herself willing to entertain more daring visions of mothering that challenge the essentialism and stark binaries favored by conceptualizations of motherhood in the early twentieth century. She does so through queering motherhood in the presentation of Cousin Jimmy.

Montgomery's fiction presents several depictions of nurturing fathers who blur the distinctions between gendered parental figures: Douglas Starr fulfills Emily's early parental needs amply and offers a model of fatherhood far removed from Archibald Murray's iron patriarchal rule, but he does not presume to fill the role of Emily's absent mother as his recalling her to Emily indicates. Following Lorna Drew's contention that "many males in the Emily Starr trilogy are . . . coded feminine" (25) and Lawson's view that the "adult males, who are nourishing of Emily's inner life, . . . [are] weak or impaired or marginal" (25), McMaster situates Emily's father, Cousin Jimmy, and Mr. Carpenter as "benevolent and nurturing but weakened men" (54). These associations between traits traditionally deemed feminine and maternal and a diminished manhood hold limited application, especially when considered in the wider context of Montgomery's other works. From early to late in Montgomery's writing life, characters like Matthew Cuthbert and Andrew Stuart show that nurturing traits do not necessarily detract from a character's masculine identity. Montgomery creates fathers and father figures who redefine the role by exhibiting traits, stereotypically associated with women, that expand and equalize the parental role. They may be designated feminized fathers, but Montgomery does not surrender their paternal status. The Emily series' Cousin Jimmy presents something different. He holds a place among the several male characters who function as father figures for Emily at New Moon, but Montgomery's presentation also allows him status among Emily's substitute mothers. He is neither exactly feminized father nor male mother. Montgomery attempts to move his identity outside of heteronormative designations to align him with maternal principles unrelated to gender specificity.

In *Queering Motherhood: Narrative and Theoretical Perspectives*, while acknowledging that "queer eludes definition," Margaret F. Gibson, following Sara Ahmed's interpretation, notes that "the designation 'queer' has," among other aspects, "something to do with sex, with gender, . . . and with disrupting the normative practices of kinship and culture" (1). Pioneer queer theorist Eve Kosofsky Sedgwick posits that concepts of queer consistently work to challenge and resist rigid mainstream categorizations that privilege heteronormativity as the benchmark in the analyses of human behaviors. Queer perspectives and behaviors are expansive, for they turn from what is accepted and established. Gibson notes that queer mothering has the potential to "destabilize existing social relations, institutions, and discourses" (2). Cousin Jimmy participates in this destabilization in multiple ways. He slips among categories. The childhood accident in which Aunt Elizabeth was involved has made him different. "He ain't quite all there . . . he's a bit simple" (*New Moon* 26), Ellen Greene bluntly tells Emily, yet his insights and advice are consistently wise. Montgomery flips traditional gender expectations concerning the New Moon establishment between Aunt Elizabeth, who is the "boss" (26), and Cousin Jimmy, who does much of the practical farming work that rural men usually do. While Aunt Elizabeth remains in charge, the domain that is exclusively Cousin Jimmy's associates him with rural women who normally tend the garden next to the house. The garden is "mine," he tells Emily: "Elizabeth bosses the farm; but she lets me run the garden" (80). Under his direction, the garden flourishes: "He could grow there plants and shrubs that would winter nowhere else in P. E. Island" (226). Although he is not the only male gardener in the Emily books, his bringing things to life and nurturing their growth associate him with traditionally female activities. In destabilizing Cousin Jimmy's gender identity in these ways, Montgomery moves maternal traits away from essentialist attributions. Through him, she suggests that the maternal is neither monolithic nor are its manifestations predictable.

Early in *Emily of New Moon*, Emily responds to Ellen Green's ideas on who among the Murrays will have her with her own wish: "I—I want somebody to love me" (25). She soon comes to know that both Aunt Laura and Cousin Jimmy answer to this need, but Cousin Jimmy seems to reflect most closely Montgomery's conceptions of the absent mother recorded in her journals. Cousin Jimmy and Emily become companions, working the garden together and sharing their thoughts like *"chums"* (*Complete Journals 1918–1921* [25 June 1918] 26). The spirit that moves Cousin Jimmy is like Emily's flash, both coming, like artistic inspiration, unbidden. They share an artistic kinship that speaks to the matrilineage of Montgomery herself and her "poetical" mother (*Complete Journals 1901–1911* [2 Jan. 1905] 117). Cousin Jimmy's queer mothering nurtures Emily's sense of self both emotionally and practically. At New Moon, the inflexible Murray ways loom as Emily's dominant, mainstream society. Cousin Jimmy understands and supports Emily's resistance to the unrelenting demands for conformity that threaten to obliterate her individuality. He stands up for Emily, anticipates her needs, and advises her sagely, helping her to negotiate her resistance successfully. He lets her know that it is acceptable not to think and act according to all the Murray ways while at the same time mediating her behavior into Murray acceptance. He consistently intervenes with Aunt Elizabeth and helps Emily problem-solve her trials with reasonable solutions. No one else among the Murray family members, or indeed in Emily's broader circle, reflects the absent mother's "fine emotions and noble impulses" as fully as Cousin Jimmy does (*Complete Journals 1901–1911* [2 Jan. 1905] 117). Emily needs little time to determine that "whatever part of him was missing it wasn't his heart" (*New Moon* 41). Cousin Jimmy's queer mothering allows Emily a place of her own at New Moon, one that does not require the complete surrender of what New Moon might consider her own queer ways. His ready and unqualified acceptance of her difference creates an environment that gives Emily the security to turn to examining her actual mother's difference to and position in the dominant Murray culture.

When Douglas Starr questions his daughter about her memory of the lost mother, Emily responds with a vivid account of seeing her mother "in a long black box . . . I wondered why Mother looked so white and wouldn't open her eyes" (*New Moon* 18). This memory of the dead mother is an appropriate introduction to the maternal figure in Montgomery's work, for the novel's most loving mothers are dead mothers. Juliet Murray Starr had considered Emily "the—only—baby—of any importance—in the world" (18), Emily's father tells her; perhaps this assurance partly explains Emily's need to believe in loving mothers not only for herself but also for her friend Ilse. Not only does Emily reclaim her own mother's position in the family that sees her as disgraced, but she also vehemently resists the image of Beatrice Burnley as a wayward woman who had "gone away of her own accord and left her dear little baby" (314). As the scandal circulating to explain the disappearance of Ilse's mother suggests, even eleven years after she vanished, these loving mothers, in the perceptions of the living, are also, to varying degrees, disreputable. They orphan their children twice, once in dying, and a second time in the lingering sense that had they lived, they may not have been fit to raise their daughters. Unable to defend herself, the deceased mother must rely on the living daughter to bring her back into the fold of social respectability. Reclaiming the mother is for Emily a responsibility intimately connected with her own developing selfhood.

While the Murray clan casts Douglas Starr as the antagonist of their family drama, it is the sins of the mother that fall on Emily's head in her life at New Moon. Montgomery gives the Murrays' attitude toward Juliet's chosen suitor a neat ironic twist by suggesting that their sense of scandal has been turned upside down. The Murrays are outraged at Douglas Starr not because he refuses to marry the woman whom he has been intensely wooing but because he eagerly does. In all three books in the series, Emily is persistently dogged by Juliet Murray's elopement with Emily's father, the man whom she loved and chose over her family. Aunt Elizabeth puts it bluntly when she allows Emily the full use of her mother's old girlhood room: "'Your mother,' she said, looking coldly at Emily over the flame of the candle . . . 'ran away—flouted her family and broke her father's heart. She was a silly, ungrateful, disobedient girl. I hope *you* will never disgrace your family by such conduct'" (*New Moon* 343). Emily from early on at New Moon must negotiate Aunt Elizabeth's inability, as Emily states, to "trust me out of her sight because my mother eloped" (*Climbs* 6). Like Aunt Elizabeth, the Murray clan generally are "firm believer[s] in heredity" much to Juliet's daughter's disadvantage (*Quest* 19). Even as Aunt Ruth begins to relent in *Emily Climbs* at rumors circulating that Emily and Ilse had been out until midnight prowling about the park with Teddy and Perry, she pointedly admonishes Emily with "you are treading in your mother's footsteps" (*Climbs* 255). The community is often only too eager to join the chorus. Gossipy Miss Potter freely opines that Emily "needs a tight rein, if *I* know anything of human nature.... She's going to be a flirt.... She'll be Juliet all over again" (73). Overheard by Emily, hiding because of her Mother Hubbard, the comments present a humorous situation, but they also reflect the easy slippage assigned to transgressive behaviors between mothers and daughters to which Ilse and her absent mother are also subject.

For Aunt Elizabeth, especially, the wayward mother's actions in the past are a threat in the present. Before Emily's father dies, he tells her that at her mother's death, the Murrays "had offered to take you and bring you up"—specifically, as Oliver Murray had put it, to "give you your mother's place" (*New Moon* 19). Emily's assuming this place when her father dies resurrects for the Murray aunts the presence of the lively, bright, young half-sister who, they feel, had betrayed them. Juliet, as the child of Archibald Murray's second wife, was a generation younger than the siblings of his first marriage, the aunts and uncles amid whom Emily finds herself. Douglas Starr reveals that Juliet's mother, Emily's grandmother, died when Juliet was born. These details indicate that the unmarried half siblings would have raised Juliet as they were now raising Emily. "They all loved and petted her and were very proud of her" (17), Emily's father tells her. Lawson, McMaster, and Sanders, like other critical commentators who discuss Aunt Elizabeth, focus on Aunt Elizabeth's relationship to Emily, but Aunt Elizabeth also had a special relationship with the motherless Juliet. "Aunt Laura says Aunt Elizabeth loved my mother very much" (218), Emily writes to her father.

Juliet's untouched, locked old bedroom, to which Aunt Elizabeth holds the keys, suggests the hidden deep hurt that Juliet's running away caused Aunt Elizabeth, a hurt too painful to revisit openly. The locked room ostensibly represents old Archibald's decree: "Cousin Jimmy says her father locked it up after she ran away with you and Aunt Elizabeth keeps it locked still out of respect to his memory, though Cousin Jimmy says Aunt Elizabeth used to fight with her father something scandalus when he was alive" (*New Moon* 115). Locked rooms, hidden secrets, and emotional hurts open to the possibility that Aunt Elizabeth guards the room not for the sake of the patriarchal domestic tyrant but because of her own mourning for the missing and missed wayward daughter/sister, still loved and cherished.

That father and daughter's "scandalus" rows may have had at their root the patriarch's blaming of one daughter, who held the position of maternal caregiver, for the sins of another becomes a subtle implication amid these details. Both Lawson and McMaster situate Aunt Elizabeth's harsh treatment of Emily in a past filled with familial aggressions, with Lawson focusing on a legacy of suppressed female rage and McMaster looking directly to the influence of Archibald Murray's abuses of power. They both connect Aunt

Elizabeth's "present fears, angers and obsessions firmly to the past" (Lawson 29), but that past has a more immediate resonance in Aunt Elizabeth's relationship with Juliet. With Juliet hovering in the background of New Moon, Aunt Elizabeth's mothering of Emily operates under her sense of deep hurts and past maternal failures. Montgomery subtly suggests Aunt Elizabeth's inner life as substitute mother. Emily, as her mother's daughter, reminds Aunt Elizabeth of a deep, life-changing emotional involvement that the elder relation still intensely feels. She also raises fears of repeating what Aunt Elizabeth believes is her own failed mothering of the beloved Juliet who defied the quasi-parental authority to marry Douglas Starr.

If Emily's taking her "mother's place" (*New Moon* 19) at New Moon resurrects for the New Moon aunts the specter of the young half-sister whom they lovingly mothered, it recovers for Emily, more openly and forcefully, the relationship with the loving missing mother. Initially, Emily acknowledges only her affiliation with the father and resists her Murray heritage. "I'm *all* Starr—I *want* to be" (55), she tells Cousin Jimmy. The aunts and uncles readily agree at first that Emily is "not a Murray" (35), but in continually designating her as "Juliet's daughter" (46), "Juliet's child" (141, 271, 379), "Juliet's girl" (290), they recognize her place in the Murray family structure while at the same time associate her with the Murray family's outlier member, a position that Emily is not adverse to occupying, even defending: Aunt Laura's attempt to comfort Emily over her aversion to wearing the terrible gingham apron with sleeves by telling her it belonged to Emily's mother elicits from Emily a prompt response that shows a subtle understanding of the challenges of New Moon girlhood: "'Then,' said Emily, uncomforted and unsentimental, 'I don't wonder she ran away with Father when she grew up'" (93).

Other objects of clothing provide more felicitous knowledge of her mother's past as Emily's sense of belonging in the Murray household intensifies. In "Worn Worlds: Clothes, Mourning and the Life of Things," Peter Stallybrass points out that "a network of cloth can trace the connections of love across the boundaries of absence, of death" (36). Clothes, he argues, "have a life of their own," presenting both "material . . . and immaterial presences. In the transfer of clothes, identities are transferred from a mother to a daughter" (38), he continues, but posits a dynamic process since clothes are also "reshaped by [their] new wearer" (35). Writing to her father about the Christmas festivities at New Moon, Emily conveys pride in her appearance, mentioning Aunt Laura's letting her "wear mother's blue silk sash with the pink daisies on it that she had when she was a little girl at New Moon" (259). These bits of clothing show Montgomery's awareness and acknowledgment of the power of what today we designate as material culture.[2] In her journal entry of December 29, 1921, Montgomery's longing for the absent mother becomes her frustration that she has nothing of her mother's "that would savour of her personality to me" (*Complete Journals 1918–1921* 361). She assuages her resentment by pasting a scrap of her mother's green silk wedding dress at the end of the entry.

Montgomery provides Emily with a sensitivity to her surroundings and to the materials in them, both organic and manufactured, and shows her lithely exercising her imagination on the material world around her. Her relationship with the Wind Woman echoes her engagements with the elusive mother. Like the Wind Woman in the natural environment, Emily's mother at New Moon seems "always around" (*New Moon* 1), yet not quite accessible. While the timing of the Wind Woman's appearances is not always predictable, her reappearances are reliable. Like Juliet at New Moon, she keeps turning up. Emily's experience in the outdoor "barrens" where the Wind Woman is "so very *real* . . . if you could just spring quickly enough around a little cluster of spruces—only you never could—you would *see* her as well as feel her and hear her" (7) is like Juliet's presence at New Moon manifesting in an object, a tradition, a memory. Like Juliet, the Wind Woman seeks out the unconventional and nonconforming, aligning with "the other gipsies of the night" (73). Perhaps most significantly, both bring comfort to the motherless daughter, offering a sense of companionship and solace.

For Emily at New Moon, this maternal support comes especially through her gaining full access to Juliet's girlhood bedroom, whose objects make the missing mother knowable. As the editors of the *Handbook of Material Culture* point out, "material culture . . . has hundreds of potential definitions and manifestations and is never just one entity or 'thing,'" but one of the entities that they cite is "the relationship of things to value systems, cosmologies, beliefs and emotions, more broadly to personal and social identities" (Tilley et al. 4). In the introduction to the section on subject-object relations, Webb Keane explains that "material things . . . not *only* express past acts, intentions and interpretations. They also invite unexpected responses. Subjects do not just realize themselves through objects, as if the fully-fledged subject were already latent . . . objects . . . may allow subjects to make real discoveries about themselves. They form the grounds for subsequent modes of action whose limits, if any, are in principle unknowable" (201).

Emily examines every object in this "room of her own" (*New Moon* 342) with its material belongings from the wallpaper and rugs to the furniture, pictures, vases, and the curtainless window that opens up to vistas both real and imagined. Her experience is immersive and multisensory. Emily locates herself in the room as she looks in the mirror, delighted at seeing her near-full reflection—"all but my boots" (344). "'I belong here,' she breathed happily" (345), in part at least because here she also locates the lost mother: "She felt deliciously *near* to her mother—as if Juliet Starr had suddenly become real to her. It thrilled her to think that her mother had probably crocheted the lace cover on the round pincushion on the table" (345). The mother that she discovers is not Aunt Elizabeth's "silly, ungrateful, disobedient girl" (343) who disgraced her family and broke their hearts but rather the "golden-haired, rose-cheeked girl" of Juliet's childhood, who crocheted, collected shells, created potpourri. As the room suggests, this person valued harmony, not tension. "The room," the narrator points out, "was full of that indefinable charm found in all rooms where the pieces of furniture, whether old or new, are well acquainted with each other and the walls and floors are on good terms" (345). Whatever challenges New Moon poses for young girlhood, it could not have been an easy decision to run, as Emily's mother did, from such a congenial space.

Through Juliet's girlhood objects and spaces, Emily identifies with her mother—she feels "perfectly at home" (345) among her mother's things—and rejects outright Aunt Elizabeth's views that Emily's mother was "wicked" to run away with her father. In beginning to write her missives to both "Dear Father and Mother" (346) after she takes over her mother's room, Emily reconciles within herself and harmonizes her parental legacies toward which she has been progressing. Her plans and actions, moreover, indicate that while her sense of being her mother's daughter is strong, she will redirect the maternal legacy toward Murray approval, dispelling the sense of disgrace that the family harbors toward the dead Juliet. That Juliet "ran away" defines her in the family as Aunt Elizabeth's summary of her sins indicates. Emily, too, holds the image of her mother as having run away as previous references suggest. Summarizing her activities at New Moon in a letter to her father, she observes: "All the New Moon brides had point lace hangkerchiefs except my mother who ran away" (217–18). As she converses with the mother that the old bedroom has made real, Emily comments, "And to think nobody has ever slept here since that last night you did before you ran away with Father" (345–46).

In contrast to the maternal runaway, Emily refuses to leave. She gives up New York at the end of *Emily Climbs*, telling Miss Royal, "I can't leave New Moon—I love it too much—it means too much to me" (363). She makes clear that she will not leave for either personal or professional reasons, although these blend together for her in the passion she holds for the writing life. Emily reverses her mother's pattern of running away and defies the Murrays' fears that she will follow in Juliet's misguided footsteps. In complete agreement with Aunt Elizabeth's determination that "there . . . be no more elopements from New Moon" (*Emily of New Moon* 369), Emily thinks, in *Emily Climbs*, that her aunt "need not be afraid I will ever elope. I have made up my mind that I will never marry. I shall be *wedded to my art*" (6).

Montgomery suggests the complexity of Emily's need to restore the mother's true and loving character through her protagonist's "second sight" (*New Moon* 394) experience in the first Emily book. Ilse's mother is another maternal runaway whose reputation of marital betrayal and child abandonment has deeply affected the family that she left behind. This image of the wayward wife and mother takes over Emily's imagination with disturbing intensity. Emily's natural curiosity is first aroused by Mr. Slade's reference to the "trick" (105) that Ilse's mother played on Dr. Burnley. She is soon writing to her father that "there is some mistery about Ilse's mother which I cannot fathum" (116). Her curiosity turns to worry as she becomes fixated on the mother's story to the point that she lies awake at night thinking about it. Emily finally hears the story from Aunt Nancy. Beatrice Burnley's sad "tale of anguish and shame" (309) devastates her. Montgomery is careful to identify the part of the story that horrifies Emily the most: "Ilse's mother had run away and left her little baby. To Emily that was the awful thing—the strange, cruel, heartless thing that Ilse's mother had done. She could not bring herself to believe it—there was some mistake somewhere" (314). Ilse's mother's story of maternal transgression becomes for Emily an "enduring anguish" (341) that forms part of her own moments of personal crisis. Hanging precariously over the rocks below when the ground beneath her gives way as she reaches for a flower, Emily lingers over thoughts of Ilse's mother, and her final prayer to God in the event of her pending death includes the petition to "*please* let somebody find out that Ilse's mother didn't do *that*" (318).

The wayward mother is central to Emily's other life-threatening crisis. Montgomery offers no scientific explanation for the "second sight" (*New Moon* 394) that overtakes Emily in her ill, fevered state when she gets the measles, but she does provide a psychological and emotional context involving the lost mother that speaks to the power of imaginative vision. Emily's worry over Ilse's mother intensifies in her fevered state to the point that it seems to worsen her condition and impede her recovery. Emily's fevered vision replaces the sinning woman guilty of abandoning her child with the loving mother eagerly returning to her baby: "'I see her coming over the fields,' she said in a high, clear voice. 'She is coming so gladly—she is singing—she is thinking of her baby—'" (389). Emily's envisioning an alternative narrative for Ilse's mother restores the lost mother to her family, and significantly, Montgomery also ties it to Emily's recovery. Whatever explanation or lack thereof Montgomery offers for Emily's "second sight," the incident affirms Emily's (and her creator's) need to make viable the presence of loving mothers, sometimes absent, in the lives of daughters.

After the restoration of Ilse's mother's reputation, Emily is able to move on. In terms of her illness, she grows calm, her fever lessens, and she begins convalescence. In the second sight incident in the next Emily book, *Emily Climbs*, Montgomery suggests that Emily is also moving beyond considering the child's need for the mother to entertain the maternal perspective and its emotional outlook. In her recent chapter in *L. M. Montgomery and Gender*, Tara K. Parmiter traces Montgomery's attention to the effect that the loss of children has on mothers—not mother loss but "mother's loss." In contrast to Emily's experience with second sight in *Emily of New Moon*, in the "psychic" events in *Emily Climbs* (240), Emily focuses on the mother's feelings for the lost child in the account of little Allan Bradshaw's disappearance. This other story of mothers separated from their children again haunts Emily as did the story of Ilse's mother abandoning her baby, taking again "almost a morbid hold on her" (*Climbs* 209), but it is the mother's pain Montgomery emphasizes: she envisions the plight of "that poor lost child" always through the perspective of "that poor mother" (221, 220). Emily's deeply affected state again leads to an unbelievable insight, but Montgomery shifts Emily's emotional involvement, her pain and worry, to align more closely with the mother's need for reunion.

Emily cannot reclaim all the maternal figures in her life. The best she can do with Dean's sad mother is avoid her fate by not marrying a Priest. Her success with the living maternal figures is also limited. While Aunt Elizabeth develops under her influence, Teddy's mother remains out of her reach. Even after Emily finds and delivers the letter to Mrs. Kent that her husband had written to her long ago, Mrs. Kent remains unforgivingly possessive about her son's love. She is at the other extreme to the maternal forebears of Emily's lineage who do not seem to need reclaiming. Named after Douglas Starr's mother, Emily is, as Cousin Jimmy suggests, "Murray and Byrd and Starr—and a dash of Shipley to boot" (*New Moon* 86), the latter from the great-great-grandmother who defied her husband's authority and established the Murrays at New Moon.

For Montgomery, the maternal becomes both a process and a product in artistic achievement. In *Emily's Quest*, Emily turns to a metaphor for her own literary achievement that several great artists have invoked before her. "Finished—complete!" she rejoices over "*A Seller of Dreams*—her first book . . . *hers*—her very own. Something to which she had given birth, which would never have existed had she not brought it into being" (*Quest* 57). In burning her manuscript after Dean's criticism, she continues the metaphor, and later, when *The Moral of the Rose* arrives as a published book, she thinks back to the *Seller of Dreams* as her "unborn" offspring (201). Emily's literary creations are a different kind of motherhood, but they are not separate from Montgomery's exploration of the mother and the maternal in the Emily books. They are its culmination. For Montgomery, the maternal, in both ideals and practice, is the power of creativity.

NOTES

1. In *The Absent Mother in the Cultural Imagination: Missing, Presumed Dead*, Berit Åström lists among "the different causes for the uses of the dead/absent mother-trope: the biography of the author" (2), which aligns with Montgomery's interest in her mother as seen in her journals. Åström warns, however, that if this interest reflects the individual author's idiosyncrasies too closely, the subject may not resonate with the public. This is not the case for Montgomery.

2. For more on this point, please see Allison McBain Hudson's chapter in this collection.

WORKS CITED

Åström, Berit. "Introduction: Explaining and Exploring the Dead or Absent Mother." *The Absent Mother in the Cultural Imagination: Missing, Presumed Dead*, edited by Berit Åström. Palgrave MacMillan, 2017, pp. 1–22.

Drew, Lorna. "The Emily Connection: Ann Radcliffe, L. M. Montgomery and the 'The Female Gothic.'" *Canadian Children's Literature / Littérature canadienne pour la jeunesse*, vol. 21.1, no. 77, 1995, pp. 19–32.

Gibson, Margaret F. "Introduction: Queering Motherhood in Narrative, Theory, and the Everyday." *Queering Motherhood: Narrative and Theoretical Perspectives*, edited by Margaret F. Gibson, Demeter Press, 2014, pp. 1–23.

Keane, Webb. "Part 3. Subjects and Objects." *Handbook of Material Culture*, edited by Tilley et al., Sage, 2006, pp. 197–202.

Lawson, Kate. "Adolescence and the Trauma of Maternal Inheritance in L. M. Montgomery's *Emily of New Moon*." *Canadian Children's Literature / Littérature canadienne pour la jeunesse*, vol. 25.2, no. 94, 1999, pp. 21–41.

McMaster, Lindsey. "The 'Murray Look': Trauma as Family Legacy in L. M. Montgomery's *Emily of New Moon* Trilogy." *Canadian Children's Literature / Littérature canadienne pour la jeunesse*, vol. 34, no. 2, 2008, pp. 50–74.

Montgomery, L. M. *Complete Journals, The PEI Years, 1889–1900*. Oxford UP, 2012.

Montgomery, L. M. *Complete Journals, The PEI Years, 1901–1911*. Oxford UP, 2013.

Montgomery, L. M. *Complete Journals, The Ontario Years, 1918–1921*. Rock's Mills Press, 2017.

Montgomery, L. M. *Emily Climbs*. 1925. Tundra Books, 2014.

Montgomery, L. M. *Emily of New Moon*. 1923. Tundra Books, 2014.
Montgomery, L. M. *Emily's Quest*. 1927. Tundra Books, 2014.
O'Reilly, Andrea. "Across the Divide: Contemporary Anglo-American Feminist Theory on the Mother-Daughter Relationship." *Mothers and Daughters*, edited by Dannabang Kuwabong, Janet MacLennan, and Dorsia Smith Silva. Demeter Press, 2017, pp. 91–111.
O'Reilly, Andrea, and Sharon Abbey, editors. *Mothers and Daughters: Connection, Empowerment, and Transformation*. Rowan and Littlefield, 2000.
Parmiter, Tara K. "Like a Childless Mother: L. M. Montgomery and the Anguish of Mother's Loss." *L. M. Montgomery and Gender*, edited by E. Holly Pike and Laura Robinson, McGill-Queen's UP, 2021, pp. 316–30.
Sanders, Joe Sutliff. *Disciplining Girls: Understanding the Origins of the Classic Orphan Girl Story*. Johns Hopkins UP, 2011.
Sedgwick, Eve Kosofsky. *Epistemology of the Closet*. U of California P, 1990.
Stallybrass, Peter. "Worn Worlds: Clothes, Mourning and the Life of Things." *Cultural Memory and the Construction of Identity*, edited by Dan Ben-Amos and Liliane Weissberg, Wayne State UP, 1999, pp. 27–44.
Tilley, Christopher Y., et al. "Introduction." *Handbook of Material Culture*. Sage, 2006, pp. 1–6.

Chapter 8

"A GHOST YOU CAN *FEEL* AND *HEAR* BUT NEVER *SEE*"

Queer Hauntings in *Emily of New Moon*

KATHARINE SLATER

The Emily of New Moon series is haunted. Redolent with psychic visions, the incorporeal sublime, possession by the dead, uncanny houses, and the unhappy weight of ancestry, these books raise ghosts that evade easy capture. This reading is nothing new to Emily scholarship; Lorna Drew, Kate Lawson, and Lindsey McMaster have previously examined these books' tribute to the gothic tradition, given their "anxious encounter with otherness, with the dark and mysterious unknown" (Anolik 1). The Emily series, Drew argues, is emblematic of the "female gothic," a genre that "leave[s] behind a residue of lost desire beyond closure" (30). For Lawson, Emily Byrd Starr's development occurs within "a troubling legacy of angry and rebellious female ancestors" who yoke "her present fears, angers, and obsessions firmly to the past" (23, 29). And in her reading of Emily's family history, McMaster notes that "the Gothic supernatural" in the Emily novels expresses "the tension characteristic of trauma narratives concerning what is known and what is suppressed" (57). Undeniably, Emily and her novels are haunted by the gothic ghosts of the Murrays' ancestral trauma and the family's legacy of abusive patriarchy. This legacy, however, doesn't walk alone. It's not the only repressed thing making itself known, nor the sole residue traceable through the cracks made by L. M. Montgomery's prose. What other spirit haunts the Emily series is stranger still.

In this chapter, I argue that the unrecognized ghost of the Emily of New Moon series—the ghost that demands recognition—is the specter of queerness. While feminist scholars have explored gender's impact on the books' narrative, critics have yet to consider how the Emily books, and *Emily of New*

Moon in particular, are antinormative novels that use haunting as a device to make queerness elusively visible. What this practice of spectral visibility achieves in the Emily series is a rejection of heteronormative futurity: a past and present dwelling that refuses or delays entry into marriage, reproduction, and linear temporalities. If the ghost is the "form by which something lost, or barely visible . . . makes itself known or apparent to us," then Emily's gothic spectrality makes known the series' tension between the rigid commands of compulsory heterosexuality and the destabilizing force of queerness, which threatens normative happiness (Gordon 8). Importantly, although the queerness of these novels is largely linked to its characters' anger and bitterness, this all-pervasive negativity does not endorse normativity. Rather, it exposes what Lee Edelman calls "the efficacy of queerness, its real strategic value," which "lies in its resistance to a Symbolic reality that only ever invests us as subjects insofar as we invest ourselves in it" (18). The "Symbolic reality" these books expose—the unshakable heteronormative order—is one that *demands* anger and bitterness, responses that are perfectly reasonable from those for whom that "reality" is not comfortable. "We must stay unhappy with this world," Sara Ahmed commands (105). Emily's characters, haunted by their queer failure to conform, obey.

The gothic qualities of the Emily series are what enable it to deconstruct the systems that wound those who resist normativity. That Montgomery's trilogy plays with gothic tropes has been well established by Lorna Drew, whose 1995 essay examines the connections between the Emily series and Ann Radcliffe's gothic romance *The Mysteries of Udolpho* (1794). Drew argues that "the gothic novel written by women" depicts a woman or girl "menaced by the very structures that are supposed to sustain her. . . . The gothic text . . . represents a critique, if not a collapse, of family and its much-touted values" (19–20). Emily's embrace of a literary career over domesticity, the series' troubling of gender norms, and the centering of supernatural and psychic elements are all, for Drew, elements of narrative rupture that link the novels to a gothic literary history.

Importantly, the gothic qualities of the Emily series are also what allow Montgomery to close the coffin on these ruptures. The resolution of *Emily's Quest* into heterosexual marriage for Emily and Teddy Kent fulfills another genre requirement for gothic fiction, which indulges "in the figurative or literal representation of difference and transgression . . . and then ultimately destroy[s] that difference only to return to the safety of the status quo" (Westengard 9). Yet the eventual destruction of difference does not erase the existence of that difference, which still takes up most of the series' narrative space: most notably in *Emily of New Moon*, the queerest of the three novels.

New Moon, focused on the relationship between long ago and now, drags us ceaselessly backward, away from the trilogy's heterosexual conclusion and into the haunted antilinear past.

The publication of the Emily series in the 1920s occurred during a historical moment of transition into broader awareness of nonnormative gender and sexuality. Mere decades after the consolidation of same-sex sexual acts into a pathologized identity—homosexuality—the early twentieth-century Canadian public was cognizant of "sexual inversion," which medical professionals attributed to mental illness (Maynard). And although the word "queer" still retained its dominant meaning of "odd" or "strange," by the end of the nineteenth century it had newly sexually charged implications (Lindemann 2). In her letters from the 1890s, Montgomery's contemporary Willa Cather consistently uses "queer" in ways that Marilee Lindemann argues are directly tied to unspoken lesbian desire. For Cather, the word queer "keeps finding its way onto the page, appearing four times in the course of a letter that contains five paragraphs . . . and occurring in a range of context that suggests its polysemous character" (Lindemann 20). "Queer" keeps finding its way onto the page in Montgomery's work too: it appears sixty-three different times across the Emily series, with more than two-thirds of the appearances in *Emily of New Moon* alone.

Like Cather's letters, the Emily books employ "queer" in ways that acknowledge its multivalent uses, including unspoken and unacceptable need. Most often, the word applies to characters who act in nonnormative ways that set them apart from other members of the community, or it characterizes the unsettling and possibly supernatural qualities of Emily's environment. Although "queer" never overtly signifies same-sex desire in Montgomery's novels, as Edelman reminds us, "queerness can never define an identity; it can only disturb one" (16). To be queer, in the Emily books, is to be haunted both by what has been and what can never be. While a gap certainly exists between the uses of "queer" in 1923 and our twenty-first-century employments of the term, the queerness of Emily's characters is nevertheless aligned with contemporary understandings, especially when examined within queer theory's antisocial thesis. In what follows, I work with Leo Bersani's and Lee Edelman's framework of reading queerness in opposition to "sociality as we know it": a way of moving through the world that is at elemental odds with the world (Bersani 7). To be queer, within the Emily series, is to live and act in stark defiance of reproductive futurism, or the positioning of heterosexual coupling and procreation as the only ethical investment to be made for cultural survival. This queer antagonism is fundamentally antinormative; it also challenges our collective social investments in futurity through a rejection of heteronormative development, contradicting familiar narratives of aging, connection, and happiness.

Emily, in particular, is marked by the possibilities of "queer," the word that most frequently characterizes her. According to her father's housekeeper Ellen Greene, Emily is "the queerest child": "You talk queer—and you act queer—and at times you look queer. And you're too old for your age—though that ain't your fault" (*New Moon* 20–21). Here, in the series' earliest use of "queer," the word does polysemic work at the intersection of the nonnormative and the uncanny. Emily speaks and acts and looks in ways that suggest her fundamental difference, but she also embodies a rejection of linear chronology that will come to define her trilogy. Emily *is* (not "acts" or "behaves") "too old for her age," and although Ellen Greene is incapable of making the connection, Emily's inherent rejection of a developmental clock is also what queers her. At the same time Western medical communities began to pathologize homosexuality, building it into an identity rather than a series of acts, scripts of temporal maturation for youth produced a new narrative of standard development. By the early twentieth century, "growing up" in the Western world meant achieving a series of prescriptive goals that facilitated young people's "placement and processing by institutions," ensuring the future growth and success of the nation-state (Lesko 97). Emily, "too old" for her age and therefore improperly temporalized, is already defying the expected chronology of her growth, a rejection that challenges normative timetables. Although much of *Emily Climbs* and *Emily's Quest* are dedicated to Emily turning down male suitors, what makes Emily queer is not primarily her rejection of heterosexuality. It's the way her development moves by countering "paradigmatic markers of life experience," refusing externally imposed notions of appropriate—and implicitly heteronormative—progress (Halberstam 2).

Emily's queerness finds a queer welcome in New Moon, the ancestral home of the Murray family, whom Cousin Jimmy proudly identifies as a "darn queer lot" (*New Moon* 70). Although Jimmy uses "lot" to mean "group," the word, like "queer," does polysemic work to invoke a plot of land; like the people who live inside it, New Moon is queer. Emily's first visit to New Moon's kitchen is as uncanny as it is welcoming:

> The sanded floor was spotlessly white, but the boards had been scrubbed away through the years until the knots in them stuck up all over in funny little bosses, and in front of the stove they had sagged, making a queer, shallow little hollow. In one corner of the ceiling was a large square hole which looked black and spookish in the candlelight,

and made her feel creepy. *Something* might pop down out of a hole like that if one hadn't behaved just right, you know. And candles cast such queer wavering shadows. (*New Moon* 53–54)

New Moon bears the sign of its female inhabitants: the material impressions of generations who have cleaned the floorboards, impressing on them "funny" convexities, "queer" concavities, and "spookish" holes. Made by women's hands, the wood's impressions simultaneously evoke the curves of pregnancy and the vacancy of bodies that will never carry children. Both, the text implies, are equally made strange. Given that the ghost is a figure "pregnant with unfulfilled possibility, with the something to be done that the wavering present is demanding," the image of "funny" protuberance gestures not just toward normative reproduction but to the swelling demand of the unspoken (Gordon 183). That unspoken *something* might, Emily understands, emerge "if one hadn't behaved just right, you know," correlating the spectral threat with nonnormative acts. Interpellating the reader with a second-person address—the "you know" that passes by in a textual instant—Montgomery's language acknowledges the extent to which spectrality refuses to be contained. The ghost won't abide by the safe distance of third-person perspective; the ghost leaks from the text to approach the reader too.

What this *something* might be that threatens Emily with its alterity becomes clearer as we consider the legacy she inherits from her female community. While Montgomery's oeuvre is populated with women who reject early-twentieth-century heteronormativity, the Emily series in particular foregrounds women queered by their choices.[1] Many of the series' major female characters, nearly all of them introduced in *New Moon*, live and act in gender-nonconforming ways. In particular, the older women of Blair Water rebuff social norms, living lives that are in direct defiance of marriage and reproduction. Aunts Elizabeth and Laura, Aunt Nancy and her long-time companion Caroline, Aunt Ruth, and Janet Royal are all, to some extent, behavioral outliers whose choices become possible through the absence of male control and the construction of a female-centric space.[2] This reading itself relies on an acknowledgment of the invisible, or spectral; Terry Castle's formulation of the "apparitional lesbian" frames the lesbian as a ghostly figure, concealed by a culture "haunted by a fear of ... women indifferent or resistant to male desire" (5). To read queer signification in the Emily series is a project of excavation that relies on what's missing as much as it relies on what's present.

In *Emily of New Moon*, Aunt Nancy Priest and Caroline Priest are perhaps the most visible ghosts of pathological sapphism, their ghoulish misandry and miserable monogamy the cords that bind them together. Like Murray sisters Aunt Elizabeth and Aunt Laura, the elderly Nancy and Caroline share a family, the "ill to marry—ill to live with" Priests (236). Their common surname first implies a sororal relation—before readers learn that Nancy is a Priest by marriage, Murray by birth—and then insinuates a marital link between the two. Caroline Priest has never married, preferring to live instead with Nancy in the decaying house of Wyther Grange. While "all the boys" fought over Nancy in her long-ago youth, Caroline "never had a beau in her life," and as Caroline herself states, she "never wanted one" (241). Their cutting remarks to one another are the overlay to their deep intimacy. In front of Emily, Nancy asks questions of her companion that don't wait for a response: "You worshipped me, Caroline, didn't you? And you worship me yet, don't you, Caroline?" (243). They sleep together in "the old wing," a statement Caroline makes that elides the question of whether or not they share a bedroom, and Emily herself notes that Nancy and Caroline "fight quite frequently but love each other very hard between times" (244, 248). It seems clear that a queer union of sorts exists between these characters, whose rejection of heteronormativity occurs within a house that Ilse Burnley notes is "haunted by a ghost you can *feel* and *hear* but never *see*" (233).

The apparitional lesbians stalk Wyther Grange. It's significant that despite substantial textual evidence, Nancy and Caroline's relationship has gone unnoticed by scholars and writers engaging with the Emily series, a fact I nevertheless find unsurprising, given that "the literary history of lesbianism ... is first of all a history of derealization.... One woman or the other must be a ghost, or on the way to becoming one. Passion is excited, only to be obscured, disembodied, decarnalized" (Castle 34). The queerness of Nancy and Caroline is possible because the text works to obscure it; their advanced age, their familial connection, and the absence of physical intimacy between them work to hide the significance of their relationship. Although *Emily of New Moon* heavily stresses the uncanny physical links between Emily and her grandfather Archibald Murray, Emily's queerness may have another ancestral connection in Archibald's sister Nancy.

The needle I seek to thread here is a delicate one. In reading the Emily series' older women through a queer lens, my goal is not to convince readers these women are empirically same-sex attracted. Given the precarity of lesbian identity in the 1920s, and given an overall lack of textual emphasis on attraction between women, it's impossible to definitively assign labels. However, as William Hughes and Andrew Smith write, "The queer thing about Gothic [literature] ... is that it refuses to be exclusively queer in the sexual sense, and the queerness of Gothic is such that its main function is to demonstrate the relationship between the marginal and the mainstream" (4). Absence is also queerly familiar; lesbian literary history is historically defined through erasure, and lesbian textual existence is paradoxically present through its low visibility, "reduced to a ghost effect . . . [that] cannot be perceived, except apparitionally" (Castle 31). A queer framework for Blair Water's spinster aunts and widowed oddities therefore allows us to consider how their alterity participates in the series' larger ruptures of normativity.

Like *Anne of Green Gables*, *Emily of New Moon*'s basic plot structure involves an orphaned child arriving at the home of unmarried relatives who constitute a "creative [alternative] to traditional, patriarchal family relationships" (Robinson 20). Emily's family of circumstance is also a family distinguished by its oddness; it rejects the gendered and heterosexual norms established by previous generations. In addition to odd Cousin Jimmy, whose "elfish face" corroborates a personality deemed not "quite right" by Blair Water, New Moon houses sweet Aunt Laura and stern Aunt Elizabeth, never-married postmenopausal sisters who share the primary responsibility of raising Emily (*New Moon* 26, 67). "Forget the Name of the Father," Eve Kosofsky Sedgwick instructs us, in her queer reframing of generational mentoring. "Think about your uncles and your aunts" (59). For Sedgwick, the avunculate offers "the possibility of alternate life trajectories," not only providing unconventional models, but also shifting our perceptions of families as inherently procreative (63).

The "darn queer" Murrays of New Moon are led by Aunt Elizabeth, whose control over the family is so firmly established that Ellen Greene, who lives in another town, can state with confidence that Elizabeth is the household "boss" (*New Moon* 22). Like the "funny little bosses" of New Moon's floorboards, Elizabeth, too, is a figure queerly pregnant with possibility. Proud and uncompromising, she's established upon her introduction as the novel's antagonist, a woman with cold "steel-blue" eyes, a "cool, appraising gaze," and a "long thin mouth" that "compressed severely" (27). Critics have acknowledged the implicit "masculinity" of Aunt Elizabeth, whom McMaster notes has "quite convincingly been dubbed a 'female-clad patriarch'" (52). And certainly, Elizabeth upholds patriarchal norms, admonishing Emily when the latter acts in ways that counter expectations for "prudence and modesty" (59). The daughter of long-dead tyrant Archibald Murray, she has internalized her father's cruelty, reproducing the trauma to which she was subjected in her father's lifetime. Yet to date, no one has considered how reading Elizabeth through a queer lens allows us to understand her rigidity as a signifier that points to her larger divergence from heteronormative happiness.

Like the temporally odd Emily, Elizabeth is set apart from others by her dismissal of linear chronology, as Cousin Jimmy notes: "Your Aunt Elizabeth doesn't like new-fangled things. In the house, we belong to fifty years ago" (*New Moon* 52). In her refusal to move forward—into the twentieth century, into heterosexual coupledom and reproduction—Elizabeth rejects what Jack Halberstam calls "repro-time," her control of New Moon shifting the domestic space from a home inhabited by "vivid brides and mothers and wives," into a "regime" of "old-maidishness" (Halberstam 5; *New Moon* 61). Despite belonging to a respectable family that's lived in Blair Water for generations, Elizabeth exiles herself from the community's sameness, her home a rejection of heteronormative hierarchies, her behavior differentiated as proud, singular, and old-fashioned. Her stubborn embrace of the past also queers the household; the gothic candles that "cast such queer, wavering shadows" are her own device, a repudiation of gas lamps: "Nothing but candles shall be burned for light at New Moon" (53, 16). Montgomery continually links Elizabeth's candles to Elizabeth's body in uncanny ways that divorce her from the normative living: the "odd shadows" cast upward by "the candle under Aunt Elizabeth's nose ... produc[e] a rather skeletonic effect"; Emily's breathless observation to Elizabeth that "when you hold the candle down like that it makes your face look just like a corpse!" (168, 284). In straying—however illusorily—from the fixity of living flesh, Aunt Elizabeth herself briefly inhabits spectrality, her body othered by its flirtation with death. Significantly, although all others, including tolerant Aunt Laura, disapprove of Aunt Elizabeth's adherence to candles, Emily herself is sympathetic: "I believe I like the candles best of all." Elizabeth's surprising praise in response—"You have some sense in you"—is one of the earliest moments of positive connection between the two, an exchange that implies their shared temporal and affinitive alterity (281).

Unlike Aunt Laura, who covers up Emily's small transgressions, or Cousin Jimmy, cheerleader of Emily's imagination, Aunt Elizabeth spends much of *Emily of New Moon* refusing any intimacy with Emily, whose very first reaction to her aunt is one of instant emotional need: "She would have liked to please Aunt Elizabeth" (27). Yet it is Elizabeth and Emily that form the series' most deeply queer relationship. The queerness of it is possible *because* the two characters are aunt and niece, which allows Montgomery's text to raise queer longings and affiliations that would be less permissible between two unrelated adult women. Elizabeth and Emily cannot—and do not—experience sexual desire for one another; paradoxically, this fact creates the conditions within which *New Moon* can produce a deeply felt love story between two female characters. Elizabeth's journey from walled solitude to increased tenderness relies not on marriage to a man but on learning to love a girl who haunts her into new understandings.³

Notably, the intimacy between Aunt Elizabeth and Emily is not always productive or sustaining. Their relationship is mired in the spectral reoccurrence of the past, and Aunt Elizabeth's emotional walls first crumble when her niece meets them with the bulldozer of Elizabeth's paternal trauma. Refusing to have her hair cut, Emily is possessed by dead Archibald Murray's likeness in her moment of deep conviction. Emily, literally haunted, dismantles her aunt's determination: "An amazing thing happened to Aunt Elizabeth. She turned pale—she laid the scissors down—she looked aghast for one moment at the transformed or possessed child before her—and then for the first time in her life Elizabeth Murray turned tail and fled—literally fled—to the kitchen" (*New Moon* 107). The gothic overtones of this haunting illuminate the profound connection between Emily and Aunt Elizabeth, already queer kin in their shared affinity for the past. Here, that fixation becomes deviant, something that resurrects what should stay dead. If the Symbolic figure of the Child is a signifier of futurity, in summoning the past Emily—a queer child—ruptures that rhetorical relationship, denying the connection between childhood and reproduction. It's the suggestive click of the scissors in Elizabeth's hand that "as if by magic, seemed to loosen something—some strange formidable power in Emily's soul," and the sound "figure[s] the fate that cuts the thread of futurity" (106; Edelman 30). The dead past, brought to life in the body of a child, insists on "haunting excess . . . on the negativity that pierces the fantasy screen of futurity, shattering narrative temporality" (Edelman 31). In summoning Archibald Murray, Emily sacrifices linear chronology for the return of the repressed, reminding Elizabeth that the past is never past, that "what is queerest about us" is the willingness "to insist that the future stop here" (Edelman 31).

Queerness disturbs as well as creates. What's queer about this scene beyond its refusal of futurity is the way it produces a connection between Elizabeth and Emily that's founded on rupture as much as it does the vulnerability of being seen. Emily's gothic possession summons a ghost that makes the implacable Aunt Elizabeth appear, for the first time, capable of being hurt, frightened, and traumatized. Certainly, this fear doesn't bring Elizabeth and Emily emotionally closer in positive or affirming ways. But Aunt Elizabeth is nevertheless newly bound to Emily through this vulnerable expression of her traumatized self, upsetting the clear hierarchy formed by age and family status. "Queer bonds," write Joshua J. Weiner and Damon Young, "are social bonds that nevertheless call into question the meaning of the 'social'" (226). For a brief moment, Aunt Elizabeth and Emily are no longer aunt and niece, but daughter and father, a perverse disruption of the familial social order that ages and empowers Emily, that de-ages and weakens Elizabeth. The disturbance dissipates, but the new affiliation lingers.

The passionate negativity of this queer bond reaches its climax toward the end of *Emily of New Moon*, when Emily discovers Aunt Elizabeth reading Emily's private letters, which include angry references to Elizabeth. Furious, Emily confronts Aunt Elizabeth, who feels both shame and anger, the latter emotion a reaction to being made to feel the first:

> For the moment they faced each other, not as aunt and niece, not as child and adult, but as two human beings each with hatred for the other in her heart—Elizabeth Murray, tall and austere and thin-lipped; Emily Starr, white of face, her eyes pools of black flame, her trembling arms hugging her letters. (311)

Here, finally, the text makes overt what has so far been implicit. Emily and Elizabeth are now defined not by their biological connection, nor their generational difference, but by their emotional resemblance. Elizabeth is no longer "Aunt Elizabeth," but "Elizabeth Murray," the use of a first and last name alone paralleled with "Emily Starr." Difference is erased, and only the shared likeness of their passion remains: a queer affinity that Edelman terms "the repetitive investment in the Same," rejecting "the value of difference in heterosexual combination and exchange" (58–59). Montgomery stresses their sameness both literally and metaphorically, given that Emily's physicality in this passage—white flesh, flaming eyes—recalls Elizabeth's candles, the signifier indicating just how thoroughly Emily embodies Elizabeth's queer rejection of temporality. Hatred here works powerfully as both a negation and a binding force. As Sara Ahmed argues, "unhappiness might involve feelings that get directed in a certain way, and even give the narrative its direction.... [T]he threads of negative affect weave together a shared inheritance" (89–90). To deviate from the cardinal signs of happiness—to express a deep unhappiness that bonds you queerly to another—is also to deviate from the straightening rod of placid assimilation that braces *New Moon*'s social community.

The "shared inheritance" of this unhappy bond is also literal, given that Emily's anger is accompanied by the "Murray look" returning to her face:

> Elizabeth Murray turned paler, if that were possible. There were times when she could give the Murray look herself; it was not that which dismayed her—it was the uncanny something which seemed

to peer out behind the Murray look that always broke her will. She trembled—faltered—yielded.

"Keep your letters," she said bitterly, "and scorn the old woman who opened her home to you." (311)

It's tempting to focus a reading of this scene on Elizabeth's emotional pain and her yielding to Emily. The "old woman" who recoils, however, is reacting *not* to the Murray look, previously implied to be the element of gothic possession and family trauma that creates Elizabeth's vulnerability. Instead, Elizabeth's dismay is in response to the "uncanny something . . . behind the Murray look," a reference that returns us implicitly to the "*something*" in New Moon's kitchen that "might pop down out of a hole if one hadn't behaved just right" (53). The ghost of the unnamable haunts Elizabeth Murray: a specter catalyzed by queer defiance. Notably, the "something" that stirs her into horror is also "uncanny," signifying a simultaneous strangeness and familiarity. Elizabeth recoils from the unnamable thing she sees in Emily, and the text implies she does so not only for its oddness but for its semblance too. What does Elizabeth see in the haunted Emily that reminds Elizabeth of what she already knows? What unspeakable, hidden feeling or inclination?

Their confrontation eventually produces a moment of catharsis, where Elizabeth, typically a pillar of impenetrability, thaws into something exposed and human.[4] Upon asking Emily's forgiveness for reading Emily's letters, Aunt Elizabeth is embraced by her niece, who begs Elizabeth to believe that she didn't mean the angry words about her aunt:

"I'd like to believe it, Emily." An odd quiver passed through the tall, rigid form. "I—don't like to think you—*hate me*—my sister's child—little Juliet's child."

"I don't—oh, I don't," sobbed Emily. "And I'll *love* you, Aunt Elizabeth, if you'll let me—if you *want* me to. I didn't think you cared. *Dear* Aunt Elizabeth."

Emily gave Aunt Elizabeth a fierce hug and a passionate kiss on the white, fine-wrinkled cheek. Aunt Elizabeth kissed her gravely on the brow in return and then said, as if closing the door on the whole incident,

"You'd better wash your face and come down to supper." (313–14)

The physical intimacy between Emily and Aunt Elizabeth is notable, especially when contrasted with a paralleled climatic moment of tenderness: the love confession between Emily and Teddy at the end of *Emily's Quest*. In that novel, Teddy tells Emily she loves him; we never witness Emily express her love directly to Teddy. Nor do they kiss or embrace on the page, suggesting a refusal to engage directly with heterosexual romance (225–27). Here, however, Aunt Elizabeth shakes in an "odd quiver" of emotion, and Emily gives her a "fierce hug" and a "passionate kiss," while Elizabeth kisses her "gravely on the brow in return," far more physicality than Emily and Teddy share in their paralleled scene. At the same time, Montgomery underscores the age difference and familial relationship between the two, with Elizabeth's "fine-wrinkled cheek" and Emily's characterization as "my sister's child," details that attempt to de-queer the temporal and relational antinormativity of their relationship. The passion and gravity of their shared embrace is only possible within this stark reminder that the two are aunt and niece, a reminder that nevertheless raises the specter of queerness through the fact of its existence. Just as *New Moon* works to obscure the intimacies of Aunt Nancy and Caroline's relationship, the novel also attempts to elide the love story of Aunt Elizabeth and Emily's connection through an insistence on years and blood.

Queerness, though, remains: a ghost we can "*feel* and *hear*," if not "*see*" (*New Moon* 233). What functions most powerfully—and queerly—in this moment of intimacy is Montgomery's refusal to substitute happiness for love. Grief, pain, and seriousness still dominate Emily and Elizabeth's exchange, providing an anchor to their new closeness that distinguishes it from easy joy. Sara Ahmed argues for "a queer definition of love" that separates "love from happiness, given how happiness tends to come with rather straight definitions" (100). Here, the love expressed between Emily and Aunt Elizabeth—a love that's only achieved through the vehicle of haunting—relies not on reaching a shared experience of happiness but on a grave commitment to working toward mutual understanding. This commitment rejects the demands of reproductive futurity—love as reproduction—instead prioritizing an ethos of consent, empathy, and communication that's valuable solely for its shared existence between two people. What's generated is in stark contrast to the easy, good life promised by heteronormative narratives: a "closing the door" that nevertheless gestures toward careful next steps.

Although *Emily's Quest* culminates in the delayed arrival of Emily Byrd Starr at acceptable heterosexuality—the "happy ending" L. M. Montgomery must deliver to readers—her trilogy nevertheless reverberates with the possibilities queerness brings, as an alternative form of connection that prioritizes understanding. A queer reading of *Emily of New Moon* and the Emily series more broadly offers us a way of disentangling unhappiness from intimacy, of releasing the assumption that anger and absence must be resolved or disappeared. Emily and the older women of Blair Water are haunted in ways that expose the frailties of linear time and matrimonial bliss. Their resistance to normative life markers asks us, as readers, to consider what emerges from that rejection of heterosexual order. If the presence of the ghost directs us to survivals and pleasures that eschew heterosexuality, then we can look at the queer intimacies established in *Emily of New Moon*—especially between Emily and Aunt Elizabeth—as affirming antinormative ways of being in relationship. "You are very hard," a feverish Emily tells her aunt, desperate to be heard, "—but *you* never lie, Aunt Elizabeth" (322). Unhappy truths mingle in Emily's words with happier ones. It's a queer amalgamation that needs a haunting to be articulated, that gestures toward a less uniform world where clear categorical boundaries become ghosts, transparent and fading.

NOTES

1. Certainly a claim can be made for the queerness of several of Emily's male characters. Dean Priest, Mad Mr. Morrison, and Cousin Jimmy Murray are all atypically masculine, rejected by their community for insufficiently conforming to normative pathways. However, given that Dean and Mr. Morrison are characterized through heterosexual romantic fixations, I believe these characters' otherness would be more productively considered through a disability lens. Dean is physically disabled, Mad Mr. Morrison is mentally ill, and Cousin Jimmy has some brain damage, all of which sideline them from acceptable masculinity in the eyes of Blair Water.

2. While this chapter restricts itself to a discussion of *New Moon*, one of the queerest subplots in the Emily series is in *Emily Climbs*. Janet Royal, an unmarried woman in her forties who edits "a big metropolitan woman's magazine," offers Emily the chance to develop her literary career in New York (*Climbs* 286). Janet, coded as lesbian, is also offering Emily entrance into a world where heterosexuality is decentered.

3. Elizabeth Rollins Epperly has discussed the extent to which Charlotte Brontë's gothic novel *Jane Eyre* "shapes much of *Emily of New Moon*," drawing numerous parallels between Emily and Jane (155). For Epperly, the possessive Dean Priest embodies the Byronic role of Edward Rochester: the "self-destructive exile who can be redeemed only by the love of a woman powerful enough to fling her soul into the void between them" (155). And while the connections between Dean and Rochester are numerous, there is another Byronic hero of *New Moon*, who, like Byron's prototypical Conrad in *The Corsair*, is one "of loneliness and mystery, / Scarce seen to smile, and seldom heard to sigh," who is "in words too wise—in conduct *there* a fool—Too firm to yield—and far too proud to stoop," who stands "exempt / From all affection and from all contempt" (175–76, 256–57, 273–74). Tortured, proud, solitary, and enigmatic, Aunt Elizabeth, too, is self-destructive, self-exiled, and only redeemable through the love of a girl powerful enough to fling her soul into the void between them.

4. Aunt Elizabeth's character arc—the emotional thawing of a cold woman—also corresponds to an archetype popular in twenty-first-century sapphic romance: the "ice queen." The ice queen, often a woman much older than her female love interest, is emotionally closed off, but "hiding flame and fury after years of repressing [her] true [self] in order to be the sort of woman [she] think[s] [she] *ought* to be" (Sinclair). In her younger, more emotionally available partner, the ice queen finds "someone who sees her for who she truly is, and who loves that person—a person who has been neglected all too long, especially by the ice queen herself.... [L]ove inspires the ice queen to take down her walls" (Sinclair). While *Emily of New Moon* is not twenty-first-century sapphic romance, the melting of a stern older woman gestures toward queer pleasures that extend beyond time and genre.

WORKS CITED

Ahmed, Sara. *The Promise of Happiness*. Duke UP, 2010.
Anolik, Ruth Bienstock. "Introduction: The Dark Unknown." *The Gothic Other: Racial and Social Constructions in the Literary Imagination*, McFarland, 2004, pp. 1–16.
Bersani, Leo. *Homos*. 1995. Harvard UP, 2009.
Byron, George Gordon. *The Corsair*. 1814. *Wikisource*, https://en.wikisource.org/wiki/The_Corsair_(Byron,_1814)/CANTO_I.
Castle, Terry. *The Apparitional Lesbian: Female Homosexuality and Modern Culture*. Columbia UP, 1993.
Drew, Lorna. "The Emily Connection: Ann Radcliffe, L. M. Montgomery and 'The Female Gothic.'" *Canadian Children's Literature / Littérature canadienne pour la jeunesse*, vol. 77, 1995, pp. 19–32.
Edelman, Lee. *No Future: Queer Theory and the Death Drive*. Duke UP, 2004.
Epperly, Elizabeth Rollins. *The Fragrance of Sweet-Grass: L. M. Montgomery's Heroines and the Pursuit of Romance*. U of Toronto P, 1992.
Gordon, Avery. *Ghostly Matters: Haunting and the Sociological Imagination*. 2nd ed., U of Minnesota P, 2008.
Halberstam, Jack. *In a Queer Time and Place: Transgender Bodies, Subcultural Lives*. New York UP, 2005.
Hughes, William, and Andrew Smith. "Introduction." *Queering the Gothic*, edited by William Hughes and Andrew Smith, Manchester UP, 2017, pp. 1–10.
Lawson, Kate. "Adolescence and the Trauma of Maternal Inheritance in L. M. Montgomery's *Emily of New Moon*." *Canadian Children's Literature / Littérature canadienne pour la jeunesse*, vol. 94, 1999, pp. 21–41.
Lesko, Nancy. *Act Your Age! A Cultural Construction of Adolescence*. 2nd ed., Routledge, 2012.
Lindemann, Marilee. *Willa Cather: Queering America*. Columbia UP, 1999.
Maynard, Stephen. "On the Case of the Case: The Emergence of the Homosexual as a Case History in Early-Twentieth-Century Ontario." *Queerly Canadian: An Introductory*

Reader in Sexuality Studies, edited by Maureen Fitzgerald and Scott Rayter, Canadian Scholars' Press Incorporated, 2012, pp. 153–70.

McMaster, Lindsey. "The 'Murray Look': Trauma as Family Legacy in L. M. Montgomery's *Emily of New Moon* Trilogy." *Canadian Children's Literature / Littérature canadienne pour la jeunesse*, vol. 34, no. 2, 2008, pp. 50–74.

Montgomery, L. M. *Emily Climbs*. 1925. Bantam Books, 1983.

Montgomery, L. M. *Emily of New Moon*. 1923. Bantam Books, 1983.

Montgomery, L. M. *Emily's Quest*. 1927. Bantam Books, 1983.

Robinson, Laura. "Bosom Friends: Lesbian Desire in L. M. Montgomery's *Anne* Books." *Canadian Literature*, vol. 180, 2000, pp. 12–28.

Sedgwick, Eve Kosofsky. *Tendencies*. Duke UP, 1993.

Sinclair, Roslyn. "Snow on Vesuvius: What I Love about Ice Queens." *Ylva Publishing*, 19 Aug. 2019, https://www.ylva-publishing.com/2019/08/19/snow-on-vesuvius-what-i-love-about-fictional-lesbian-ice-queens/.

Weiner, Joshua J., and Damon Young. "Queer Bonds." *GLQ*, vol. 17, no. 2–3, 2011, pp. 223–41.

Westengard, Laura. *Gothic Queer Culture*. U of Nebraska P, 2019.

Part Four

Time

Chapter 9

THE ROMANCE OF HISTORY IN THE EMILY NOVELS

E. HOLLY PIKE

Two kinds of history are at play in L. M. Montgomery's Emily trilogy: the family history and traditions that Emily learns once she arrives at New Moon and the record of publicly significant events that she learns in school. While the trilogy forms a Künstlerroman,[1] it is also an account of Emily's life as an individual belonging to a particular place with a particular history that influences how the characters live in the present. As Emily claims when she chooses not to move to New York and work in publishing, her development as a writer is tied to her life at New Moon: "Some fountain of living water would dry up in my soul if I left the land I love" (*Climbs* 366[2]). This love of her mother's ancestral home is grounded largely in her sensitivity to the natural world of the farm, sea, and woods,[3] but also resides in the history and traditions of the place that Emily learns from her Murray relations. In her discussion of the traumatic elements of Emily's maternal history, Kate Lawson identifies "the force of inheritance, of personality as determined not by conscious choice but as driven by unconscious patterns of behaviour related to the past rather than to the present"; she argues that Emily shares with Aunt Elizabeth "an inter-generational family drama which links her present fears, angers and obsessions firmly to the past" ("Adolescence" 29). While Emily's experiences significantly differ from those of her maternal female ancestors, she lives in a world created by the choices they made in the past and by her actions she generates ongoing family history.

The construction of the past and how the study and transmission of history are depicted are thus important aspects of both the content and the structure of the Emily trilogy. The introduction of historian Francis Parkman as a possible literary model in *Emily Climbs* and passing references to the novels themselves as biography and history raise the question of exactly what constitutes history. Emily discusses with Dean Priest the "crimson and purple pages in history" that she prefers but cannot defend in light of the individual suffering Dean says they cause. The narrator relates that Emily will later describe these heroic events as "an inspiration to humanity," apparently assuming that no "squabble around a ballot-box" can ever be inspirational. Dean's assertion that history is made through "pain—and shame—and rebellion—and bloodshed and heartache" and that "the happiest countries, like the happiest women, have no history" (*New Moon* 332–33) effectively eliminates both peaceful and successful existence and women's experiences from history; he thinks of history as broad movements and great events. However, this understanding of what constitutes history is contested throughout the trilogy through Montgomery's focus on the private experiences of women, both historically and in the present of the novel. I will argue that over the course of the trilogy both through references to historical events and through the structure of the novels, Montgomery engages with family history as domestic experience and public history as a romantic record of dramatic events to privilege an understanding of history as grounded in the local and personal—a version of history that values women's activities, peace, and continuity rather than conflict and disruption.

That women's private experiences are central to the presentation of New Moon as a place in *Emily of New Moon* is indicated in the narrator's description of Emily's first view of the house, which refers exclusively to women's roles: "It was a house which aforetime had had vivid brides and mothers and wives, and the atmosphere of their loves and lives still hung around it, not yet banished by the old-maidishness of the regime of Elizabeth and Laura" (74). Cousin Jimmy Murray's stories focus on women too: Emily's great-great-grandmother Mary Shipley Murray refused to get back on the ship that brought her to North America when it stopped at Prince Edward Island for water (*New Moon* 86), and great-great-grandmother Elizabeth Burnley Murray was so homesick that she refused to remove her bonnet for weeks before accepting her lot (*New Moon* 87–88). Emily's father, telling her about the Murrays shortly before his death, emphasizes the length of their history at New Moon, telling her that they have been there "since the first Murray came out from the Old Country in 1790" (*New Moon* 16), a phrasing that provides continuity with the family's history in the British Isles. Elaborating on the Murray heritage, Cousin Jimmy links his stories to spots such as the graveyard, Lofty John Sullivan's bush, and the garden (*New Moon* 85–91), emphasizing the Prince Edward Island aspects of the family's past. The events he recounts have family rather than public significance though they are tied to the European settler history of the region, through the feud between the neighboring Roman Catholic Sullivans and the Presbyterian Murrays, for instance. Despite the specificity of 1790, the narrative gives little attention to the political history of Prince Edward Island, ignoring such facts as the displacement of Indigenous people and the Acadian expulsion. These historical events receive only indirect and dismissive or negative mention later in the trilogy, through the place name Indian Head (*Climbs* 201), allusion to a "scalping" story (130), the title of Evelyn Blake's plagiarized poem "A Legend of Abegweit" (303), and reference to the local "French" people in *Emily of New Moon*.[4]

Emily's first view of New Moon further suggests that the land-family connection is reciprocal: "She saw a big house peering whitely through a veil of tall old trees—no mushroom growth of yesterday's birches but trees that had loved and been loved by three generations." The personification that depicts trees as loving the family that occupies the land is echoed in the descriptions of the house "peering" and the "friendly" dormer (*New Moon* 64), naturalizing the Murrays' historical occupation of the space. The narrator's account of Emily's response to Lofty John Sullivan's threat to cut down the bush that protects New Moon from wind and storms (225) encapsulates Emily's feelings about the relationship between the geographical place she inhabits, its settler history, and the lived experience of her family. Her love of New Moon encompasses the natural world ("every stick and stone and tree and blade of grass"), the built environment ("every nail in the old kitchen floor"), and the intangible cultural heritage ("every 'tradition' of its history") (226). That the continuation of this place in its current form depends on the actions of a neighbor draws attention to both the historical acts of the family—Archibald Murray selling the land to Lofty John's father fifty years earlier (80)—and the settler history that established individual ownership of land. The importance of continuity to the Murray sense of self is demonstrated in the New Moon "traditions" that are often domestic necessities of the past maintained in the present in spite of technological change. Emily defends Aunt Elizabeth's insistence on candles as "a Murray tradishun" rather than an old-fashioned practice (115); the same is implied about the farm's continued use of the pot imported from England rather than a modern boiler-house for preparing the pigs' potatoes (171). Other Murray traditions also center on what was traditionally women's domestic work: keeping the jampots filled (119), a sausage recipe from "the Old Country" (207), sanding the kitchen floor (*Climbs* 68), and pickles packed in jars to form patterns (248). The "traditions" of New Moon and the Murray family that Emily comes to love are by definition linked to a reverence for the past, but they specifically support both the Murray sense of difference from the other settler families and the ongoing value of the private activities of women.

This private continuity created through tradition is contrasted with the romantic "crimson and purple pages" that Dean refers to and Emily finds "enthralling" (*New Moon* 332). History as taught by Mr. Carpenter adheres to the latter pattern by focusing on dramatic interpretation of events. To make history memorable, he employs the re-creation of individual experiences, so the students "play the different characters and enact the incidents" of the British history they must learn (355–56), in contrast to Miss Brownell's apparent method of reading and memorization (197, 256). The narrator's reference to *Emily of New Moon* as "this history" (373) shortly after the description of Mr. Carpenter's teaching continues to privilege individual experience by eliding academic generic distinctions between fiction and history in an echo of Emily concealing from Aunt Elizabeth her knowledge that *The History of Henry Esmond* is a novel (269).

In the narrator's construction, personal life is history as much as is the broad march of public events. Emily's musing about "the histories written in mysterious hieroglyphics" on the faces of the congregation at prayer meeting (*Climbs* 44) makes the same assumption. The narrator's self-identification as Emily's "biographer" in *Emily Climbs* (17, 137, 194, 271, 333) similarly links fiction to literary forms that are assumed to be nonfictional. Emily's conception of what is truly interesting in the study of the past further reflects this thinking, as her ruminations on the Tudor period focus on what is not in "that pageant of kings and queens and geniuses and puppets"; she wonders about the interior lives of the queens of the period, the things that historians "*can't* tell you" (292).

The practice of history as a literary form becomes more significant in the series with the references in *Emily Climbs* to American historian Francis Parkman, author of the multivolume history *France and England in North America*.[5] He is first mentioned when Emily records in her diary that "a complete set of Parkman" is being offered as a prize for "the best poem, written by a pupil of Shrewsbury High School" (299). While a monumental work of history may not be an obvious choice as a prize for poetry, in the context of Parkman's reception and fame in the nineteenth and early twentieth centuries it is understandable. The level of Parkman's renown is indicated in Emily's diary reference to him by surname only, with the clear expectation that the name needs no more explanation than Shakespeare's.[6] However, Parkman is particularly significant as a writer model because of the style of history he wrote: twentieth-century historiographers consider Parkman a "romantic" historian. Nicholas Carr elaborates on the romantic approach:

The depiction of a world struggling to bring itself into accord with spirit formed the definitive core of romantic history (or, what amounts to the same thing, history written as a romance). The stylistic traits that have sometimes been taken as its hallmarks—color, vitality, grandeur, stirring heroes, nature, ideas of national genesis or progress—might better be seen as elaborations of romanticism's central concern with the relationship between the real and ideal worlds. (8)

According to Richard C. Vitzthum's analysis of *Montcalm and Wolfe*, Parkman's narratives suggest that history is created through heroic deeds. Vitzthum argues that in Parkman's depiction, George Washington, like most of his heroes, "bravely confronts and finally overcomes immense obstacles" (479). W. J. Eccles says of Parkman's volumes, while acknowledging the tendentiousness of his argument, "As literature they rate very highly indeed ... they are endowed with the epic qualities of Greek tragedy" (164). These descriptions indicate that Parkman's method is that of the "crimson and purple pages" that "enthrall" young Emily and that Mr. Carpenter has his pupils act out.

Montgomery read Parkman's *Montcalm and Wolfe* in 1900, at a point when she expressed a preference for history and biography rather than fiction. In her journal she notes that she found the work "fascinating," stating that "fiction no longer satisfies me. I want to read what *real* men and women have done and thought and endured." She adds that reading Parkman led to her rereading James Fenimore Cooper's *The Last of the Mohicans* (Montgomery, *Complete Journals 1889–1900* 453) but does not record whether that choice resulted from some shortcoming in the historical narrative or from an association of subject. Nonetheless, turning from fiction to history and back to fiction searching for "*real* men and women" suggests that she sees little formal distinction. Parkman himself in an early essay on Cooper admits that fiction is more memorable than history as it is generally written, but he decries Cooper's "needless liberties" with historical fact, clearly expecting fiction that references historical events to function like history as a genre ("Works of James Fenimore Cooper" 153).

Ellen Donovan specifically links Parkman's acknowledgement of the power of fiction to his practice as a historian: "While one cannot insist that Parkman is consciously imitating Cooper or Scott, because Parkman uses the same ideas to praise Cooper and Scott as he does to describe his own goals for his history, an influence may be surmised" (277). Wilbur T. Jacobs similarly focuses on Parkman's novelistic style and associates it with the creation of drama: "Parkman understood that history could be made dramatic and interesting enough to be read by everyone. It is no easy task to pick out and label economic, political, diplomatic, or institutional history in his works because they are woven into a dramatic fabric by the hand of an artist" (251–52). These analyses suggest that Parkman believes fiction and history must necessarily share narrative strategies.

While Parkman focuses on great men and public events, his method as a historian could allow development of the kind of interior history Emily seeks when she thinks of the Tudors and that Montgomery provides in the trilogy. David Levin, for instance, notes Parkman's "increased reliance on letters and journals to carry parts of his narrative" by the time he writes *Montcalm and Wolfe* (210). Parkman himself refers to accessing unpublished archival documents from France and England amounting to thousands of pages, listing "great numbers of autograph letters, diaries, and other writings of persons engaged in the war" and "books, pamphlets, contemporary newspapers and other publications" among his sources (*Montcalm and Wolfe* xxxi–xxxii). Certainly, some of these sources express states of mind—Parkman notes that the personal rather than official letters of Montcalm and Bourlamaque "throw the most curious side-lights on the persons and events of the time" (*Montcalm and Wolfe* xxxi–xxxii)—but his phrasing relegates the personal correspondence to a secondary function as a "side-light." In *Emily of New Moon* Emily's letters to her father are included without comment by the narrator, but in *Emily Climbs*, in a passage that Elizabeth Waterston calls "an odd and awkward intrusion" (130), the narrator specifically refers to Emily's diary as an external source. While the passage does intrude, it also defines a method of composition similar to Parkman's and in doing so similarly separates the minor from the major events of a life: "By way of linking up matters unimportant enough for a chapter in themselves, and yet necessary for a proper understanding of [Emily's] personality and environment, I am going to include some more [extracts]" (*Climbs* 17).

For both Parkman and Montgomery, personal records lead to an understanding of environment and personality. Eccles claims that Parkman's "willingness to consult all the available source material" helps him accumulate enough detail to re-create the past environment so the reader can "live in the past for a brief spell" (174), while an unsigned contemporary review of *Montcalm and Wolfe* asserts Parkman's interest in the individual: "The persons who make history are dearer to him than the forces which the philosopher discovers at work" ("Mr. Parkman's *Montcalm and Wolfe*" 269). For both Montgomery and Parkman, the complete picture of the individual, whether a great man who "makes" world events or a woman writer working quietly in Prince Edward Island, is the center of interest in the narrative. Montgomery shares the method used by Parkman in *Montcalm and Wolfe* but uses fictional rather than historical sources and makes Emily's family history and interior experiences the center rather than a sidelight.

Most of Montgomery's trilogy constructs the narrative of Emily's life as a chronicle, a form of historical record that presents events in order of occurrence rather than necessarily analyzing the relationships between events or considering them thematically or by some other system. This structure is clearest in *Emily Climbs* and *Emily's Quest*, where Montgomery's choice to feature Emily's diary entries provides dates that allow readers to track the passage of time. The opening lines of *Emily Climbs*, like the reference to the year 1790 in *Emily of New Moon*, suggest that Montgomery intends the series to be grounded in real-world history; "the olden years before the world turned upside down" (*Climbs* 1) is surely a reference to the first world war.[7] The references to the death of Queen Victoria and to the young prince's age at the time of the spanking recounted by Mrs. McIntyre further tie Emily's experiences to "real-world" events even though the dates in Emily's diary indicate only that it is the twentieth century.[8]

The tie between the chronologies of history and of fiction seems the more significant in that the datable references are connected to a fictional eyewitness account, told by a woman character, of the private life of a historical monarch. Mrs. McIntyre describes the royal family as wanting "a quiet, nice time like common folks" during their summer visits to Balmoral, creating a version of Queen Victoria outside of her political role (*Climbs* 225). The spanking of Bertie, the heir to the throne, could form part of a full understanding of Edward VII's personality and environment, like the "unimportant" events depicted only through the narrator's inclusion of Emily's diary entries, but as a domestic event without a written record its inclusion in the kind of history Emily learns in school and discusses with Dean is unlikely. In Mrs. McIntyre's life, however, it is such an important event that it rivals only the death of her favorite son in significance (230, 236).

The specific and roughly datable references to Queen Victoria in *Emily Climbs* are replaced in *Emily's Quest* with Emily's and Ilse Burnley's dismissive or critical references to things being "Victorian."[9] The characters use the term as one of those "synthesizing constructs" that, as historian David Lowenthal notes, "harden and reify thought about the past" (254), thus reducing the likelihood of reflection on the complexity of the actual period referenced, as Lawson also argues ("Victorian Sickroom" 243–44). Emily pushes against this synthesizing when she snaps at Ilse, "You call every nice, simple, natural emotion Victorian. The whole world today seems to be steeped in a scorn for things Victorian. Do they know what they're talking of?" (*Quest* 241).

Emily's remark opens up the question of what is really understood about the past and asserts the continuity of ordinary human feelings as a historical force, a construction of history that privileges individual experience and domestic relations over the public and political actions that create dramatic events. Once she is engaged to Perry Miller, Ilse describes Emily's wish for her happiness as "blessedly Victorian" (259), supporting Emily's belief in the ongoing value and relevance of attitudes associated with the past. Emily and Ilse's exchange on Lucrezia Borgia similarly questions the certainty of our knowledge of the past. Ilse prefers to retain the "picturesque" version of Borgia as a poisoner while Emily describes her as "an excellent and rather stupid woman beloved for her good works" and therefore not a suitable subject for the type of "picturesque" history Ilse admires (131–32). However, if she was a woman devoted to good works, Borgia may have had an influence on the lives of those around her rivaling that of more dramatic individuals and events.

Other possible historical references are dismissed or fictionalized in *Emily's Quest*. There is a passing reference to the Boxer Rebellion, suggesting real-world historical time for Dean's travels (*Quest* 90), but the sinking of the *Flavian* after striking an iceberg (which Teddy Kent escapes through Emily's psychic intervention), an apparent allusion to the *Titanic*, must occur several years before the historical event, since Emily is not yet twenty years old (82, 105). Here, real-world history has been recast to suit the needs of the fictional life story. Late in the novel, rather than presenting a chronicle, the narrator merely notes that time passes: "Year after year the seasons walked by her door" (260). The gap between Ilse and Teddy's aborted wedding and Ilse and Perry's marriage is not recorded, and we learn only that "one autumn" Perry brings her back from Montreal (261). Emily's career is similarly glossed over; there has been enough time for her to have published "those books"—plural—before "one winter" Mrs. Kent dies (262–63), but readers are not told how many books or how many winters have passed.

This separation of the narrative from both chronicle form and real-world chronology may be signaled in the opening pages of *Emily's Quest*, where the narrator describes Emily as "one of the ladies of New Moon, where nothing had ever changed since her coming there" (2). The seemingly unchanging nature of the place, rather than indicating lack of history in Dean's terms, asserts the importance of the continuity that New Moon's traditions support. The summary account of Emily's suitors similarly emphasizes continuity and preservation of tradition. Waterston aptly notes that the "Blair Water gossip" (152) about Emily's suitors is "accurate as social history" as "the small community has a stake in continuation and therefore in courtships" (147);

however, the comments on the individual suitors are mostly those of Emily's clan and reflect family rather than community values.

The three unmarried women living at New Moon cannot inherit the farm and house and choose not to change their domestic practices, but as they all understand, Emily's cousin Andrew, when he inherits, will want to change things in order to either make the farm profitable or prepare it for sale (*Quest* 176–77). They nevertheless have a role in New Moon's continuity despite what the narrator calls the "old-maidishness" of Elizabeth and Laura's "regime," which might "banish" the history of "brides and mothers and wives" that provided the continuity of new generations (*New Moon* 74). Elizabeth and Laura continue the traditions established by those earlier women to maintain the Murray sense of difference and deliberately pass those traditions on to Emily. Through her literary success, Emily is able to buy Lofty John's bush (*Quest* 185), reversing an act of her grandfather's that had put the farm at risk (*New Moon* 80, 225), so she now has the power to determine whether or not New Moon will remain protected from the elements, and thus has a role with Andrew in its future.

Dean's gift to her of the Disappointed House allows her to remain close to the land occupied historically by her settler ancestors and to retain a home in contact with the physical landscape to which she is emotionally attached. The desperate choice to stay to avoid further ocean travel made by one great-great-grandmother and the reluctance to stay evinced by another result, after generations have passed, in Emily, who has the power to choose freely between staying and going and actually does both, as it is suggested that the Disappointed House will be only a "summer home" for her and Teddy after they marry (*Quest* 269). Emily's inheritance of both the furniture and dishes that her grandmother brought to her marriage (89) and some of Aunt Nancy's belongings (93–94) reinforces the connection between traditions, history, and women's roles. The unusual items that Dean brings into their planned home, including a prayer rug, jades and ivories, and a dragon teapot, have their own histories, but Dean does not tell the stories of their acquisition (89–90), and their histories are neither family history nor the settler history of Prince Edward Island, as he has acquired his belongings through travel. The origins of Emily's inherited pieces may in fact be just as exotic, the mahogany table and willow pattern china, for instance, being products of colonialism, but they have been passed down through the women of the family rather than being mementos of adventurous travel. Their importance lies in their role within the family home, where they are used and cared for and create and participate in traditional practices.[10]

Near the end of *Emily Climbs*, Parkman comes up again, now as a personal role model for Emily. When Janet Royal points out the difficulties Emily may have to overcome to have a successful writing career while remaining at New Moon—lack of material and atmosphere, local jealousies and misunderstandings, the disdain of important editors for rural postmarks (*Climbs* 364–65)—Emily refers to Miss Royal having told her that Parkman "was unable to write for more than five minutes at a time—that he took three years to write one of his books—six lines per day for three years" (366). Emily argues that if Parkman could succeed despite illness, she will be able to succeed despite the limitations of her location.[11]

Emily does face some of the difficulties Miss Royal predicts, but her real struggle, as Elizabeth Epperly argues, is "our consuming human struggle with meaning and despair" ("*Emily's Quest*" 229). While Emily experiences dramatic events—her fall and rescue by Dean, her fall on the stairs, and her psychic experiences, for instance—the diary entries and letters establish her interior history, her struggles with the conditions of her own life. As Epperly argues, "Emily's happiness depends on continuing engagement with a process" (229), a statement that suggests private daily experience rather than the dramatic breakthrough as the source of happiness and creativity. Epperly also argues that Montgomery is "too astute a writer" not to understand how the unmarked and uneventful passage of time between Ilse and Teddy's and Emily and Teddy's engagements would be "challenging" to her readers; Epperly recognizes the "wasted time" as a necessary period during which Emily and Teddy "learn about their respective gifts" and Emily "recognizes the power of her inner voice" (*Fragrance* 190), the voice presented both in her works, which we do not see, and in her diaries. As Miss Royal admits after the publication of *The Moral of the Rose*, Emily could not have written it had she gone to New York (*Quest* 210) because her writing process is firmly based in her life at New Moon. Whether or not she has the "*thrilling* career" that she hoped for as a child (*New Moon* 332), Emily's success depends on her history, which continues and builds on her family's traditions and ties to New Moon.

Lowenthal argues that "historical knowledge, no matter how consensually verified, is necessarily shaped by both narrator and audience" so "for the most part we remain at historians' mercy" (338). We understand, however, that history occurs whether or not incidents are dramatic or are even recorded. The years of Emily's life skipped over in *Emily's Quest* include events, such as the publication of subsequent books and the marriage of her dearest friend, that are not described, even though the publication of Emily's first book and Ilse's first planned wedding are recounted at length. Those events are nonetheless significant, as are unrecorded events in the lives of Emily's great-great-grandmothers—not the refusal to leave or the refusal to remove the bonnet but the daily, repeated activities that create the traditions that bind Elizabeth, Laura, and Emily to life at New Moon and make it possible for Emily to write. The supposed "old-maidishness" of New Moon under Elizabeth and Laura's occupation (*New Moon* 74) becomes a representation of the continuity they provide when Mr. Carpenter, assessing thirteen-year-old Emily's writing, asks, "What do you know of the hungry world?—you in your New Moon seclusion of old trees and old maids" (402). The reciprocal relationship of the trees with the family history identified in Emily's first examination of the farm (64) suggests seclusion to Mr. Carpenter, but it actually is a different aspect of the "hungry world," less frequently described in histories, in which success comes after private struggle.

The two concepts of history that run through the series ultimately both give value to individual experience, but the dramatic version that focuses on great men and great events leaves out the experience of the vast majority of people, the experience of women in particular. By presenting Parkman as a literary model, Montgomery draws attention to what is valuable in his method while still demonstrating that a "great man" or "romantic" approach only tells part of the story. The removal of *Emily's Quest* from detailed chronology and real-world historical time both asserts the fictionality of the narrative and points to the limitations of a history that focuses on big events rather than accounting for the undramatic activities that shape daily experience of both public and private life. Parkman may remain a literary model for Emily because he overcomes personal difficulties and for Montgomery because he understands the importance of personal records, but the "faded and frayed" set of Parkman that Emily bought with her earnings from "The Woman Who Spanked the King" that are "dearer to her than all the other volumes in her library" (*Climbs* 307–8) are dear not because of their contents but because they are symbols of her own achievement.

NOTES

1. For discussion of the Emily novels as a Künstlerroman, see Campbell, "Wedding Bells and Death Knells"; Epperly, *The Fragrance of Sweet-Grass*; MacLulich, "L. M. Montgomery and the Literary Heroine" and "L. M. Montgomery's Portraits of the Artist"; Menzies, "The Moral of the Rose"; Pike, "The Heroine Who Writes and Her Creator," "Reading the Book as Object and Thing," and "(Re)Producing Canadian Literature"; Sardella-Ayres, "Under the Umbrella: The Author-Heroine's Love Triangle"; and Waterston, *Magic Island*.

2. All citations of *Emily of New Moon*, *Emily Climbs*, and *Emily's Quest* (hereafter *New Moon*, *Climbs*, and *Quest*, respectively) in this chapter are from the Tundra editions, based on the original McClelland and Stewart editions.

3. For Emily's connection to nature, see for instance Epperly, "*Emily's Quest*: L. M. Montgomery's Green Alternative to Despair and War?"

4. See Emily and Ilse's invention of a language to counter the French boys' "jabbering" (*New Moon* 241) and Emily's account of local francophone naming practices (348–49).

5. Parkman's history consists of *The Pioneers of France in the New World* (1854), *The Jesuits in North America* (1867), *La Salle and the Discovery of the Great West* (1869), *The Old Régime* (1874), *Count Frontenac and New France under Louis XIV* (1877), *Montcalm and Wolfe* (1884), and *A Half-Century of Conflict* (1892) (Farnham 359).

6. An online search suggests that Parkman's collected works were widely available in the first decade of the twentieth century. One seller website lists multiple printings by Little, Brown (1899, 1902, 1905) and a Canadian edition by Morang (Toronto, 1899) (The Works of Francis Parkman Frontenac Edition 16 Volumes Parkman Francis—AbeBooks, accessed 12 Jan. 2022).

7. Epperly raises this issue in "*Emily's Quest*: L. M. Montgomery's Green Alternative to Despair and War?"

8. The prince is "no more than nine years old" (*Climbs* 224) at the time of Mrs. McIntyre's story, which must therefore take place around 1850. In Emily's diary entries, years are in the form "19—".

9. See pages 14, 42, 72, 81, 131, 149, 206, 224, 227, 241, 243, 251. The only uses of "Victorian" in *Emily Climbs* refer to Mr. Carpenter's dislike of italics (*Climbs* 3, 25). The adjective is not used at all in *Emily of New Moon*. For more on this point, please see Kate Lawson's chapter in this collection.

10. For more on this point, please see Allison McBain Hudson's chapter in this collection.

11. This account of Parkman's difficulties was widely disseminated after his death in 1893 when his career was celebrated in American journals. See for instance Winsor in *Atlantic Monthly* (1894) and Ward in *McClure's Magazine* (1894). Montgomery was certainly familiar with *McClure's*, having had a story accepted by them but apparently never published (*Complete Journals 1901–1911* [29 May 1903] 72; *Green Gables Letters* 68). Parkman described how he overcame his limitations in a letter to Dr. George E. Ellis that other writers reproduced (Farnham 315). Since this conversation takes place in the spring following Emily's autumn encounter with Mrs. McIntyre, who refers to the queen "dying two years ago" (*Climbs* 228), presumably it is 1904.

WORKS CITED

Campbell, Marie. "Wedding Bells and Death Knells: The Writer as Bride in the *Emily* Trilogy." *Harvesting Thistles: The Textual Garden of L. M. Montgomery, Essays on Her Novels and Journals*, edited by Mary Henley Rubio, Canadian Children's Press, 1994, pp. 137–45.

Carr, Nicholas. "'I Have Not Abandoned Any Plan': The Rage in Francis Parkman," *Massachusetts Historical Review*, vol. 17, 2015, pp. 1–34.
Donovan, Ellen. "Narrative Voices in Francis Parkman's *Montcalm and Wolfe*." *Clio*, vol. 18, no. 3, 1989, pp. 275–90.
Eccles, W. J. "The History of New France According to Francis Parkman." *William and Mary Quarterly*, vol. 18, no. 2, April 1961, pp. 163–75.
Epperly, Elizabeth Rollins. "*Emily's Quest*: L. M. Montgomery's Green Alternative to Despair and War?" *L. M. Montgomery and War*, edited by Andrea McKenzie and Jane Ledwell, McGill-Queen's UP, 2017, pp. 214–33.
Epperly, Elizabeth Rollins. *The Fragrance of Sweet-Grass: L. M. Montgomery's Heroines and the Pursuit of Romance*. U of Toronto P, 1992.
Farnham, Charles Haight. *A Life of Francis Parkman*. Little, Brown, 1900. Canadiana.ca.
Jacobs, Wilbur T. "Some of Parkman's Literary Devices," *New England Quarterly*, vol. 31, no. 2, June 1958, pp. 244–52.
Lawson, Kate. "Adolescence and the Trauma of Maternal Inheritance in L. M. Montgomery's *Emily of New Moon*." *Canadian Children's Literature / Littérature canadienne pour le jeunesse*, 94, summer 1999, pp. 21–41. https://ccl-lcj.ca/index.php/ccl-lcj/article/view/4575.
Lawson, Kate. "The Victorian Sickroom in L. M. Montgomery's *The Blue Castle* and *Emily's Quest*: Sentimental Fiction and the Selling of Dreams." *Lion and the Unicorn*, vol. 31, no. 3, 2007, pp. 232–49.
Levin, David. *History as Romantic Art: Bancroft, Prescott, Motley, and Parkman*. Stanford UP, 1959.
Lowenthal, David. *The Past Is a Foreign Country—Revisited*. Cambridge UP, 2015.
MacLulich, T. D. "L. M. Montgomery and the Literary Heroine: Jo, Rebecca, Anne, and Emily." *Canadian Children's Literature / Littérature canadienne pour la jeunesse*, vol. 37, 1985, pp. 5–17. https://ccl-lcj.ca/index.php/ccl-lcj/article/view/1822.
MacLulich, T. D. "L. M. Montgomery's Portraits of the Artist: Realism, Idealism, and the Romantic Imagination." *English Studies in Canada*, vol. 11, Dec. 1985, pp. 459–73.
Menzies, Ian. "The Moral of the Rose: L. M. Montgomery's Emily." *Canadian Children's Literature / Littérature canadienne pour la jeunesse*, vol. 65, 1992, pp. 48–61. https://ccl-lcj.ca/index.php/ccl-lcj/article/view/4744.
Montgomery, L. M. *Complete Journals of L. M. Montgomery: The PEI Years 1889–1900*, edited by Mary Henley Rubio and Elizabeth Hillman Waterston, Oxford UP, 2012.
Montgomery, L. M. *Complete Journals of L. M. Montgomery: The PEI Years 1901–1911*, edited by Mary Henley Rubio and Elizabeth Hillman Waterston, Oxford UP, 2013.
Montgomery, L. M. *Emily Climbs*. 1925. Tundra Books, 2014.
Montgomery, L. M. *Emily of New Moon*. 1923. Tundra Books, 2014.
Montgomery, L. M. *Emily's Quest*. 1927. Tundra Books, 2014.
Montgomery, L. M. *The Green Gables Letters from L. M. Montgomery to Ephraim Weber, 1905–1909*. 1960. Edited by Wilfrid Eggleston, Borealis Press, 2001.
"Mr. Parkman's *Montcalm and Wolfe*," *Atlantic Monthly*, vol. 55, Feb. 1885, pp. 265–70.
Parkman, Francis. *Montcalm and Wolfe*. 1884. Foreword by C. Vann Woodward, Viking Press, 1984.

Parkman, Francis. "The Works of James Fenimore Cooper." *North American Review*, vol. 74, no. 154, 1852, pp. 147–61.

Pike, E. Holly. "The Heroine Who Writes and Her Creator." *Harvesting Thistles: The Textual Garden of L. M. Montgomery, Essays on Her Novels and Journals*, edited by Mary Henley Rubio, Canadian Children's Press, 1994, pp. 50–57.

Pike, E. Holly. "Reading the Book as Object and Thing in L. M. Montgomery's *Emily* Series." *Journal of L. M. Montgomery Studies*, 15 Dec. 2020, https://doi.org/10.32393/jlmms/2021.0003.

Pike, E. Holly. "(Re)Producing Canadian Literature: L. M. Montgomery's Emily Novels." *L. M. Montgomery and Canadian Culture*, edited by Irene Gammel and Elizabeth Epperly, U of Toronto P, 1999, pp. 64–76.

Sardella-Ayres, Dawn. "Under the Umbrella: The Author-Heroine's Love Triangle." *Canadian Children's Literature / Littérature canadienne pour la jeunesse*, vol. 105-6, Spring/Summer 2002, pp. 100–113. https://ccl-lcj.ca/index.php/ccl-lcj/article/view/3849.

Vitzthum, Richard C. "The Historian as Editor: Francis Parkman's Reconstruction of Sources in Montcalm and Wolfe." *Journal of American History*, vol. 53, no. 3, Dec. 1966, pp. 471–86.

Ward, Julius H. "Francis Parkman." *McClure's Magazine*, Jan. 1894, pp. 185–98.

Waterston, Elizabeth. *Magic Island: The Fictions of L. M. Montgomery*. Oxford UP, 2008.

Winsor, Justin. "Francis Parkman." *Atlantic Monthly*, vol. 73, May 1894, pp. 660–64.

Chapter 10

ENCROACHING DARKNESS

L. M. Montgomery's Books about Emily

CAROL L. BERAN

Both Alice Munro and Margaret Laurence name Lucy Maud Montgomery's books about Emily as books that mattered to them. Munro specifies her interest in Emily's development in these novels:

> But what's central to the story, and may be harder to write about than sex or confused feelings in families, is the development of a child—and a girl child, at that—into a writer. Emily says at the end of the book, that she has to write, she would write no matter what, and we have been shown not only how she learned to write, but how she discovered writing a way of surviving as herself in the world. (Afterword 359)

Laurence speaks of her love for *Anne of Green Gables*, but goes on to say that

> the other of Montgomery's books that stirred me was *Emily of New Moon*. Both Anne and Emily were rebels—intelligent, talented girls who were not about to be put down. Emily had the added appeal of wanting to become a writer—no, of actually *being* a writer, as I myself was, even as a child, although I never dreamed I would someday be published. ("Books" 163)

Obviously, Emily's need to write appealed to Munro and Laurence as they were discovering their similar predilection. However, this simple formulation marginalizes factors such as Montgomery's experiences in the fifteen years between the publication of *Anne of Green Gables* and *Emily of New Moon* that darkened the tone of the later books, Montgomery's presentation of Emily's visionary experiences in a way that questions gender roles, and Montgomery's use of both first person and third person narrators to create gaps that challenge readers to engage actively in the story. Changes in tone, theme, and narrative patterns enriched the books about Emily with a complexity that may have drawn readers as sensitive to writing as Munro and Laurence.

CONFLICTS AND COMPLEXITY

In the years between Anne and Emily, success as an author, marriage, motherhood, and the First World War brought additional conflicts into Montgomery's life, making her later, less famous series darker in tone and more complex than her first published novel.

In June 1908, Montgomery's life transformed with the publication of *Anne of Green Gables*, which sold quickly and whose popularity continued to grow. In July 1911, Montgomery married Ewen MacDonald, a Presbyterian minister, after a long engagement that predated the publication of her first novel. MacDonald's work took Montgomery away from Prince Edward Island, away from the locales so important in her books.

At the time of her marriage, Montgomery already knew that she had a calling similar to the calling that would beckon Emily on her path to becoming a professional writer. In her memoir, *The Alpine Path*, originally published as essays in the years between Anne and Emily, Montgomery describes her own transcendental experiences in similar terms to those she uses to describe Emily's:

> It always seemed to me, ever since early childhood, that, amid all the commonplaces of life, I was very near to a kingdom of ideal beauty. Between it and me hung only a thin veil. I could never draw it quite aside, but sometimes a wind fluttered it and I caught a glimpse of the enchanting realm beyond—only a glimpse, but those glimpses have always made life worth while. (Installment III; compare *New Moon* 7, 29)

Before marrying, Montgomery was already translating those glimpses beyond the veil into an income from her writing. Whereas most women at that time needed to marry for financial support, the successful author probably could have supported herself. Friction between her roles as wife and author created conflicts that contribute to the differences between Anne and Emily. Excerpts from her journals indicate that Montgomery "felt so miserable at her wedding banquet that she had to repress the urge to rip the ring off her finger" (see Lefebvre 101). A woman used to being independent would be aware of how much control of her life a married woman of that time gave up to her spouse and to children. With the birth of children, the roles and responsibilities of her married identity expanded. In 1912 Montgomery's son Chester was born. In 1914 she experienced a stillbirth. In 1915 her son Stuart was born. In less than a decade, Montgomery had become a published novelist, a wife, a mother, and a grieving mother.

Although Montgomery's mixed emotions about her marriage have been amply discussed with materials from her journals, her public statements express a strong belief that marriage and bearing children is the central purpose of a woman's life; writing had to be fit into the edges of life as a wife and mother. Montgomery tells an interviewer, "I would say that a woman may successfully combine a profession of her own with the oldest one in the world, that of wifehood and motherhood but only if she be able to pursue the career at home. It doesn't seem to me possible for a mother to be to her children what she should if they are only recipients of her left over time, and are, for the major part, under the care of paid help" (Muir 225). These statements reveal her inner conflict as she tried to reconcile a received ideal of motherhood with her sense of her vocation as a writer.

When the First World War began in 1914, the Dominion of Canada became involved in the war effort. The Canadian Parliament gave unanimous consent, and the country seemed united in support of participation. "Most English Canadians viewed the war in simple terms: good versus evil; democracy versus autocracy; the Anglo-Saxons versus the 'Huns.' Recruitment propaganda, including statements by church leaders, reinforced this image" (Francis et al. 177). However, reports of the horrors of the front—poison gas, sickening trenches, foolishly ordered offensives that led to many deaths—caused many Canadians to reevaluate their beliefs about the war (187–95).

The war produced conflicts that become evident in Montgomery's writing during these years. In 1915 Montgomery published a letter in the *Boston Evening Transcript*, writing, "This horrible waiting—waiting—waiting every day for the war news—the dreadful uncertainty—the casualty lists—it all seems to me as if I were crushed under an ever-increasing weight" ("[This Hideous War]" 149). Montgomery began writing the books about Anne before the First World War; the series progresses into the time of the war. Three of Montgomery's sequels to *Anne of Green Gables* before the Emily series, as Elizabeth Waterston puts it, are "shadowed by war" (62): *Anne's House of Dreams* (1917), *Rainbow Valley* (1919), and *Rilla of Ingleside* (1921). Montgomery's heroic vision of the war is complicated by the time she publishes *Rilla of Ingleside*. Although Anne collapses into grief when a son dies in Europe, Anne's daughter Rilla shows how women on the home front supported the war, not just verbally but through actions such as caring for a war baby. A double view of the war is encapsulated in the reactions of mother and daughter: incredible grief at the deaths on foreign soil, and the need to carry on valiantly in spite of this. Andrea McKenzie explains, "What Montgomery shows us is both a dominant ideology and a subversion of it: a nation welded by sacrifice, but a sacrifice made by both the men who fought and the women who mourned them" (343).

The complexity that the war experience brought about in Montgomery's thinking and writing surfaces in the Emily books. *Emily Climbs* begins with a sentence in which Montgomery acknowledges the trauma of World War I as she specifically places her story prior to the war: "Emily Byrd Starr was alone in her room, in the old New Moon farmhouse at Blair Water, one stormy night in a February of the olden years before the world turned upside down" (1). Montgomery includes additional commentary about war by having characters comment about a central controversy. Dean Priest insists on the horrors of war, reminding Emily that "defeated people had mothers, sisters, and sweethearts. If they could have fought a bloodless battle at the polls wouldn't it have been better—if not so dramatic." She responds "confusedly" that she "can't feel that way"; the narrator comments that ten years later she would have said, "The heroes of Thermopylae have been an inspiration to humanity for centuries. What squabble around a ballot-box will ever be that?" (*New Moon* 274). Montgomery leaves a gap, a disjunction to prod readers to think about assenting to Dean Priest's view or revising this in the way the more mature Emily does.[1]

That conflict between Dean and Emily finishes quickly, and the story moves on, but in general, the Emily books tend to linger over periods of disillusionment and inner turmoil in ways that the Anne books do not. The books about Anne and about Emily are both generally episodic. The adventures of the heroines are told mostly in discrete, self-contained stories, loosely held together by the girls growing up as the books continue. Episodes from *Anne of Green Gables* cohere around the ideas of proving a girl is as important to the family as a boy would be and Anne's repeated efforts to become a valued member of the family and community. Episodes in the books about Emily connect because Emily seeks an identity that reflects both her Starr inheritance and her Murray heritage while struggling to fulfill her calling as a writer. Furthermore, whereas Anne generally does not change inwardly, although "she talks less, though more thoughtfully, but that's about it" (Atwood, "Afterword" 2008, 90), Emily demonstrates a sustained change after many of her adventures. For example, when Anne falls from a roof and breaks her ankle, a few paragraphs cover her recovery and seven-week absence from school (*Anne* 224–26). When Emily trips on the steps, her injuries keep her inactive for a long period, and the story lingers over her shifting relationship to her family, place, and calling. Inner conflict exists in both stories, but in the later books, that conflict becomes more prominent than in *Anne of Green Gables*.

That sustained period of inner turmoil following her injury produces a more vulnerable and depressed Emily. She no longer experiences the flash, and she says she is "done" with writing (*Quest* 76, 86). Whereas Anne heals largely off-stage, Emily's prolonged physical recovery makes her susceptible to Dean Priest's attentions to such an extent that she accepts his offer of marriage (*Quest* 74–93). Dean Priest is not simply a false romantic lead but, as Elizabeth Waterston puts it, "her own dead father's friend, who brings her back to life again, at the cost of possessing her soul" (Waterston 64). He offers a mature but jaded, cynical view that threatens, in Elizabeth Epperly's words, the deepest parts of Emily's identity, the vocation to which she has dedicated her life and genius:

> Emily's apparent love struggle with Dean Priest is nothing less than the female writer's fight for survival. . . . Montgomery makes the apparently conventional love story of Emily and Teddy actually a triumph of the female artist over the crippled and crippling constraints of male authority and domination. Emily wins, keeps her voice, and is true to the imaginative influences that have enriched her individuality. (148; see also 183)

That victory, however, comes only after emerging from a long period of self-doubt and disillusionment that takes root in the extended period of introspective recovery that has no prolonged parallel in Anne's story.

VISIONARY EXPERIENCES

If the years between *Anne of Green Gables* and *Emily of New Moon* brought turmoil and conflicts on a personal level, they also brought reaffirmation of Montgomery's sense of Vocation as she published her autobiographical essays, *The Alpine Path*. Many readers, no doubt including Margaret Laurence and Alice Munro, have felt an emotional attachment to a kindred spirit of the sort Brenda R. Weber talks about in her essay as they read the stories of the joys and obstacles Emily experiences on her way to becoming a published writer. Laurence writes, "These two fictional girls gave me, I think, the sense that a woman could be—and it was *all right* for her to be—an intelligent, independent-minded person who was determined to pursue her own vocation, as well as being a wife and mother" ("Books" 163). Munro as a child found the story of the developing writer "a revelation" (Ross, *Alice Munro* 43–44). In an interview, she told Catherine Sheldrick Ross, "I remember when I read *Emily of New Moon* I realized that I was reading something different. Emily to me was the watershed book of my life" (16).

In the novels Dean Priest, by imposing the gender role definitions of the period on Emily, threatens her vocation as a writer. Just as Montgomery had to struggle with traditional gender roles and her vocation as a writer in the period between *Anne of Green Gables* and *Emily of New Moon*, the girl writer she created following those difficult years had to struggle with the ways in which masculinity pervaded inherited literary models. Emily takes her writing seriously—as a man would be expected to—rather than limiting herself to the socially acceptable woman's roles centering on children, kitchen, and church.

The masculine literary traditions within which Emily works permeate the trilogy. Emily's visionary experiences and their relationship to Emily's calling to become a writer are emphasized from the beginning of the series. In the third paragraph of the first chapter of *Emily of New Moon*, Montgomery writes, "And then there was 'the flash' too. She never knew when it might come, and the possibility of it kept her a-thrill and expectant" (1). A few pages later the narrator emphasizes how the flash has been part of Emily's experiences since early childhood in a passage that echoes Montgomery's description of her own experiences in *The Alpine Path*, quoted above: "It had always seemed to Emily ever since she could remember, that she was very, very near to a world of wonderful beauty. Between it and herself hung only a thin curtain; she could never draw the curtain aside—but sometimes, just for a moment, a wind fluttered it and then it was as if she caught a glimpse of the enchanting realm beyond—only a glimpse—and heard a note of unearthly music" (7). The flash is fleeting: "This moment came rarely—went swiftly, leaving her breathless with the inexpressible delight of it. She could never recall it—never pretend it, but the wonder of it stayed with her for days" (7). Her response to the flash is to feel "all agog to get home and write down her 'description' before the memory picture of what she had seen grew a little blurred" (7). For Emily, the flash is a barometer of her mental health, a source of inspiration for her writing, an integral part of her identity, and a sign of her Vocation as a writer.

The term "flash" and the idea of a moment outside time that brings joy to the person who experiences it may come from William Wordsworth's poem "I Wandered Lonely as a Cloud," where the poet speaks of memories that "flash upon that inward eye" when he is away from the scene that inspired the flash (334–35; see Beran 159). If so, this literary inheritance is distinctly gendered in a way that excludes a female artist. We know that Wordsworth's sister Dorothy accompanied the poet on the walk that gave rise to "I Wandered," but Dorothy's journal entry about that day celebrates the beauty of nature without evoking a flash on the inward eye (D. Wordsworth 409–10). Having the flash is apparently an experience reserved for men in the minds of both Wordsworth siblings. Emily's flash is empowering for her, and Montgomery claims it is just as available to Emily as it was to William Wordsworth.[2]

Another literary model provides a more complicated gendered reference. An incident of clairvoyance in the Emily saga follows closely the experiences of Charlotte Brontë's character Jane Eyre:

> My heart beat fast and thick: I heard its throb. Suddenly it stood still to an inexpressible feeling that thrilled it through, and passed at once to my head and extremities. The feeling was not like an electric shock; but it was quite as sharp, as strange, as startling: it acted on my senses as if their utmost activity hitherto had been but torpor; from which they were now summoned, and forced to wake. They rose expectant: eye and ear waited, while the flesh quivered on my bones.
> ...I saw nothing, but I heard a voice somewhere cry—Jane! Jane! Jane! Nothing more. (373–74)

Later, Mr. Rochester affirms that he called aloud as "the Alpha and Omega of my heart's wishes broke involuntarily from my lips in the words—'Jane! Jane! Jane!'" He heard a voice saying, "'I am coming: wait for me' and a moment after went whispering on the wind the words—'Where are you?'" (398), Jane's exact replies at the moment they each had the experience.

In a parallel scene in *Emily Climbs*, Montgomery's heroine, locked in the church alone at night during a storm and fearful she is being pursued by Mad Mr. Morrison, screams to Teddy to save her, though "she did not know why she called for Teddy—she did not even realize that she had called him" (49). Teddy says, "I heard you call me," and Emily acknowledges, "I called for you when I saw Mad Mr. Morrison first. But, Teddy, you couldn't have heard me—you *couldn't*. The Tansy Patch is a mile from here" (52). Asked how he knew where she was, Teddy admits, "I just seemed to know you were in the church when I heard you calling me" (53). Emily occupies Rochester's role:

hers is the voice that calls out across the distance to her rescuer. There is no feminine visionary reply, only Emily's call in a masculine position. Although Dean Priest suggests Emily's second sight might be an inheritance from her Scottish grandmother (*Quest* 128–29), the parallels with Rochester associate her with a power that this literary model reserved for men.

Whereas the flash signals and reaffirms Emily's vocation as a writer because it connects her with William Wordsworth and Rochester in *Jane Eyre*, it also places her in a masculine tradition of visions. The visions that Emily experiences link her to St. Paul, definitively placing her even as a young girl in a male, Christian tradition valued by Emily's community. That tradition was one with which Montgomery was deeply familiar, not only as a Protestant herself but as the wife of a working minister. Still, Christianity was not simply something that surrounded Montgomery throughout her life; it was also something with which she struggled, specifically during the years between the publication of *Anne of Green Gables* and *Emily of New Moon*, as a particular strain of what she called "damnable theology" had infected her husband with shattering doubts about his own salvation (qtd. in Rubio 212). The Christian idea of Vocation is grounded in a masculine New Testament tradition. In the biblical account, when the man then called Saul, a persecutor of Christians, travels to Damascus, "suddenly there shined round about him a light from heaven" (Acts 9:3). Saul hears Jesus speaking to him: "Saul, Saul, why persecutest thou me?" (Acts 9:4). This event leads Saul to change the direction of his life. Emily's calling to be a writer mirrors through her visions the Apostle's calling to preach the gospel. Like the Apostle, Emily also has visions that reveal important things to her: Paul's vision calling him to "Come over into Macedonia and help us" (Acts 16:9) is reflected in Emily's experiences of seeing what happened to Ilse's mother years ago, of being able to call out to Teddy psychically when she gets locked in the church during a storm, and of being able to reach out across the ocean to Teddy to prevent his boarding a ship that sank.

Both Emily's psychic abilities and the flash are powers coming from outside the everyday world. St. Paul's Vocation is imposed by God unexpectedly, is given to a male as was Wordsworth's flash, and brings a spiritual outcome. The connection with St. Paul allows Emily to move outside feminine roles considered appropriate at the time, and hints that her calling is supernaturally affirmed rather than, as her friends and relatives too often insist, an example of her own willfulness.

Drawing from the biblical tradition, the tradition of the Victorian novel, and the British romantic tradition gives the narrative a serious tone commensurate with an author who has experienced an additional fifteen years of trauma beyond what the woman who wrote *Anne of Green Gables* had experienced. Emily's saga points to gaps between male and female roles and between a mere desire to enter a profession and a calling to a profession. Like Paul's, Emily's calling has a spiritual aspect; even as Paul preached and converted people to faith in Christ, Emily learns to forgo fanciful if entertaining plots of knights or fairies in order to write stories that perpetuate goodness, justice, and belief, not specific religious doctrines, but moral living as Montgomery saw it.

Emily's sense of Vocation provides a focus for the series about her: whereas finding a home, a place to belong, was paramount to Montgomery's narratives about Anne's experiences, even in the final book about Emily, Montgomery leaves ambiguous whether the protagonist's quest signaled in the title is to marry a man she loves or to achieve success as a writer. Because readers learn of Emily's sense of a calling to be a writer early in the first novel of the series and because her efforts at writing and publishing continue throughout all three volumes, her Vocation not merely distinguishes Emily from Anne, but also gives her a calling that many people in her community would have considered a career for males only.

Munro and Laurence each told interviewers that the need to write—a feeling Emily expresses often—was central to their lives. Munro told Graeme Gibson, "I can't imagine living without writing" (244), adding later that to be a writer, "you have to think that your work is more important than almost anything else and you have to start thinking this when you're very young" (253). Lois Wilson says Laurence told her, "I think that almost all serious writers experience a sense of vocation. When young writers say, 'Do you think I should become a writer?' I say, if you don't have to be, then don't do it" (153).

NARRATION

Both Laurence and Munro were drawn to Montgomery's sophisticated writing in the Emily books. Munro told Catherine Sheldrick Ross that "there's a literary aspect to *Emily* that I had not found in any other book before. So when I was finished with it, I was rather upset and didn't like it. Then in about two years I went back to it and then read it again, because those satisfactions were the ones that I was now seeking" ("An Interview" 16). For Munro, ultimately "what mattered to me finally in this book, what was to matter to me in books from then on, was knowing more about life than I'd been told, and more than I can ever tell" (Afterword 361). Like Montgomery, Laurence chooses narrative point of view very carefully. She notes that she often writes in the first person, and when she uses third person limited, she is in a way still writing from the character's point of view. In either case, "The character is not a mask but an individual, separate from the writer" ("Time" 16). However, she notes "one difficulty of first person narration—the lack of external viewpoint" ("Gadgetry" 33).

A striking difference between *Anne of Green Gables* and the Emily books is the latter's frequent use of first-person narration. The dovetailing of and contrast between first and third person provides a complexity at the level of reader engagement by challenging readers to fill in gaps between the narrative voices in ways that aren't demanded of readers of *Anne of Green Gables*. This greater complexity may reflect the inner turmoil Montgomery endured between Anne and Emily. It also might have drawn sensitive readers like Munro and Laurence to the later series.

In *Emily of New Moon*, Emily writes letters to her father after his death; as she grows older, she begins journal writing. In an essay on writing, Montgomery expresses her preference for narrative very close to the character:

> Personally I prefer writing in the first person, because it then seems easier to *live* my story as I write it. Since editors seem to have a prejudice against this, I often write a story in the first person and then rewrite it, shifting it to the third. As a reader, I enjoy a story written in the first person far more than any other kind. It gives me more of a sense of reality, of actually knowing the people in it. The author does not seem to *come between* me and the characters as much as in the third-person stories. ("From *Fiction Writers*" 195)

The idea that the choice of narrator might "come between" is an insight into Montgomery's understanding of how to foster reader empathy and emotional synchronicity between reader and character. This insight plays out in the books about Emily both in the segments told directly by Emily and in segments that use a third-person narrator at various distances from Emily.

Sometimes the third-person narrator sees only the outside of characters, including Emily. For example, when the Japanese prince leaves without their becoming engaged, the narrator asserts, "Nobody ever knew just what he said to her one night at moonrise in the garden. Emily was a little white and strange and remote when she came in, but she smiled impishly at her aunts and Cousin Louise" (*Quest* 190). Montgomery chooses to obscure the matter by keeping the narrator at a distance from Emily. Emily says, "So I'm not to be a Japanese princess after all," and the narrator notes she was "wiping away some imaginary tears" (190). The distancing creates gaps for readers to fill. Did he propose? Did she refuse him? Are the imaginary tears an act for her relatives? A satiric gesture giving them what they expect with a twist? How is she actually feeling? Why is she "white" and "remote"? Are the imaginary tears covering up deeper emotions? By not granting full access to Emily's emotions in this scene, Montgomery's third-person speaker refuses to allow us to draw close to Emily while enticing us to become cocreators with Montgomery as we think of alternative possibilities.

Montgomery's third-person narrator in the Emily years is not at a consistent distance. By using at times a limited narrator who knows only what Emily knows, Montgomery invites readers up close to Emily to share her thoughts and emotions in ways we do not after the moments with the Japanese prince: "Sheer panic shattered Emily's trance. She bounded to her feet with a piercing scream of terror" and "shrieked madly" to Teddy to save her (*Climbs* 49). The scene could have been told from Emily's point of view, to bring us even closer to Emily. When Emily experiences the storm and pursuit by Mad Mr. Morrison, we do learn about her emotions, but we are also invited to read the scene in a way Emily cannot. The narrator tells us, "The thunder and lightning were almost incessant: rain blew against the windows, not in drops but sheets, and intermittent volleys of hail bombarded them. The wind had risen suddenly with the storm and shrieked around the church" (45). For Emily this is a frightening storm. For readers when *Emily Climbs* was published and after, words like "volleys" and "bombarded" evoke battlefields of the First World War, even as Emily's pursuit by Mad Mr. Morrison reflects enemy armies pursuing the British and Canadian troops. The scene thus invites us to remember fears experienced during war even as we might say to Emily, it is only a storm that will pass. When Emily gets control of her emotions, the limited narrator speaks briefly with omniscience: "I think it was at that moment Emily wholly ceased to be a child" (47). We both are and are not Emily as the momentarily omniscient narrator in her own voice indicates how to evaluate Emily's experience.

Emily's narration in her letters and journals enables readers to connect closely with the character and her emotions, yet because we have read scenes from the point of view of a more adult speaker, we can interpret experiences in ways the child or young girl does not. When Emily tells how a friend betrays her, a slightly condescending yet sympathetic narrator pulls us back from Emily and asks for a complex response: "It was a child's tragedy—and all the more bitter for that, since there was no one to understand" (*New Moon* 104). When Emily writes in her diary, "Aunt Elizabeth says silk stockings are immoral. I wonder why—any more than silk dresses" (*Climbs* 4), readers see both sides of the story as the girl's question reveals contradictions at the heart of the adult code. When the narrator indicates that Aunt Ruth would have seen one of Emily's actions as "an added proof of slyness," she switches to first person to add, "Remember that I am only Emily's biographer, not her apologist" (*Climbs* 118), leaving a space for readers to disagree with Aunt Ruth but refusing herself to be the final arbiter.

By including several narrative voices in the text, Montgomery creates gaps for readers to fill. Reflecting on discrepancies among the voices makes readers aware that life is more complex even in these seemingly simpler times in the past.

CONCLUSION

Margaret Atwood, after mentioning qualities in *Anne of Green Gables* that make it a book for "preadolescents," goes on to assert that "*Anne* draws on a darker and, some would say, a more respectably literary lineage": books about orphans. If she had not been accepted at Green Gables, "Anne's fate would have been to be passed around as a cheap drudge from one set of uncaring adults to another. In the real world, as opposed to the literary one, she would have been in great danger of ending up pregnant and disgraced, raped [. . .] by the men in the families in which she had been placed" ("Afterword" 1992, 116–17).

In contrast, the three books about Emily do not merely draw on a darker reality outside the fiction but incorporate a darker view. The series appeals to nostalgia for childhood and for a simpler life: candles rather than gaslight, a dairy in the home, a lost time and place. However, the experiences Montgomery had of literary success, marriage, motherhood, and the First World War between writing *Anne of Green Gables* and the Emily series influenced the tone of the later books. The way Montgomery presents vocation and uses narrative distancing complicates the seeming simplicity of the novels as they involve readers in actively creating the story, making these books rich enough that later writers such as Alice Munro and Margaret Laurence credit the Emily books as influential.

By alluding to William Wordsworth, Emily Brontë, and St. Paul, Montgomery turns what might seem like a child's willfulness into a serious and gender role–defying Vocation. By using narrators that present Emily and her story at different distances, Montgomery provokes readers to address gaps and disjunctions individually, making creating a full text a challenge. An active reader, one invited by the story to think, is likely to experience more pleasure in the text than a more passive one. The Emily series offers not just Canadian gothic and Canadian romanticism and Canadian local color but demonstrates how writing about a small community in Canada can push readers to engage in a project of becoming aware of a darker, more complex world that coexists with a happier one presented by the beauty of rural Canada and with the joyous one glimpsed in the flash.

NOTES

1. For more on this point, see E. Holly Pike's chapter in this collection.
2. See also Jessica Wen Hui Lim's chapter in this collection.

WORKS CITED

Atwood, Margaret. "Afterword: *Anne of Green Gables* by Lucy Maud Montgomery." 1992. Reprinted in Margaret Atwood, *Writing with Intent: Essays, Reviews, Personal Prose 1983–2005*, Carroll and Graff, 2004, pp. 115–20.

Atwood, Margaret. "Afterword to *Anne of Green Gables* by L. M. Montgomery." McClelland and Stewart, 2008, pp. 355–61. Reprinted in Margaret Atwood, *Burning Questions: Essays and Occasional Pieces 2008–2020*, O. W. Toad, 2022, pp. 83–91.

Beran, Carol L. "Beautiful Girlhood, a Double Life: Lucy Maud Montgomery, Margaret Laurence, and Alice Munro." *American Review of Canadian Studies*, vol. 42, no. 2, 2011, pp. 148–60.

Brontë, Charlotte. *Jane Eyre*. 1847. Norton Critical Edition, edited by Deborah Lutz. Norton, 1971.

Epperly, Elizabeth Rollins. *The Fragrance of Sweet-Grass: L. M. Montgomery's Heroines and the Pursuit of Romance*. U Toronto P, 1992.

Francis, R. Douglas, et al. *Destinies: Canadian History since Confederation*. Holt, 1988.

Gibson, Graeme. "Alice Munro." *Eleven Canadian Novelists interviewed by Graeme Gibson*. Anansi, 1973, pp. 237–64.

The Holy Bible. Authorized King James Version, 1611. World, n.d.

Laurence, Margaret. "Books That Mattered to Me." *Margaret Laurence: Recognition and Revelation, Short Nonfiction Writings*, edited by Nora Foster Stovel. McGill-Queen's UP, 2020, pp. 161–70.

Laurence, Margaret. "Gadgetry or Growing." *Margaret Laurence: Recognition and Revelation, Short Nonfiction Writings*, edited by Nora Foster Stovel. McGill-Queen's UP, 2020, pp. 28–37.

Laurence, Margaret. "Time and the Narrative Voice." *Margaret Laurence: Recognition and Revelation: Short Nonfiction Writings*, edited by Nora Foster Stovel. McGill-Queen's UP, 2020, pp. 15–19.

Lefebvre, Benjamin. Editor's Preface to "[The Marriage of L. M. Montgomery]." *The L. M. Montgomery Reader: Volume One, A Life in Print*, edited by Benjamin Lefebvre. U of Toronto P, 2013, p. 101.

McKenzie, Andrea. "Women at War." *The L. M. Montgomery Reader: Volume Two, A Critical Heritage*, edited by Benjamin Lefebvre. U of Toronto P, 2014, pp. 325–49.

Montgomery, L. M. *The Alpine Path: The Story of My Career. Everywoman's World*, vol. 8, no. 2, 1917. University of Pennsylvania Digital Library. https://digital.library.u.penn.edu/women/Montgomery/alpine/alpine.html.

Montgomery, L. M. *Anne of Green Gables*. 1908. Edited by Cecily Devereux. Broadview Press, 2004.

Montgomery, L. M. *Emily Climbs*. 1925. Random House Canada, 1998.

Montgomery, L. M. *Emily of New Moon*. 1923. Random House Canada, 1998.

Montgomery, L. M. *Emily's Quest*. A. Burt, 1927.

Montgomery, L. M. "From *Fiction Writers on Fiction Writing*." *The L. M. Montgomery Reader: Volume One, A Life in Print*, edited by Benjamin Lefebvre, U of Toronto P, 2013, pp. 189–96.

Montgomery, L. M. "[This Hideous War]." *The L. M. Montgomery Reader Volume One, A Life in Print*, edited by Benjamin Lefebvre, U of Toronto P, 2013, pp. 148–50.

Muir, Norma Phillips. "Famous Author and Simple Mother." *The L. M. Montgomery Reader Volume One, A Life in Print*, edited by Benjamin Lefebvre, U of Toronto P, 2013, pp. 224–29.

Munro, Alice. Afterword. *Emily of New Moon*, by L. M. Montgomery. McClelland and Stewart, 1989, pp. 357–61.

Ross, Catherine Sheldrick. *Alice Munro: A Double Life*. ECW Press, 1992.

Ross, Catherine Sheldrick. "An Interview with Alice Munro." *Canadian Children's Literature / Littérature canadienne pour la jeunesse*, 53, 1989, pp. 14–24.

Rubio, Mary Henley. *Lucy Maud Montgomery: The Gift of Wings*. Anchor Canada, 2008.

Waterston, Elizabeth. "Lucy Maud Montgomery 1874–1942." *The L. M. Montgomery Reader: Volume Two, A Critical Heritage*, edited by Benjamin Lefebvre. U of Toronto P, 2014, pp. 5–74.

Weber, Brenda R. "Confessions of a Kindred Spirit with an Academic Bent." *Making Avonlea: L. M. Montgomery and Popular Culture*, edited by Irene Gammel. U of Toronto P, 2002, pp. 43–57.

Wilson, Lois. "Faith and the Vocation of the Author." In *Margaret Laurence: Critical Reflections*, edited by David Staines. U of Ottawa P, 2001, pp. 151–62.

Wordsworth, Dorothy. "From the Grasmere Journals." *The Norton Anthology of English Literature, The Romantic Period*, Vol. D, 9th ed., edited by Stephen Greenblatt et al., Norton, 2012, pp. 404–15.

Wordsworth, William. "I Wandered Lonely as a Cloud." *The Norton Anthology of English Literature, The Romantic Period*, Vol. D, 9th ed., edited by Stephen Greenblatt et al., Norton, 2012, pp. 334–35.

Chapter 11

READING EMILY OUT OF TIME AND PLACE

Breaking Chronology and Space

MARGARET STEFFLER

In 1998 I wrote an article entitled "The Canadian Romantic Child: Travelling in the Border Country, Exploring the 'Edge'" in which I argued for the vibrancy of borders that marked the liminal space between two expanses such as field and forest, mountain and valley, or ocean and land. Using environmental terms and theories, particularly those associated with bioregionalism and permaculture, along with postcolonial concepts of contact zones, I argued for the productivity of these margins in which I confidently placed what I called the "Canadian Romantic child." Emily Byrd Starr was one of those children. My analysis assumed that the vitality required to move forward and "progress" depended on sustaining a tension between centers and margins to ensure that colliding forces would produce the energy needed to challenge the stagnant conditions of the staid and insular center.

My 2003 article "Brian O'Connal and Emily Byrd Starr: The Inheritors of Wordsworth's 'Gentle Breeze'" examined how Emily's flash, like a Wordsworthian spot of time, generates "insight and inspiration." In this article I argued that it was through Emily's temperament and imagination that an "insular and judgemental" Canadian society was tempered (95). My argument assumed a chronological and transatlantic movement through time and space in a type of literary displacement and replacement of the Wordsworthian child from the English lake district to Prince Edward Island. As in the argument in the earlier article, I assumed a separation between child and adult, with the persistence of divisional lines establishing the necessary entrenchment of difference that set the child's depth against the superficiality of adult society.

My current reading dismantles the divisions of time and space on which my earlier readings depended. In the spirit of Wai Chee Dimock's theory of resonance, I now consider Montgomery's Emily novels as texts that travel, participating in a "diachronic historicism" that benefits from the "dynamics of endurance and transformation that accompany the passage of time" ("A Theory" 1061). As such, *Emily of New Moon*, *Emily Climbs*, and *Emily's Quest* cannot claim an "indwelling identity" but depend on "a relation, a form of engagement, between a changing object and a changing recipient, between a tonal presence and the way it is differently heard over time." Dimock argues that "a text cannot and will not remain forever the same object" ("A Theory" 1064, 1062). The shift from my former view of Emily ministering to a needy society to my current view of Emily as a character who does not presume or strive to know, understand, or influence is a result of dynamic changes in the relation between text and reader. Rather than depending on designs of centers and margins, on chronological ages and stages, and on transatlantic movements, my current reading of Montgomery's Emily releases tensions of opposing spaces while breaking a reliance on one-way progressions from past to present in literary history and individual lives. In my current reading, Emily no longer explores the edge or serves as a source of corrective imaginative power, and neither does she move definitively from childhood through adolescence into adulthood, leaving behind each stage of life as she matures. The point of Emily is that she challenges the existence and efficacy of divisions of time and space, along with the genres of the Bildungsroman and Künstlerroman.

In my current discussion, the concepts of "texts in motion" and "deep time" join the "theory of resonance" in loosening Emily from static divisions and borders. Katherine Bergren's *The Global Wordsworth: Romanticism Out of Place* explores ways in which reading backward and reading globally set texts in motion, encouraging the emergence of dynamic qualities that lift literary works from positions fixed in time and place. Similarly, in *Through Other Continents: American Literature across Deep Time*, Dimock persuasively appeals to "deep time" as a context in which to read literature, particularly national literatures. She advocates an approach that views time as "a set of longitudinal frames, at once projective and recessional, with input going both ways, and binding continents and millennia into many loops of relations, a densely interactive fabric" (3–4). Reading with an openness to texts in motion, deep time, and resonance opens up placelessness and timelessness, along with a recognition of the value of fluidity, vagueness, and the ineffable.

From *The Fragrance of Sweet-Grass: L. M. Montgomery's Heroines and the Pursuit of Romance*, published in 1992, to the recent "Reading Time: L. M. Montgomery and the 'Alembic' of Fiction" (2019), critic Elizabeth Epperly has considered ways in which time and space are challenged and transformed in the Emily novels. In her early discussion of *Emily's Quest*, Epperly contextualizes Emily's (and Montgomery's) easy recall of Wordsworth, arguing that he is "woven into Emily's understanding of her own depressions and transcendent joys, reminding her . . . of the enduring blessing of nature." Epperly also points out that "Tintern Abbey" is "the one poem most in tune with [Emily's] need to look, with a loving eye, backwards and forwards" (*Fragrance* 200, 199). In her chapter "Natural Bridge: L. M. Montgomery and the Architecture of Imaginative Landscapes," Epperly proposes that "Montgomery's writing creates a natural bridge across cultures and time" and "[spanning] a spatial or temporal gap . . . may link states of mind, places, or both" (94).

In the same chapter she develops Montgomery's textual conversations with earlier writers, studying ways in which "Montgomery, like Wordsworth, Emerson, and Irving," believes in "the kinship of all things in relation to each other" (91). Wordsworth's sense of a presence in nature, Emerson's "neo-Platonic theories of the ideal harmony and unity of Nature behind nature" (91), and Irving's deep affinity to the arch (97–100) link Montgomery to these writers and their philosophies, demonstrating, in Epperly's view, that texts "which appeal to readers across time and cultures, as Montgomery's texts do, are ones that fire the neurons, despite changes in taste and time, and in so firing activate archetypal patterns that also support cultural meaning and relationships." She further argues that "there is no 'or' in binary opposites unless there is always first an 'and' bridging the two" (100).

Finally, in her analysis of the middle chapters of *Emily's Climbs* in "Reading Time," Epperly emphasizes the importance of Emily's description and experience of "expanded time": "Such moments come rarely in any life, but when they do come they are inexpressibly wonderful—as if the finite were for a second infinity—as if humanity were for a space uplifted into divinity—as if all ugliness had vanished" (*Climbs* 177). Such expansions of earthly time and physical spaces, along with the requisite "and" to join binaries, emphasize a fluidity in Emily's development that resonates beyond her personal sphere to a larger realm.

I argue that Emily's uncanny experiences lead to a deconstruction of binary oppositions between child and adult, past and present, naivete and wisdom, mortality and immortality, pointing to a grand and pervasive fluidity based in "deep time" and expansive space. The result of Emily's "flash" and mystical moments involves the dismantling of chronological distinctions, such as those that define the Bildungsroman, national literatures, and literary periods. In addition, spatial distinctions, particularly those distinguishing body, mind, and soul, the physical and the divine, the local and the global, are blurred. Through Emily, Montgomery sees and offers a world and a life that value vagueness over certainty, thus reassuring characters and readers that the ineffable is indeed unknowable and should be valued as such.

Like Wordsworth, who spent his life "rewriting, reshaping, reinterpreting [his] early experiences" (Plotz 168), Montgomery copied, rewrote, and revised her childhood diaries and her journals, particularly during the period when she was writing the Emily novels (Rubio 273–78). Such a process emphasizes the mutability and flexibility of the course of a human life as made apparent in the adjustment of the past by the present. This fluidity challenges assumptions that human development is divided into progressive ages and stages. The impact of this foundational challenging of chronological time is clearly seen throughout the three Emily novels and leads to the breaking of other divisions and distinctions. *Emily of New Moon*, for example, repeatedly refers to the body, mind, and soul in ways that subvert conventional separations of the physical, intellectual, emotional, and spiritual aspects of being human. *Emily Climbs* questions the measurement of life in stages and the separation of life from death. Finally, *Emily's Quest*, with its focus on memory and looking back, confronts the barriers between human and divine time and space, moving through spontaneous and temporary leaps initiated by the "flash" into more substantial and permanent shifts.

READING FLASHES AND THE UNCANNY INTO FLUIDITY

The "flash" in *Emily of New Moon*, that sudden moment "when soul seemed to cast aside the bonds of flesh and spring upward to the stars" (*New Moon* 91), is familiar in its similarity to a Wordsworthian transcendental "spot of time" (*Prelude*, 1805, XI, ll. 257–315; 342–88) with its perception "of all the mighty world / Of eye, and ear,—both what they half create, / and what perceive" ("Tintern Abbey" ll. 105–7). Like the flash, the uncanny moments when Emily is possessed by an external force or person take her out of herself as seen, for example, in the way her maternal grandfather works through her to save the trees bordering New Moon (*New Moon* 121). This uncanny possession reconfigures the vertical lines of the conventional family tree, suggesting radical connections based in complex kinship rather than straightforward generational succession. Emily moves back in time to become her grandfather or, viewing it another way, her grandfather moves forward to inhabit Emily. He does not simply pass down qualities through a one-way inheritance. Inheritance also reaches out horizontally beyond humans to include the trees themselves in Emily's fight to protect the "bush of spruce and hardwood [that] had *always* been there," that "belonged to

New Moon *morally*" (*New Moon* 213). Emily's appeal to the Roman Catholic priest, Father Cassidy, to persuade the trees' owner, Lofty John Sullivan, to preserve the trees rather than take them down reaches back to earlier eras at New Moon and addresses the "Murray-Sullivan feud of three generations" (*New Moon* 215). Emily's thoughtful walks to and from Father Cassidy's house bridge other relationships broken over an even longer period of time—the rivalry between Catholics and Protestants in Emily's part of the world as well as the chasm separating the young and the old.

Relationships between the physical, emotional, and spiritual in *Emily of New Moon* include less startling experiences than those instigated by the flash and the uncanny. Most basic are those that connect the body with the emotions. The teacher's slap on Emily's face, for example, leaves not only a "smitten cheek" of "crimson," but a "wound . . . in her heart." Miss Brownell's slap is a reaction to Emily's "rapt, uplifted face where great purplish-grey eyes were shining with the radiance of a divine vision" as "an exquisite echo in her soul" responds to the sound of the words of the *Bugle Song* (*New Moon* 103). The movement is the reverse of the upward trajectory of the "flash." Emily is pulled down from the spiritual realm into a suffering heart. The conduit for the fall from the divine to deeply hurt feelings is the body—specifically the skin of the cheek—demonstrating how physical sensations are directly connected to the emotions.

The reaction of the physical body to emotions is also apparent in Emily's fingertips becoming cold when she is excited and in the way the story of the death of Ilse's mother "gnawed at her with an almost physical pain" (*New Moon* 293, 296). The emergence of these physical phenomena reverses the movement from the slapped cheek inward to the heart. In these cases, the emotions of excitement and sadness felt in the heart travel to the extremities of the physical body—to the fingertips and the edge of pain, both lying at the surface of the skin, which functions as a layer that both protects and connects the individual with the world in which she lives. The movement between the emotional and the physical travels both ways—inward or down as in the slap resulting in humiliation and outward or up as in the cold fingertips reflecting excitement.

The physical body is also connected to the spirit as manifested in the relationship between the ill body and the soul. Emily's delirium resulting from the fever caused by the measles is explicable through medical science and is discernable in its emergence to the surface of her body. The flushed face and pulse rate alert those observing Emily to the danger, while the hurting eyes are a sign to Emily herself. Complicating and exacerbating the symptoms of the physical illness is Emily's distraught worry about the mysterious death of Ilse's mother years before. Aunt Elizabeth responds to Emily's wandering words, worry, and vision that Ilse's mother fell down the well by reassuring her that she will search the old well for the body of her friend's mother. Aunt Elizabeth's promise affects Emily to the point of relieving the physical manifestations of fever and delirium, resulting in "the wild glare [leaving] [Emily's] eyes" and "a great sudden calm [falling] over her anguished little face" (*New Moon* 366).

Significantly, it is through the physical disturbances caused by the illness that Aunt Elizabeth realizes that "she really did not know much about the child's mind" (*New Moon* 366, 363), having limited her care to Emily's body. Not only does Aunt Elizabeth witness the connections between the physical and intellectual in the way Emily's body affects her mind, but she is also opened to the possibility of further connections to the spiritual or what she calls "second sight" (*New Moon* 370). Strict distinctions separating body, mind, and soul, ministered to by the home, school, and church respectively, each institution dedicated to a single strand of human development, are challenged, breached, and connected through Aunt Elizabeth's surprising response to Emily's condition and request.

The narrator continues to make distinctions between body, mind, and soul in descriptions of Emily's growth, noting both unevenness—"Emily *had* grown, taller and older, in soul, if not in body"—and harmony: "Emily grew rapidly that summer in body, mind and soul" (*New Moon* 321, 359). Although there are delays and inconsistencies, each "part" of Emily is seen to bring along and encourage the others: "Physically she recovered with normal celerity but a certain spiritual and emotional languor persisted for a time" (373). It is Aunt Elizabeth who perceptively articulates the lifting of such distinctions between child and adult when she states that "there was not one law of fairness for children and another for grown-ups" (358). The powerful interactions between the physical, intellectual, emotional, and spiritual parts of Emily during her illness lead to the crucial realization by Aunt Elizabeth and the reader that society's imposed and artificial separations are unsustainable. Dean Priest, however, in his observation that Emily has "left the childhood of her soul behind, though she is still a child in body" (375), continues to insist on dividing Emily into irreconcilable parts.

The novel's reference to the "doctrine of the transmigration of souls" (*New Moon* 315) introduces the possibility of radical challenges to assumed separations between earthly and divine spaces and experiences, borne out in Emily's uncovering of Ilse's mother's fate. Montgomery's attachment to Wordsworth's "Ode: Intimations of Immortality," particularly her "lingering over the lines 'Our birth is but a sleep and a forgetting'" (*Complete Journals*,

1930–1933 259), highlights her attraction to the Neoplatonic belief in preexistence, which is less extreme than a belief in the transmigration of souls. Significantly, Montgomery arranges for the idea of the transmigration of souls to be voiced by Dean as a way for him to "explain" or "explain away" Emily's wisdom and insight, which, in his opinion, are at odds with her chronological age. Although the transmigration of souls may be an appealing theory to Montgomery and Emily, Dean's view of the doctrine discredits Emily in its erroneous assumption that she is too young to experience the feelings and insight she has displayed.

The distinctions challenged by *Emily of New Moon* are mainly those demarcating body, mind, and soul, but they anticipate the challenges to the division of human development into ages and stages that emerge in *Emily Climbs*. The narrator of *Emily Climbs* notes the porous border between childhood and adulthood in Emily's effort, "unchildlike in its determination," to regain self-control when locked in the church. That fluidity is lost in the subsequent declaration that "at that moment Emily wholly ceased to be a child" (47), which assumes a permanent transition from one stage and age to another. Childlike Cousin Jimmy, however, reinforces the persistence of a porous two-way membrane between child and adult. Similarly, Emily and Ilse's pact to come back to one another after death (176) and Teddy's belief that he previously existed in a star further challenge barriers constructed by chronological time and the subsequent closing down of previous states of being.

In contesting divisions of time and limitations of space, these thoughts break distinctions between the earthly and the sacred, "as if humanity were for a space uplifted into divinity" (*Climbs* 177). Wordsworth's "Ode: Intimations of Immortality" again reverberates here in its reminder that previous states of existence are accessible: "Though inland far we be, / Our Souls have sight of that immortal sea / Which brought us hither" (528, ll.163–65). Such an expansion of time and space is initiated and prolonged by Emily in the garden on a November evening when she feels that "the future was mine—and the past, too" and that she "had been alive here always ... shared in all the loves and lives of the old house ... would live always—always—always—," leading her to proclaim: "I was sure of immortality then. I didn't just believe it—I *felt* it" (*Climbs* 214–15). In responding to the past life of the garden and house with faith, imagination, and feeling, Emily ushers in a sense of time that is fluid and expansive in reference to her own existence.

The liminal space between childhood and adulthood in this middle novel is described by Emily as "betwixt-and-between"; it affords her the opportunity to "be childish" with "none daring to make [her] ashamed" while also allowing her "to behave maturely," based on "the authority of [her] extra inches" (*Climbs* 155). The liminality and fluidity of time take on more profound qualities. When Emily and Ilse have no choice but to sleep on a haystack under the moon and stars, Emily experiences that moment of ecstasy, in which the finite is raised to the infinite and humanity into divinity, leaving only beauty. She looks back at her haystack night as one of those moments when "the soul slips over into eternity for a little space" (220) and senses in retrospect a distortion of time, which made the "night under the moon" seem "like a year of some strange soul-growth" (199). Despite the soul-growth, Emily feels "childish" (202) soon after the haystack experience when she and Ilse seek shelter in the Bradshaw home. Emily is persuaded by Ilse to show the Bradshaw family the picture of the Scobie cottage she seems to have drawn in her sleep, complete with automatic writing locating the family's lost son, Allan.

Emily resists the feeling of being possessed by the Scobie house where, thanks to her drawing, lost Allan is found. She hopes she will "grow out of it" (207), "it" being these moments of possession accompanied by uncanny insight. Just as Emily's body was a conduit for a "current of beauty" (177) during the night under the stars, so it has been a vehicle for the discovery of lost Allan during the night of drawing. The former's sublimity brings ecstasy whereas the latter's uncanniness instills fear and dread. Emily's awareness of these possessions of her body, whether uplifting or disturbing, is accompanied by a sense of fluid time that belies the minutes and hours on the clock, liberating her from a dependence on the literal and linear world. Emily does not grow out of her past or the effects of the sublime and uncanny; she embodies them. It is not a matter of a child leaving behind unusual gifts, but a matter of Emily's temperament being receptive at all ages to forces that lead to higher planes of consciousness.

In *Emily's Quest*, which focuses on memory and the past, Emily not only senses other worlds and times related to her own existence but travels between the human and divine more generally, sustaining a relationship with both realms. After growing apart from Teddy, she turns to written words from the past, including his old letters with their "terrible resurrective power," which surround her with "bitter fancies and unbidden ghosts—the little spectral joys of the past" (161). Like Montgomery, Emily reads over her old journal entries, wondering if the "gay, light-hearted entries" were "really written by me, Emily Byrd Starr" (106). Most significantly, "on her twenty-fourth birthday Emily [opens] and [reads] the letter she had written 'from herself at fourteen to herself at twenty-four'" (167). Weariness and regret move her to self-pity as she vanquishes "foolish little Fourteen" to its "shadowy past" (169) and eventually feels that "for the first time in her life death seemed a friend" (183). When Emily experiences the flash during these "dreary months," she wonders whether she "will lose it altogether as [she] [grows] old" (165).

Despite Emily's attempt to segregate her past hopes, literally boxing away "old, foolish letters, full of dreams and plans," she does not box away her dreams to write, both the dreaming and the writing absorbing her to a point that takes her soul away from the earth and from the overbearing Dean. When Dean dismisses her writing, Emily's emotional response is one "she had not felt ... since the night Ellen Greene had told her her father must die" (*Quest* 86, 58). Words written on pages can be sequestered and allocated to boxes, but the emotions attached to those words insist on emerging. Similarly, the "horrible power or gift or curse," which Emily hoped she "had outgrown" and "left ... behind forever," persists. In a state of sleep-delirium she moves "like a haunted, driven creature in a weird, uncanny half-lit kingdom" (96, 95) to warn Teddy, who is traveling home from England, of impending danger. She later learns that at that moment of her warning Teddy had chased a vision of Emily, thus missing his booked voyage and what would have been his death by drowning on the doomed ship, the *Flavian*. Emily wonders whether it is her love for Teddy that allows her "to set at naught the limitations of time and space to save him" (107).

In this third Emily novel, Emily articulates her feeling that "all her life she had grown ... by these fits and starts." She describes these spurts in terms of space, moving through change and loss from "some 'low-vaulted past'" into "some 'new temple' of the soul more spacious than all that had gone before" (*Quest* 32). Moving against this entry into a spacious temple, however, is the drive to move backward into childhood, a desire shared by Ilse, who wants to return to the state of the child "for just one blissful summer" and who urges Teddy and Emily to "be mad, crazy, happy kids again." For Teddy returning home that summer, "time has stood still" and "nothing seems changed," whereas Emily maintains that "they might have been children together again," but acknowledges that "childhood had never known this wild, insurgent sweetness—this unconsidered surrender" (114, 113). It is Ilse who openly admits that they have only been pretending to be children again. Although Emily agrees that "we can't go back to childhood" (130), the essence and depth of childhood, as opposed to Ilse's version of its light playfulness, persists in the growing and grown Emily.

Emily, in her time alone at New Moon, enjoyed "hours of rapture and insight that shed a glory *backward and forward*" and "slipped mentally back into childhood and had delightful adventures she would have been ashamed to tell her adult world" (*Quest* 40, emphasis added). But she also "seemed to herself to grow ... old and wise" (63). Emily's body and age are at odds as she tells Aunt Laura with a sense of acceptance: "It's only my body that is young. My soul is a hundred years old" (67). For Cousin Jimmy, who "never grew up—not in [his] head" (110), body and age do not match in conventional ways and never will. With an emphasis on aging in all characters from Ilse and Teddy to Cousin Jimmy and Aunt Elizabeth, the novel conveys Emily's impulses and moves through the past, change, and loss into timelessness—into eternity and spacious temples of the soul where ages and stages do not exist.

DEEP TIME, RESONANCE, AND TEXTS IN MOTION

By the time Montgomery's Emily novels were published in McClelland and Stewart's New Canadian Library (NCL) series in 1989, the texts in the series were followed by an essay afterword rather than preceded by an academic introduction. Montgomery's work was commented on in essays by Alice Munro for *Emily of New Moon*, Jane Urquhart for *Emily Climbs*, and P. K. Page for *Emily's Quest*. These afterwords provide a conversation between twentieth-century writer-fans and Montgomery's work. Looking back at the novels and their own earlier readings, Munro, Urquhart, and Page put the texts in motion in terms of their lives, considering the novels as "diachronic objects" (Dimock, "A Theory" 1060).

I see these afterwords, as well as works published by Munro, Urquhart, and Page, as examples of the powerful ways in which Montgomery's work has traveled over time and space. Quoting a number of critics in her argument for "reading globally,"[1] Bergren includes Robert Kiely's 1993 comment that "temporal boundaries, like geographical borders, have always been crossed in two directions" (Kiely 5). Bergren argues that "a dominant national literature that travels these interconnected global networks cannot remain very insular" and that "cultural forms do not flow merely in one direction from dominant to dominated, influence to influenced, past to present" (10). She also refers to Vilashini Cooppan's definition of "globalized reading," which is based in a dialogue between texts that are "locally inflected and translocally mobile" (Cooppan 33).

The afterwords to the NCL editions of Montgomery's Emily novels provide examples of Emily traveling and being "repurposed" by later writers just as Montgomery read and repurposed Wordsworth. Montgomery's work has, of course, traveled globally in astonishing ways (Ledwell and Mitchell).[2] In this context of transnational travel over time, Bergren talks of the advantages of reading backward and out of context—of reading Wordsworth and understanding him differently after reading Jamaica Kincaid's *Lucy*, for example

(1–3). Reading Wordsworth after reading Montgomery's Emily trilogy, reading Montgomery after reading Munro's short stories is to read with an awareness of texts in motion, reverberating with relevance and evolving in meaning.

Alice Munro concludes her afterword to *Emily of New Moon* by emphasizing the "life spreading out behind the story," noting that "there's so much going on behind, or beyond, the proper story" (391). Referring to a kind of palimpsestic layering, she emphasizes degrees of depth but also alludes to expanding space. In noting layers and expansions, Munro challenges prescribed and limited settings and locales as well as chronological time. In her concluding sentence she focuses on the ineffability of experience that can be sensed or "known" in the deepest of manners but cannot be put into words or "told" (391). Like Emily and Montgomery, Munro suggests and reveals meaning through showing lives "unfathomable—deep caves paved with kitchen linoleum" (*Lives* 236) rather than attempting to articulate meaning that, in its very nature, is elusive. For Munro, the ineffable and uncanny simply exist, arousing wonder, and are subject to reduction when probed for answers and explanations that are not forthcoming.[3]

In her afterword to *Emily Climbs*, Jane Urquhart speaks in terms of reflection, emphasizing ways in which the "immensely fertile and heartbreakingly fragile" (334) condition of the young writer reflects the land around her. Urquhart considers the Emily books as "mirrors" in which she "could see not only who girls such as myself had been, who we were now, but who we might eventually come to be" (330). Urquhart speculates that Montgomery, in writing Emily, is "building the past as she [Montgomery] would have liked to experience it" (333). The adult Urquhart refers to "the child in me" (331), acknowledging the futility of dividing lives into ages and stages and generally challenging the concept of time as progressive, as well as space as defined, singular, and finite.

In P. K. Page's afterword to *Emily's Quest*, Page, like Urquhart, refers to reflection, the "fidelity" and "willingness to serve or care for another" reflecting a higher love (239). Page's focus on the flash and what she calls Emily's "physic powers" (237) places her interest in the otherworldly—the paranormal. In "Reading Time: L. M. Montgomery and the 'Alembic of Fiction,'" Epperly reminds readers that the pact made by Emily and Ilse that the one who dies first will try to come back to the other (*Climbs* 176) is based on the pact made between Montgomery and her cousin Frederica Campbell.[4] Page also made such a pact with her friend Gertrude Tomalin Ross, who, according to Page, did appear to her after she died. Page described this visitation to her biographer Sandra Djwa as "a whole lot of little specks of light dancing, like a little molecular dance, like a lot of illuminated gnats. And they danced and danced and they coagulated and got bigger and bigger, and it became an outline of a human being, all in this molecular light" (Djwa 60). These "vibrating atoms" and this "molecular dance," yearned for by Montgomery and experienced by Page, provide a powerful image of texts, forces, times, people, and places in motion.

Texts in motion, texts resonating, texts reaching across time and space break the borders and barriers I depended on in my earlier readings of Emily. I now read with an impulse to allow time to travel in all directions and with a willingness to permit space to expand in any way it chooses. Bringing Emily into conversation with Wordsworth, reading Emily back into Wordsworth, I move through the mystical and transcendental flash-like spots of time; through the "growth of the poet"[5] and development of the young writer on the Alpine Path; through the contemplative and retrospective "inward eye" of "I Wandered Lonely as a Cloud" (l. 21) and the dreams of Emily; through the return memory narrative of "Tintern Abbey" and the reading of the letter addressed by the fourteen-year-old to the twenty-four-year-old—pushing into the Neoplatonic flavor of preexistence in "Ode: Intimations of Immortality," the possibilities of the transmigration of souls, and the depth of the uncanny.

Reading Emily in conversation with Wordsworth, who precedes her, and with Munro, Urquhart, and Page, who follow her, encourages fluid reading backward and forward as well as global reading across nations. What Bergren claims for Wordsworth—"what emerges when we read Wordsworth alongside his diverse afterlives is a poet whose representations of local, natural landscapes came to invoke a broader global context as he aged—not in order to expand the boundaries of the local or juxtapose its sphere with that of the world but rather in order to detail the entanglement of the two" (10)—readers of Montgomery can claim for her.

Emily's uncanny experiences converse and become entangled with the mysticism explored by Page, especially in her writings in Brazil and Mexico; with Irish mythology incorporated by Urquhart in much of her fiction, notably in *Away*; and with the history and tales of Scotland that form the layers of Ontario's rock and land in many of Munro's short stories, particularly those in *The View from Castle Rock*. These conversations encourage an acceptance and celebration of the unknown and the unknowable. The "entanglements" and resonances that result from global readings of texts in motion within deep time cause the borders, distinctions, and contact zones of nations, postcolonialism, and bioregionalism to fade in favor of a fluidity that suggests possibilities as opposed to solutions and answers.

The childlike qualities of Emily are not separate from or superior to the mature characteristics of the adult. The child does not correct, temper, or mitigate the adult world. The child and adult partake of each other and intersect with each other in ways that deconstruct the border between them on which my earlier readings depended. Readers of Montgomery's Emily novels, like Emily herself, are moved to accept an "entanglement" of time and place that yields neither certitude nor knowledge but a reverence for the value and persistence of vagueness, the uncanny, and the ineffable.

NOTES

1. Bergren refers to work by Hans Robert Jauss, who asserts that "a literary work is not an object that stands by itself and that offers the same view to each reader in each period. It is not a monument that monologically reveals its timeless essence. It is much more like an orchestration that strikes ever new resonances among its readers and that frees the text from the material of the words and brings it to a contemporary existence" (Jauss 21). Bergren also incorporates Jerome Christensen's concept of Romantic anachronism, specifically the inability of the past "to seal itself off as period or epoch or episode with no or necessary consequences for our time" (Christensen 3).

2. Ledwell and Mitchell's edited collection studies Anne, but the travels of Emily are not far behind as is apparent in the many translations of *Emily of New Moon* and in the 2007 anime *Kaze no Shoujo Emiri [Emily, Girl of the Wind]* in Japan.

3. See Munro, "What Do You Want to Know For?"

4. See *L. M. Montgomery's Complete Journals, The Ontario Years, 1918–1921*, p. 102.

5. Wordsworth's poem was titled *The Prelude, or Growth of a Poet's Mind* when it was published in 1850.

WORKS CITED

Bergren, Katherine. *The Global Wordsworth: Romanticism Out of Place*. Bucknell UP, 2019.

Christensen, Jerome. *Romanticism at the End of History*. Johns Hopkins UP, 2000.

Cooppan, Valashini. "World Literature and Global Theory: Comparative Literature for the New Millennium." *simplokē*, vol. 9, no. 1–2, 2001, pp. 15–44.

Dimock, Wai Chee. "A Theory of Resonance." *PMLA*, vol. 112, no. 5, Oct. 1997, pp. 1060–71.

Dimock, Wai Chee. *Through Other Continents: American Literature across Deep Time*. Princeton UP, 2009.

Djwa, Sandra. *Journey with No Maps: A Life of P. K. Page*. McGill-Queen's UP, 2012.

Epperly, Elizabeth. *The Fragrance of Sweet-Grass: L. M. Montgomery's Heroines and the Pursuit of Romance*. U of Toronto P, 1992; with a new preface 2014.

Epperly, Elizabeth. "Natural Bridge: L. M. Montgomery and the Architecture of Imaginative Landscapes." *L. M. Montgomery and the Matter of Nature(s)*, edited by Rita Bode and Jean Mitchell, McGill-Queen's UP, 2018, pp. 89–111.

Epperly, Elizabeth. "Reading Time: L. M. Montgomery and the 'Alembic of Fiction.'" *Journal of Montgomery Studies*, Collection: L. M. Montgomery and Reading, 6 May 2019. https://doi.org/10.32393/jlmms/2019.0002.

Jauss, Hans Robert. *Toward an Aesthetic of Reception*. Translated by Timothy Bahti, U of Minnesota P, 1982.

Kiely, Robert. *Reverse Tradition: Postmodern Fictions and the Nineteenth-Century Novel*. Harvard UP, 1993.

Ledwell, Jane, and Jean Mitchell. Introduction. *Anne Around the World: L. M. Montgomery and Her Classic*, edited by Jane Ledwell and Jean Mitchell, McGill-Queen's UP, 2013, pp. 3–24.

Montgomery, L. M. *Emily Climbs*. 1925. Seal Books, 1983.

Montgomery, L. M. *Emily of New Moon*. 1923. McClelland and Stewart NCL, 2007.

Montgomery, L. M. *Emily's Quest*. 1927. McClelland and Stewart NCL, 1989.

Montgomery, L. M. *L. M. Montgomery's Complete Journals, The Ontario Years, 1918–1921*. Edited by Jen Rubio, Rock's Mills, 2017.

Montgomery, L. M. *L. M. Montgomery's Complete Journals, The Ontario Years, 1930–1933*. Edited by Jen Rubio, Rock's Mills, 2019.

Munro, Alice. Afterword. 1989. *Emily of New Moon*, McClelland and Stewart NCL, 2007, pp. 387–91.

Munro, Alice. *Lives of Girls and Women*. Penguin, 2005.

Munro, Alice. "What Do You Want to Know For?" *The View from Castle Rock*, McClelland and Stewart, 2006, pp. 316–40.

Page, P. K. Afterword. *Emily's Quest*, McClelland and Stewart, 1989, pp. 237–42.

Plotz, Judith. *Romanticism and the Vocation of Childhood*. Palgrave, 2001.

Rubio, Mary Henley. *Lucy Maud Montgomery: The Gift of Wings*. Doubleday, 2008.

Steffler, Margaret. "Brian O'Connal and Emily Byrd Starr: The Inheritors of Wordsworth's 'Gentle Breeze.'" *Windows and Words: A Look at Canadian Children's Literature*, edited by Aïda Hudson and Susan-Ann Cooper, U of Ottawa P, 2003, pp. 87–96.

Steffler, Margaret. "The Canadian Romantic Child: Travelling in the Border Country, Exploring the 'Edge.'" *Canadian Children's Literature / Littérature canadienne pour la jeunesse*, vol. 24, no. 1, Spring 1998, pp. 5–17.

Urquhart, Jane. Afterword. *Emily Climbs*, McClelland and Stewart, 1989, pp. 330–34.

Wordsworth, William. "I Wandered Lonely as a Cloud." *William Wordsworth: The Poems*, vol. 1, pp. 619–20.

Wordsworth, William. "Lines Composed a Few Miles Above Tintern Abbey." *William Wordsworth: The Poems*, vol. 1, pp. 357–62.

Wordsworth, William. "Ode: Intimations of Immortality from Recollections of Earliest Childhood." *William Wordsworth: The Poems*, vol. 1, pp. 523–29.

Wordsworth, William. *The Prelude, 1799, 1805, 1850*, edited by Jonathan Wordsworth, M. H. Abrams, and Stephen Gill, Norton, 1977.

Wordsworth, William. *William Wordsworth: The Poems*, vol. 1, edited by John O. Hayden, Penguin, 1977.

Chapter 12

EMILY'S AFTERLIVES

Trauma, Repetition, and (Re)Reading
in *Emily of New Moon* and *Russian Doll*

ANASTASIA ULANOWICZ

"Everybody loves Anne, but I love Emily. She's dark." So proclaims Nadia Vulvokov, the protagonist of the Netflix series *Russian Doll*, shortly before she dies for the twelfth time.[1]

Released by the popular streaming service in 2019, *Russian Doll* immediately received critical and popular acclaim for its depiction of a hardened New Yorker (Natasha Lyonne) who repeatedly dies, and is just as soon revived, on the evening of her thirty-sixth birthday—the age her mother achieved before her own tragic death. Reviewers praised the series for its "raw, affecting themes about mortality and grieving" (Nussbaum) as well as for Lyonne's stirring turn as a woman whose "guilt over leaving her mother drives her to try to save everyone, even before herself" (H.).

Significantly, the series earned an especially appreciative audience in devotees of L. M. Montgomery for its recurrent allusions to the author's novel *Emily of New Moon*—which, as Nadia's pronouncement suggests, has been long eclipsed by the enduringly popular *Anne of Green Gables*. Soon after the series' release, fans of both *Emily* and *Russian Doll* rushed to conjecture the significance of Montgomery's "dark" heroine to the program's enticingly mysterious plot. Readers on platforms like Reddit, as well as writers for sites such as IndieWire and Vox, were quick to point out hidden allusions, or "Easter eggs," in the Netflix series that draw a connection between Nadia and Emily. For instance, they noted how both characters are orphans who have aunts named Ruth, seek consolation in mirrors and companionable relationships with cats, undergo significant transformations after falling from great heights, and experience moments of clairvoyance that allow them to assist friends with whom they have strong and even fated bonds. In a particularly insightful essay published by Vox, Constance Grady argues that Emily becomes an avatar for Nadia—herself a video game creator whose own image appears as an avatar in a game she is trying to "de-bug." Emily's story, Grady maintains, "is about someone surviving trauma and becoming stronger and quippier and more heroic for it." To that end, Grady maintains, "it's only when Nadia fully embraces the idea of a heroic Emily that she is able to begin to let go of her guilt over what happened to her mother, and finally close the loop" of childhood trauma to which she has been consigned.

To be sure, responses such as Grady's offer greater insight into the motivations of a complex character who—as the title of its final episode, "Ariadne," suggests—weaves her way through a labyrinthian plot. And yet it may be equally valuable to consider how this Netflix series may contribute to rereadings of Montgomery's novel, not least because it premiered shortly before the centennial of *Emily of New Moon*'s publication. Indeed, as I will argue, *Russian Doll*—insofar as it is a meditation on repetitions, false starts, and the promise of coming to terms with a dark past—offers a critical lens through which to (re)examine rereadings of beloved childhood texts such as *Emily*. Drawing on Alison Waller's concept of "remembered reading" and Pierre Bayard's counterintuitive term "nonreading," I maintain that the program's structure of repetition places into relief the endless possibilities afforded by successive returns to a text.

READING *RUSSIAN DOLL* THROUGH *EMILY OF NEW MOON*

Often compared to Harold Ramis's 1993 hit film *Groundhog Day*—in which a cynical television weather reporter (Bill Murray) awakes repeatedly on the idiosyncratic American holiday that at once marks the continuation of winter and the anticipation of spring—*Russian Doll*'s major narrative conceit involves a time loop. In the first episode, Nadia Vulvokov (Lyonne)—a hard-drinking, chain-smoking, street-smart denizen of New York's East Village who also happens to be a gifted video game designer—leaves a raucous birthday party thrown by her best friend Maxine (Greta Lee). Shortly thereafter, she is hit by a car after leaving an unsatisfying one-night stand in search of her lost cat. Mysteriously, she finds herself in Maxine's cavernous bathroom and discovers that she has returned to the (nearly) exact set of events that preceded her mortal accident. Bewildered—and careful to avoid oncoming traffic—Nadia relives the same night, only to die hours later by falling from a pier and returning again to Maxine's bathroom. In the six episodes that follow, Nadia dies in increasingly extravagant ways: falling into sidewalk cellars, plummeting from staircases, perishing from winter exposure in an alley ("That was dark!"), being swarmed by bees, perishing from a faulty gas-jet explosion, and choking on shards of glass. After each mortal event, she returns to the benighted night of her birthday party. And yet, in the hours that span between each of her deaths and returns, Nadia manages to meet Alan Zaveri (Charlie Barnett), a fellow New Yorker who has been mysteriously consigned to a similar series of brutal deaths and sudden resurrections. Although the garrulous Nadia and the fastidious Alan have little in common save for their inclination to die suddenly and return to life in bathrooms—the former in a repurposed bohemian loft and the latter in an antiseptic flat—they eventually discover that their lives are somehow intertwined. Ultimately, Nadia and Alan overcome their respective time loops by intentionally intervening in the events that precipitated each. Nadia soothes the anxious and jealous Alan and thus prevents him from taking a suicidal leap from his apartment roof, while Alan talks Nadia out of pursuing the last of many toxic affairs. In the final scene of the first season, Nadia's and Alan's timelines converge as the two join a carnivalesque parade of punks and indigents in Tompkins Square Park: as if, as Sarah Kessler conjectures, "they've risen, impromptu, to protest the conditions of the loop that entraps them all" (28).

At first glance, such a sleek and thoroughly twenty-first-century Netflix series would seem to have little in common with a comparatively antiquated and lesser-appreciated text such as Montgomery's *Emily of New Moon*. And yet as its very title suggests, *Russian Doll* manages to incorporate various, and often surprising, cultural and literary allusions in ways that intensify its themes. Much like a *matryoshka*—or nesting doll produced not only in Russia but throughout Eastern and Central Europe, including Nadia's site of maternal heritage, Hungary—the narrative of *Russian Doll* prompts viewers to excavate layers of significance.

Indeed, it might be that, as antiquated as it may appear, *Emily of New Moon* is more relevant to contemporary readers than it was to its original readers. As Joe Sutliff Sanders argues in his book on orphan girl fiction, Montgomery's novel "may be more at home now than it was in the age it was written" (141). This is in part, Sanders explains, because *Emily* was published at a moment when the orphan girl narrative was waning, and books featuring modern urban girls were beginning to achieve popularity. In effect, the novel was published at a time that was out of joint: insofar as it "embraces both the charm of the sentimental narrative and the irony of the twentieth century" it is at once of, beyond, and before its time (241). This appears to be an insight shared by the producers of *Russian Doll*, whose own protagonist experiences the disjointedness of time.² Through its allusions to *Emily*, then, the program offers contemporary audiences a familiar story of inherited trauma that is certainly more "at home" now than it was in 1923 when Montgomery's novel was first published.³

Emily is first introduced in the fifth episode, when Nadia and her newfound friend Alan confess their mutual love for Montgomery's "darker" children's novel. Subsequently, Nadia visits her childhood caregiver, Aunt Ruth (Elizabeth Ashley), who has preserved a box of her beloved objects, including a well-worn copy of *Emily of New Moon*. As the series progresses, its allusions to Emily intensify. The seventh episode, for instance, features a flashback in which Young Nadia's (Brooke Timber) reading of *Emily* is interrupted by an altercation between Aunt Ruth and her increasingly unstable mother (Chloë Sevigny). When, in the same episode, Nadia begins to suspect that she might break the time loop by repairing relationships she has broken, she gives her well-worn childhood edition of *Emily* to Lucy (Tatiana E. Rivera), her jilted lover's daughter—a leather jacket–clad preteen whose precocious, worldworn demeanor mirrors her own and whose long dark hair and porcelain skin resemble that of Montgomery's heroine.

To be sure, *Russian Doll*'s allusions to Emily enrich Nadia's characterization. If Emily is an orphan, Nadia is practically one: her father is absent and her mother is dead.⁴ Likewise, if Lyonne's iconic mane of ginger hair renders her character more similar to Montgomery's Anne Shirley,⁵ her heavily kohled eyes and black-leather ensembles suggest a resemblance to the dark-haired Emily, whom Lorna Drew has argued functions as a gothic heroine.⁶ Moreover, Nadia, like Emily, demonstrates a rare combination of stubborn determination, tenderness, and a spark of artistic genius. Although she affects the persona of a world-worn party girl—whose trenchant quips cut as deeply as Emily's terrifying Murray glare—Nadia, like Montgomery's heroine, nevertheless interacts with animals and marginalized people with remarkable gentleness. Likewise, despite the rough demeanor befitting an orphan with little formal education, Nadia is actually a gifted (and presumably self-taught) video game programmer who, like the young writer Emily, strives to perfect her self-hewn craft. Ultimately, *Russian Doll*, much like *Emily*, suggests that its protagonist's compassion and aesthetic prowess are amplified by a profound sense of intuition, if not a supernatural sensibility. Just as Emily is taken by Wordsworthian reveries she calls "the flash" and experiences a prophetic fever dream during which she envisions the tragic death of her companion Ilse's unjustly maligned mother, Nadia engages in uncanny experiences of time and mortality whose reality and significance remain inscrutable to her closest friends.

Indeed, *Russian Doll*'s apparently deliberate depiction of Nadia as an early twenty-first-century version of Emily places into starker relief both texts' central themes of trauma and grief. As scholars such as Kate Lawson and Lindsey McMaster have argued, *Emily* is largely a narrative about the inheritance of family trauma—and as such, it is concerned with the repetition of trauma through consecutive generations.[7] This becomes immediately evident in the beginning of the novel, when the recently orphaned protagonist loses her loving father years after having mourned the loss of her mother, whom she remembers only as a corpse in a "long black box" (15). Begrudgingly adopted by maternal relatives who consider her a burden, Emily is conscious that her relatives resent her because her mother, the appropriately named Juliet, fled her tightly bound family after pursuing a forbidden love match with her father. Significantly, as Lawson observes, Emily is not immediately aware of the *reason* for this elopement: that is, she initially does not understand that Juliet was escaping a puritanical family ruled by her ruthless grandfather Archibald (33). Emily's reincorporation into the Murray clan, however, makes evident the legacy of violence her mother fled and attempted to spare her progeny. Throughout *Emily of New Moon*, the titular protagonist is emotionally abused by her primary caregiver, the frigid Aunt Elizabeth, whose acts of hostility involve drowning newborn kittens (and accidentally almost drowning her cousin in a fit of rage); demanding that Emily destroy her beloved manuscripts; and insisting on cutting the raven-colored tresses that Emily considers her "one beauty" (106). Although, as McMaster argues, Aunt Elizabeth is a clearly "strong-minded, assertive, and competent woman," she has nevertheless "internalized [the] repressive dictates" of her father to such a degree that she redirects her "feminine rage" at the comparatively free-spirited Emily (52).

Significantly, it is only when Emily stuns her aunt with Archibald's dreaded "Murray glare" that Elizabeth begins to "register some degree of horror at the results of her own outbursts" (58). In this remarkable passage, Aunt Elizabeth's ominously clicking scissors "seemed to loosen something—some strange formidable power in Emily's soul" and the protagonist feels an "uprush as from unknown depths of some irresistible surge of energy" (106). Fixing her gaze directly at her aunt, Emily categorically states, "*My hair is not going to be cut off*. Let me hear no more of this" (107, emphasis in original). This response frightens both Elizabeth and Emily. The former blanches, lays down her scissors, and flees the room in horror when she sees "Father [. . .] looking from [Emily's] face" (107). The latter, for her part, has an "uncanny sense of wearing somebody else's face instead of her own" and registers that she has just delivered the infamous "Murray look" (107). In this moment, Emily (as well as her aunt) recognizes that she possesses the ability to channel the past, which is itself the product of the echoing traumas of the past. Although this passage, like later ones, is tinged with the supernatural in ways befitting a gothic narrative, it also suggests how Emily's stay in the tension-filled Murray household has caused her to absorb and mimic gestures of frustration and rage of which, up to this point, both she and Aunt Elizabeth had been unaware.

In *Russian Doll*, Nadia is similarly haunted by a traumatic maternal legacy. This becomes abundantly clear in a flashback at the beginning of the seventh episode, in which Nadia's manic young mother piles watermelons into a recently purchased sports car as her young daughter looks on in bewilderment; when a bodega owner expresses concern about Nadia's well-being, her mother coerces her into getting him fired. Significantly, Young Nadia's fresh red tresses in this scene rhyme with her mother's frazzled ginger mane: not unlike Emily, whose elders remark her uncanny likeness to bygone members of the Murray clan, Nadia's resemblance to her mother suggests her potential to inherit her mental illness as well. Likewise, a flashback in which her mother shatters a mirror in a manic rage is repeated, with a difference, when the adult Nadia begins to choke to death on shards of glass. This flashback and corresponding death scene—which, as fans have observed, allude to mirror imagery in *Emily*—places into relief McMaster's insights regarding the relationship between trauma and uncanny mirroring in Montgomery's novel. Since trauma involves an "inability to integrate the traumatic event into consciousness in a way that would render it accessible and acceptable to the self"—and thus traumatic "memories appear in the repetitive, intrusive forms of visualization of the trauma scene"—its ultimate "working through"[8] may be precipitated by events or images that propel it to consciousness (57).

If, in Montgomery's novel, Emily's mirroring of the "Murray glare," as well as her perception of the similarities between her mother's fate and that of Ilse's, mark moments in which Aunt Elizabeth and the protagonist respectively register unspoken and repeated traumas, then Nadia's bloody regurgitation of mirror shards signals her own increasing consciousness of the traumatic toll incurred by her mother's illness and abuse. This scene marks a moment in which Nadia not only begins to see how she has quite literally internalized and mirrored her mother's self-destruction but also intuits that she may only save herself by reconstructing shards of memory she has repressed. If, in *Emily*, the protagonist merely intuits that her embodiment of Archibald's "Murray look" is the sign of a repressed past that demands reckoning, the heroine of *Russian Doll* becomes dramatically more aware of her need to face, and extricate herself from, a traumatic maternal legacy. Not insignificantly, however, Nadia's bloody epiphany immediately follows her gifting of her copy of *Emily of New Moon* to her ex-lover's young daughter. Here, it appears as though Nadia channels her childhood literary idol—as though she realizes that, in order to repair and sustain a potential maternal relationship, she must continue the struggle Emily had only begun.

Notably, the Netflix series also draws on, and places into stark relief, the themes of intergenerational trauma implicit within *Emily*. In the sixth episode of the first season, Nadia matter-of-factly states that her maternal grandmother was a Holocaust survivor.[9] This proclamation suggests that her mother's manic episodes may not be merely the result of biological inheritance but rather the result of inherited, second-generation trauma—or, in fact, a combination of both.[10] Indeed, in both the flashback scenes and in the present, Nadia wears a necklace with a gold coin, which she tells Alan is one of the 150 South African Krugerrands into which her maternal grandmother converted her life savings after fleeing war-era Europe. (Holocaust survivors, she informs Alan in the sixth episode, were "paranoid" about investing their money in banks, not least because their savings and property were appropriated by Nazis[11]). Her mother used the remaining coins—totaling exactly $152,780.86—to purchase luxury goods, including the aforementioned sports car, and so Nadia wears the remaining one as a talisman. This coin, then, functions not only as a literal inheritance but also as a figure of the generational trauma that the protagonist has inherited. Moreover, it suggests all she has both lost and managed to preserve precisely because of this trauma: that is, as the last of a profligately exploited sum, it serves as an indexical image of what has survived, or has been salvaged from, a traumatic historical legacy. To a certain extent, this Krugerrand corresponds with Emily's own diary, which was gifted to her by her father and remains her only tangible connection to a family bond that is disrupted by her incorporation into the benighted Murray clan. Significantly, however, Nadia's Krugerrand plays a much more explicit symbolic role in *Russian Doll* than Emily's diary does in Montgomery's novel. Indeed, in the final episode, Alan is able to save Nadia from self-destruction, and thus close the time loop in which they are both imprisoned, by calling out the exact sum of her cherished coin. In effect, he reminds her of the potential she still possesses, even despite the various losses she has endured.

READING *EMILY OF NEW MOON* THROUGH *RUSSIAN DOLL*

To be sure, *Russian Doll*'s deft allusions to *Emily* amplify its characterization of Nadia and its overarching themes of individual and multigenerational trauma. And yet even as it is valuable to consider how familiarity with Montgomery's novel enriches an appreciation of the Netflix program, it is just as important to question how *Russian Doll* might permit new insights into *Emily*—especially a hundred years after the novel's relatively muted debut.

If *Russian Doll*'s treatment of trauma has so resounded with audiences, this is in part because not only its plot but its very structure depends so crucially on repetition. As I have demonstrated above, Nadia's recurrent deaths dramatize the long and difficult process of unconsciously repeating a past trauma; gradually recognizing such a pattern of repetition and its implications; and eventually "working through," or actively and productively mourning, the loss instantiated by such trauma. Significantly, however, the series' depiction of such repeated deaths also bids its audience to sympathize with its protagonist by prompting them to participate in a similar—or, as it were, mirroring—pattern of repetition and gradual recognition. That is, the viewer must return to visual and narrative details they may have initially overlooked in order to better grasp the heretofore mysterious reasons for the protagonist's repeated deaths and revivals. For instance, although viewers immediately know that Nadia dies and is revived on her thirty-sixth birthday, it is only later that they register the coincidence of Nadia's death and that of her thirty-six-year-old mother and thus the traumatic legacy they share. Indeed, even such seemingly inconsequential details such as the mother-daughter pair's similarly untamed ginger manes take on greater significance once the audience begins to register their correspondences. Likewise, the narrative logic and affective charge of the final episode—in which Nadia and Alan must independently save one another on the night of their respective first deaths—depends on the audience's ability to recall earlier minor characters and sequences they might have initially forgotten or dismissed but whose reappearance becomes suddenly critical to the ultimate unfolding of the plot. For that matter, even the series' repeated and accumulating references to *Emily* challenge careful viewers to become mindful of even the most apparently casual cultural and literary allusions and thus to revisit the plot with additional perspective.

In the end, then, *Russian Doll* is as much a meditation on the process of (re)reading as it is one on the process of mourning traumatic loss. This is not least because, as a series whose episodes were released simultaneously on a popular subscription streaming service, it invites immediate consumption of an entire production followed by closer and slower viewings of discrete episodes that might deliver details and nuances that were overlooked in a first pleasurable "binge."[12] To be sure, the series' enticement toward multiple viewings is in the direct interest of its service platform, which profits not only from retained interest but also from the potential of further and similarly lucrative installments. And yet even once one admits the more cynical, profitable interests behind a corporately produced series like *Russian Doll*, it is nevertheless possible to consider the insights its structure of repetition affords with respect to the process of rereading childhood books, and *Emily* in particular.

Rereading, as Alison Waller observes in *Rereading Childhood Books: A Poetics* (2019), "forms its own sub-genre of writing about children's literature": indeed, she cites at least ten bibliomemoirs published in the past fifteen years about the pleasures of rereading books for young people (16).[13] Such attention to a return to childhood's books is prompted in part, she argues, because "remembering and rereading are imaginative processes for reclaiming the private relationships that child selves once had with these texts" (2). Drawing on a series of interviews she conducted with adults from the UK—in which she asked participants to recall, among other things, narrative details of books, memories of initial encounters, and affective responses during both initial and subsequent encounters—Waller theorizes rereading as a "poetics" (19). That is, she qualifies rereading as a "creative act of discovery" (20). Such "making"—or "poesis"—she argues, "takes place both in terms of the cognitive, subjective, and affective processes involved for each individual reader when they remember and revisit, and in terms of the written and oral accounts they might create to record such actions" (20).

Like Waller, the French psychoanalyst and literature professor Pierre Bayard, in his provocatively titled book, *How to Talk about Books You Haven't Read* (2007), identifies (re)reading as an ongoing process in which readers coparticipate with the text, and with one another, in endless combinations of cultural and material circumstances. Crucially, for Bayard, books and the conditions in which they are read[14] are so rich that any act of (re)reading can never be complete. "We do not," he insists, "retain in memory complete books identical to the books remembered by everyone else, but rather fragments surviving from partial readings, frequently fused together and further recast by our private fantasies" (56). Thus, any act of reading, however close and however repeated, is always one of "*nonreading*": the most an individual can do is to "skim" a text with the understanding that their effort is always incomplete or partial. Certainly, Bayard's claim is provocative, especially to those scholars and bibliophiles for whom such terms as "nonreading" and "skimming" imply passivity, laziness, or even anti-intellectualism. And yet Bayard's concept of nonreading—which should not be confused with *not*-reading—should be ultimately refreshing and liberatory. Too often, he insists, we are encouraged "from our school years onward to think of books as untouchable objects" and consequently "feel guilty at the very thought of subjecting them to transformation" (181). Thus, the recognition that any book can never be mastered, or any reading can ever be complete, allows us "to begin to truly listen to the infinitely mobile object that is a literary text" (181).

Russian Doll, insofar as its structure of repetition forces viewers to reckon with moments of inattention and misrecognition—and insofar as its complex literary and cultural allusions forbid any final or exhaustive interpretation—thus serves as a vehicle through which to consider a beloved childhood text like *Emily of New Moon*. That is, much like Bayard, this series suggests that any (re)reading of *Emily* (or in fact, its own narrative inspired by Montgomery's novel) will always be incomplete, and thus can only at best be considered what Bayard calls a "nonreading." And yet instead of forbidding audiences from plumbing the depths of its narrative or its early twentieth-century literary source, *Russian Doll* rather insists that the humbling and radically contingent experience of "nonreading"—that is, a necessarily partial reading that demands the reader's creative coparticipation in the shaping of the narrative—ultimately allows for endless interpretations of an "infinitely mobile object that is a literary text."

One might begin to appreciate the possibilities of incomplete or "non" (re)reading by recognizing the context in which a text is read. For example, *Russian Doll*'s viewers' pleasure[15] in coparticipating with Nadia in her reconstitution of a previously repressed past is in large part dependent on their being "at home" with psychoanalytic discourse that was largely unfamiliar to *Emily*'s original early twentieth-century readers. To be sure, many Netflix viewers may not be acquainted with, say, Freud's distinction between melancholia and mourning or Lacan's articulation of the mirror stage—both of which arguably achieve substantial significance in the series.[16] And yet most twenty-first-century audiences *are* familiar with the rituals of psychotherapy and thus with such concepts as "consciousness," "the unconscious," and "working through trauma." Terms such as "trauma" and "repression" have so permeated contemporary quotidian discourse that their Freudian origins are often forgotten or otherwise deemed irrelevant. Ultimately, such unconscious or otherwise unattributed fluency in (popular) psychoanalytic discourse has permitted audiences to grasp the significance of Nadia's traumatic maternal legacy.

In turn, *Russian Doll*'s allusions to *Emily* might prompt viewers—both devotees of Montgomery and first-time readers who may have been intrigued by the show's references to her "dark" novel—to (re)read Emily with particular attention to its similar themes of the repression and gradual working through of intergenerational trauma. In this way, their appreciation of the text is substantially different from that of its original readers, who most likely were not as familiar with discourses of trauma. Of course, this does not mean that early twentieth-century readers were not sensitive to *Emily*'s themes of grief and its overcoming—or that Montgomery herself did not intend to explore them. After all, grief is arguably a universal theme in literature—and what's more, the publication of the novel coincided with the post–First World War moment in which Freud developed his theory of trauma and in which psychoanalysis gained traction in North America. And yet most early readers of *Emily* did not possess the vocabulary—beginning in fact with the very term "trauma"—or conceptual framework that contemporary readers do to more fully appreciate, say, how Emily's "Murray glare" forces into Aunt Elizabeth's consciousness a traumatic instance she previously could not integrate, or how Emily's reconciliation of Ilse and her father potentially forecloses a cycle of trauma. For that matter, although *Emily*'s earliest readers were surely sensitive to how Archibald Murray's tyrannical reign over his family stunted the spirits of his female descendants, the language of second- and third-wave feminism—which is now as omnipresent in popular Western discourse as that of psychoanalysis—may permit contemporary readers to identify the repressive patriarchal structure of the Murray clan and, more generally, provincial North American culture. Thus, ever-shifting discourses, and the cultural and material conditions that produce them, permit new insights that, as Bayard argues, subject a text to "transformation."[17]

The question remains, then: What might *Russian Doll* contribute to the gradually evolving (re)reading—or, in effect, nonreading—of *Emily*? Perhaps one place to begin might be the final episode of the first season, in which Nadia and Alan discover that the only way they might overcome their respective time loops is to intercede on behalf of the other: Nadia must prevent Alan from committing suicide (the death that inaugurated his subsequent mortal series) and Alan in turn must convince Nadia not to pursue a toxic one-night stand that continues her mother's legacy of self-destructive behavior. Drawing on the imagery of the nesting doll evoked in the series' title, Kessler maintains that "the two must acknowledge the nesting of their lives—their symbiosis in the face of their disparate experiences of loss, loneliness, and despair, the condition of life that Kierkegaard called the 'sickness unto death'—to escape the loop" (27). To this end, Kessler maintains, *Russian Doll*'s "portrait of Nadia and Alan as unwillingly connected individuals forced to accept their symbiosis and work together in order to survive might be read as an argument in favor of communal interdependence over neoliberal independence" (24).

Kessler's reading of *Russian Doll*, like the series itself, is predicated on its production in the early twenty-first century during which conditions of globalization, climate change, and technologies of communication have placed into relief tensions between discourses of self-sufficiency and radical connectedness. At first glance, then, such a reading would hardly seem to apply to *Emily*—which, as Sanders suggests, was revolutionary in its own right precisely because it champions its protagonist's right to privacy and development as an "emerging individual" at a historical moment when the prospect of girls' and women's independence was entirely new (132). Thus, it would seem as though *Russian Doll*'s critique of "neoliberal independence" would be at best presentist, and at worst intellectually irresponsible or even irrational, if it were to be considered with respect to *Emily*, one of its foundational sources.

I would like to argue that, through its critique of individual self-sufficiency, *Russian Doll* identifies similar, anticipatory critiques that are immanent—or, as it were, nested within—Montgomery's novel. After all, Nadia's supernatural intercession on behalf of Alan (and vice versa) is hardly new. Indeed, it is preceded, and perhaps even inspired, by Emily's own mystical intervention on behalf of her closest friend, Ilse. If Emily possesses the ability to embody, and bring into consciousness, traces of past traumas, she also demonstrates the potential to intercede in a newly developing cycle of trauma. This is most evident when, during a fever dream, she has a vision of the true, tragic fate of her friend Ilse's mother, whose memory was tarred by the "cruel" rumor of her infidelity. Up to this point, Ilse's father has been so traumatized by his lost wife's ostensible betrayal that he revisits this trauma on his daughter, whom he neglects and berates[18]—and whose own blunt demeanor and tendency to slight Emily and others demonstrate her repetition of her father's woundedness. When, however, the protagonist discovers, during her reverie, that Ilse's mother fell into a well as she purposefully sought to be reunited with her husband and the infant Ilse, Emily is able to broker a reconciliation between father and daughter that forecloses the kind of intergenerational traumatic memory that haunts the Murray clan and threatens to consume her as well. What is more, Emily's intervention allows her to maintain a close relationship with Ilse, whose increasing ability to become vulnerable and engage in intimacy sustains the protagonist in a continuing drama of self-development. In this way, then, a recognition of more contemporary themes of "symbiosis" and "communal interdependence" in *Russian Doll* might allow readers to discover their traces, as though for the first time, in Montgomery's early twentieth-century novel. This, arguably, is evidence of Bayard's concept of "nonreading," insofar as it suggests evolving insights and perspectives that are not constrained by an initial or final reading of the original text, but rather enlarged and enriched by ever-shifting cultural perceptions and encounters with intersecting texts.

CONCLUSION

In the penultimate episode of *Russian Doll*'s first season, Nadia gives her ex-lover's daughter, Lucy, a copy of *Emily of New Moon*. She does so, however, with a caveat. The book, she states, "isn't really a present"; rather, it's "more like something we share." By stating that the book is not simply a gift, Nadia suggests that the well-worn novel is not a mere object or token whose value depends on its symbolic exchange but rather the bearer of a narrative that Lucy can consume and interpret on her own terms. And yet Nadia's characterization of the novel as "more like something we share" suggests a certain intergenerational solidarity[19] in their mutual appreciation of Montgomery's text. Even though Nadia and Lucy are two distinct individuals separated by at least twenty years of experience—and even if they experience at best a tenuous relationship that may or may not result in Nadia's reunion with Lucy's father and eventual adoption of the young girl[20]—they may still share discrete but nevertheless intersecting responses to the novel that ultimately enrich its significance. Indeed, it is not insignificant that the protagonist of *Russian Doll*—Nadia—bears a name that means "hope" in Russian and other Slavic languages. If there is any hope promised in *Russian Doll*, or for that matter *Emily of New Moon*, it is that their repeated readings and intergenerational sharing might allow for new perspectives and insights that exceed the intentions of their authors or the conditions of their respective moments of production.

NOTES

1. "Superiority Complex," season 1, episode 5.
2. In the first season, to which this chapter is devoted, Nadia experiences the disjointedness of time within the present: that is, she experiences multiple scenarios within a single chronotope (New York's East Village in the second decade of the twenty-first century). In the second season, however, Nadia experiences such disjointedness as she literally shuttles (via an errant New York subway car) through discrete moments of history.
3. See Carol L. Beran's chapter in this collection on insights on how Montgomery changed between *Anne of Green Gables* and *Emily of New Moon*.

4. The program makes clear that Nadia's mother has died—in fact, it makes clear Nadia repeatedly dies on the evening of her thirty-sixth birthday, which was the age at which her mother died—but it does not disclose the causes of her mother's death. Nadia's (ostensible) biological father appears in season 2 of *Russian Doll*, which premiered on April 20, 2022, although the nuances of his relationship to the protagonist remain unresolved.

5. Or, for that matter, Sylvia Plath's red-headed Lady Lazarus, who states that "dying is an art" that she does "exceptionally well."

6. Drew performs a comparative analysis of Ann Radcliffe's *The Mysteries of Udolpho* and *Emily of New Moon*—both of whose protagonists are named Emily—to argue that they exemplify the "female gothic." The female gothic, she argues, "may be understood as the genre that documents female uneasiness within the social order" and reintroduces the "maternal/natural realm as a source of plenitude and pleasure" (20).

7. Not unlike the plot of *Wuthering Heights*, written by another gothic Emily.

8. In his landmark study, "Remembering, Repeating, and Working Through" (1914)—published, significantly, in the same year as the beginning of the Great War—Freud argues that individuals incorporate lost objects (including both people and ideas) into their egos and thus repeatedly "act out" these losses until they are gradually able to disentangle themselves from such losses in a process of mourning, or "working through." Freud revisits his arguments about the repetition of yet-unassimilated losses in his foundational work, *Beyond the Pleasure Principle*, in which he explicitly refers to the experiences of First World War–era soldiers in order to theorize the repetitive mechanisms of trauma. Notably, Holocaust scholars such as Dominick LaCapra have drawn on Freud's concepts of melancholic repetition and mourning/working through in order to theorize collective responses to historical trauma. As I suggest, *Russian Doll*'s depiction of the intersection of individual and historical trauma appears to draw from Freudian psychoanalysis and its adoption by Holocaust/trauma scholars.

9. As Mira Fox notes in an essay on *Russian Doll* in the Jewish periodical *Forward*, Lyonne's own maternal grandparents were Holocaust survivors.

10. This question becomes of central importance in the second season, in which Nadia travels back in time—first, to her own conception, and later, to her grandmother's experience in Second World War–era Hungary—and considers how her own selfhood has been shaped by maternal inheritance. Significantly, in the second episode of the second season, Nadia briefly mentions epigenetics—the theory that radical changes to an environment affect DNA, which has informed conjectures that subsequent generations of trauma survivors (e.g., of the Holocaust) bear genetic traces of their forebears' experiences.

11. This detail becomes central in the second season of *Russian Doll*, which addresses the "Gold Train" and Nazi appropriation of Jews' savings and property.

12. Such re-viewings are further encouraged by social media platforms such as YouTube and Reddit, in which fans post responses and reviews.

13. Of the many texts that Waller cites, perhaps the most significant is Margaret Mackey's *One Child Reading: My Auto-Bibliography* (2016) in which the esteemed Canadian children's literature scholar recalls the books she read as a child in Newfoundland in the 1950s and '60s in order to theorize how texts construct readers, and vice versa.

14. For Waller, this is both the "reading scene" ("a conceptual space shaped and defined by remembering in which activities of lifelong reading take place") as well as the "life space" ("a temporal and spatial zone in which encounters with books take place and are linked to other actors and real-world contexts") (20).

15. In the famous "fort-da" passage of Freud's *Beyond the Pleasure Principle*—in which he describes and analyzes a repetitive game his young grandson devises in order to cope with his mother's necessary withdrawal—Freud suggests that works of art intended to offer pleasure similarly perform the child's "greatest achievement" of reckoning with loss.

16. Lacan's concept of the "mirror stage" involves the child's ability to recognize themselves as a discrete, yet imperfect, subject who is separate from their mother and/or the Other. Arguably, *Russian Doll* alludes to the mirror stage in flashback scenes in which Nadia's mother breaks mirrors—thus disallowing her daughter from perceiving herself as a distinct subject—as well as in the scene in which Nadia regurgitates pieces of a broken mirror and begins the slow process of disentangling herself from her mother.

17. This becomes abundantly clear in the CBC's 1998 television adaptation of Emily, which, as Christopher Gittings demonstrates, makes critical changes to the plot to redress Montgomery's "caricatures of Irish difference" and her "absenting of Micmacs from the social terrain of the trilogy" (23). By daring to reimagine, and arguably enrich, the plot and characters according to emerging discourses of Canadian national identity for "a late twentieth-century Canadian audience" (23), the producers of the CBC adaptation demonstrated what Bayard counterintuitively calls "nonreading." That is, they resisted "think[ing] of books as untouchable objects" and rather regarded the beloved novel as an "infinitely moveable object" whose resonance necessarily shifts in relation to the cultural and material moment in which it is re-presented to a new generation of readers. The same might be said of another popular Netflix series, *Anne with an E* (2017–19), which places into relief, among other things, the trauma presumably experienced by the heroine of Montgomery's *Anne of Green Gables* when she was interned in an orphanage.

18. Most likely, it is implied, because he suspects Ilse is not his legitimate, or biological, daughter.

19. For an elaboration of "intergenerational solidarity," see Justyna Deszcz-Tryhubczak and Zoe Jaques's introduction to their edited volume, *Intergenerational Solidarity in Children's Literature and Film*.

20. Notably, no mention is made of Lucy or her father in the second season of *Russian Doll*. Counterintuitively, this might amplify, rather than detract from, Nadia's gifting of Emily to Lucy: the young girl is free to appreciate the novel's depiction of maternal legacy without the additional constraints imposed by a domineering red-headed stepmother.

WORKS CITED

Bayard, Pierre. *How To Talk about Books You Haven't Read*. Translated by Jeffrey Mehlman. Bloomsbury, 2007.

Deszcz-Tryhubczak, Justyna, and Zoe Jaques, editors. *Intergenerational Solidarity in Children's Literature and Film*. UP of Mississippi, 2021.

Drew, Lorna. "The Emily Connection: Ann Radcliffe, L. M. Montgomery, and 'The Female Gothic.'" *Canadian Children's Literature / Littérature canadienne pour la juenesse*, no. 77, Spring 1995, pp. 19–32.

Fox, Mira. "In *Russian Doll*, Inherited Holocaust Trauma Spills through Generations—Through Time Travel." Forward, 20 Apr. 2022, https://forward.com/culture/500200/netflix-russian-doll-time-travel-holocaust/.

Freud, Sigmund. *Beyond the Pleasure Principle*. Edited and translated by James Strachey. W. W. Norton, 1990.

Freud, Sigmund. "Remembering, Repeating, Working Through (Further Recommendations on the Technique of Psychoanalysis II)." *The Standard Edition of the Complete Psychological Works of Sigmund Freud: Volume 12*. Edited and translated by James Strachey. Hogarth P, 1958. 145–56.

Gittings, Christopher. "Re-Visioning *Emily of New Moon*: Family Melodrama for the Nation." *Canadian Children's Literature / Littérature canadienne pour la juenesse*, vol. 24, no. 3–4, 1998, pp. 22–35.

Grady, Constance. "Why Netflix's *Russian Doll* Keeps Referencing *Emily of New Moon*." *Vox* 16 Feb. 2019, https://www.vox.com/culture/2019/2/16/18223862/netflix-russian-doll-emily-of-new-moon.

H., Marissa. "*Russian Doll* Is about Many Things. For Me, It's the Need to Protect an Unwell Parent." *Glamour*, 22 Feb. 2019, https://www.glamour.com/story/russian-doll-mothers.

Kessler, Sarah. "Alone Again Tonight: *Russian Doll*." *Film Quarterly*, vol. 73, no. 2, 2019, pp. 23–30.

Lawson, Kate. "Adolescence and the Trauma of Maternal Inheritance in L. M. Montgomery's *Emily of New Moon*." *Canadian Children's Literature / Littérature canadienne pour la juenesse*, vol. 25, no. 2, 1999, pp. 21–35.

Mackey, Margaret. *One Child Reading: My Auto-Bibliography*. U of Alberta P, 2016.

McMaster, Lindsey. "The 'Murray Look': Trauma as Family Legacy in L. M. Montgomery's *Emily of New Moon*." *Canadian Children's Literature / Littérature Canadienne pour la juenesse*, vol. 34, no. 2, 2008, pp. 50–74.

Montgomery, L. M. *Emily of New Moon*. 1923. Seal Books/McClelland-Bantam, 1998.

Nussbaum, Emily. "The Clever Thrill Ride of *Russian Doll*." *New Yorker*, 28 Jan. 2019, https://www.newyorker.com/magazine/2019/02/04/the-clever-thrill-ride-of-russian-doll.

Plath, Sylvia. "Lady Lazarus." *Collected Poems*. HarperCollins, 1992.

Russian Doll. Series created by Natasha Lyonne, Leslye Headland, and Amy Poehler. Netflix, 2019–2022.

Sanders, Joe Sutliff. *Disciplining Girls: Understanding the Origins of the Classic Orphan Girl Story*. Johns Hopkins UP, 2011.

Waller, Alison. *Rereading Childhood Books: A Poetics*. New York: Bloomsbury, 2019.

ABOUT THE CONTRIBUTORS

Yoshiko Akamatsu is a professor at Notre Dame Seishin University, Okayama, Japan. She translated Montgomery's posthumous collection of short stories, *Akin to Anne: Tales of Other Orphans*, in 1989. Her most recent works include a book of her collected essays, *From Red-Haired Anne to Black-Haired Emily* (English translation), 2022; "An Overview of *Anne* Books in 21st Century Japan" in the 2022 digital exhibition "The *Anne of Green Gables* Manuscript"; and "The Problems and Possibilities Inherent in Adaptation: *Emily of New Moon* and *Emily, Girl of the Wind*" in *Children and Childhoods in L. M. Montgomery: Continuing Conversations*, 2022.

Carol L. Beran's essays on works by Canadian writers such as L. M. Montgomery, Alice Munro, Margaret Laurence, Aritha van Herk, Margaret Atwood, Michael Ondaatje, Robert Kroetsch, and Hugh MacLennan have appeared in Canadian and American journals. Beran's two books are *Living Over the Abyss: Margaret Atwood's Life before Man* and *Critical Insights: Contemporary Canadian Fiction*.

Rita Bode is professor of English literature at Trent University, Canada. She has coedited three volumes of essays on L. M. Montgomery, the latest of which, *Children and Childhoods in L. M. Montgomery: Continuing Conversations* (McGill-Queen's University Press, 2022), includes her chapter, "Vulnerable Situations: Boys and Boyhood in the *Emily* Books." Her maternal scholarship includes essays on Montgomery and Sandra Cisneros, and she also works and publishes on American women writers of the long nineteenth century, with a special interest in their transatlantic literary relationships. She is currently editor of the *Edith Wharton Review*.

Lesley D. Clement, past visiting scholar of the L. M. Montgomery Institute (University of Prince Edward Island) and consulting editor of the *Journal of L. M. Montgomery Studies*, has held teaching and administrative positions at various Canadian universities. She has published on visual literacy, visual culture, empathy, and death in picture books and Montgomery's writings. Her work on Montgomery appears in *Studies in Canadian Literature*, *L. M. Montgomery and the Matter of Nature(s)*, and *L. M. Montgomery and Gender*. She coedited and contributed to *Children and Childhoods in L. M. Montgomery: Continuing Conversations* (McGill-Queen's University Press, 2022), *L. M. Montgomery's Rainbow Valleys: The Ontario Years, 1911–1942* (McGill-Queen's University Press, 2015), and *Global Perspectives on Death in Children's Literature* (Routledge, 2016).

Yan Du is a PhD candidate and a Cambridge Trust scholar in children's literature in the Faculty of Education at the University of Cambridge. She has presented and published on topics including young adult literature and media culture, Chinese girls' literature, gender and sexuality in Chinese adolescent fiction, girl's authorship, and verse novels.

Allison McBain Hudson is a PhD candidate at Dublin City University, researching material culture in the novels of L. M. Montgomery. Originally from Alberta, Canada, she obtained a BA in English from the University of Calgary in 1995 and moved to Ireland in 1997. She earned an MA in children's and young adult literature from Dublin City University in 2019 with a focus on Montgomery's unique Romanticism and "everyday magic." She is married to an Irish sculptor and lives on the outskirts of Dublin with their two daughters.

Kate Lawson is associate professor in the Department of English Language and Literature at the University of Waterloo, Waterloo, Canada. She is the editor of the Broadview edition of Charlotte Brontë's *Villette*, coauthor of *The Marked Body: Domestic Violence in Mid-Nineteenth-Century Literature* (State University of New York Press, 2002), and author of numerous articles on Victorian fiction and L. M. Montgomery.

Jessica Wen Hui Lim teaches English at St Andrew's Cathedral School in New South Wales. She previously taught English literature at the University of Cambridge and was a director of studies in English at Lucy Cavendish College. Her research centers on women's writing and children's literature from the eighteenth and nineteenth centuries, with a focus on literary explorations of theological and pedagogical concerns. She coedited *Women's Literary Education c. 1690–1850* (Edinburgh University Press, 2023) with Louise Joy, and her articles have appeared in the *Journal for Eighteenth Century Studies*, the *Charles Lamb Bulletin, Notes and Queries*, and *Oxford Research in English*.

Lindsey McMaster is a scholar of English Studies at Nipissing University in Ontario, Canada. She teaches undergraduate courses on writing, creativity, children's literature, and Canadian literature, specializing in the history of women writers. Her book, *Working Girls in the West: Representations of Wage-Earning Women*, charts the rise of the working heroine, a touchstone figure of social change in the Canadian West.

E. Holly Pike taught literary history, women writers, and children's literature at Grenfell Campus, Memorial University of Newfoundland. She has published on the works of L. M. Montgomery in edited collections and journals and has presented papers on Montgomery at numerous conferences. She is coeditor with Laura M. Robinson of *L. M. Montgomery and Gender* (McGill-Queen's University Press, 2021) and with Rita Bode, Lesley D. Clement, and Margaret Steffler of *Children and Childhoods in L. M. Montgomery: Continuing Conversations* (McGill-Queen's University Press, 2022). Now retired, she serves on the editorial board of the *Journal of L. M. Montgomery Studies* and continues her research.

Joe Sutliff Sanders is a specialist in children's media in the Faculty of Education at the University of Cambridge and a fellow at Lucy Cavendish College. Among his books are *Disciplining Girls: Understanding the Origins of the Classic Orphan Girl Story* and *A Literature of Questions: Nonfiction for the Critical Child*.

Katharine Slater is an associate professor of English at Rowan University, where she teaches courses on children's and young adult literature. Her recent articles and book chapters include "Dearly Departed: *The Arrival*'s Spectral Refugee," "Daisy Ashford and the Child Writer's Use of Scale," and "'Lurched Forward and Stopped': *Last Stop on Market Street* and Black Mobility." Her current book project looks at the geographies of gender and sexuality in young adult literature, arguing that queer female characters grow and move in ways that trouble sequential development.

Margaret Steffler is professor emerita in the Department of English Literature at Trent University. Her areas of research include Canadian women's fiction and life writing, the construction of girlhood in Canadian and global narratives, and Canadian Mennonite/s Writing, particularly the work of Miriam Toews. She is active in L. M. Montgomery Studies and is the editor of P. K. Page's *Mexican Journal* and *Metamorphosis: Selected Children's Literature* in The Collected Works of P. K. Page. She has also published on the work of Sylvia Fraser, Alice Munro, Carol Shields, Catharine Parr Traill, Susan Frances Harrison, Rudy Wiebe, David Bergen, and Al Purdy.

Anastasia Ulanowicz is an associate professor of English at the University of Florida, where she researches and teaches in the areas of children's literature, comics and visual rhetoric, memory studies, and historical fiction. Her book, *Second-Generation Memory and Contemporary Children's Literature: Ghost Images* (Routledge, 2013), received the Children's Literature Association Book Award in 2015. Her current book project explores the representation of Eastern Europe in North American and Western European comics.

INDEX

adults and adulthood, 23, 31–32, 112, 131, 185, 189, 194–95, 200–201
Alpine Path, The (Montgomery), 105, 111, 176, 179–80
anime, 123–26, 201n2
"apparitional lesbian," 148–49
authenticity (authentic self), 15, 31, 55, 58–61, 63–64

banality, 25–34
Bayard, Pierre, 211–14
belonging (state of being), 13, 54–57, 60–64, 137. *See also* objects
Bergren, Katherine, 190, 198–200
books, as objects, 75–81
boundaries, 4, 14, 55, 57, 62–65, 156, 198, 200
Brontë, Charlotte, 10, 24–25, 28, 31, 34, 181, 186
Burnley, Ilse, 5, 25, 29–31, 46, 55, 58, 60–64, 87, 92–95, 114, 123, 135–36, 140–41, 149, 167–68, 170, 182, 193–94

candles, 6, 27, 71, 73–75, 85, 135, 147–48, 151, 153, 163, 186
cats, 90, 203–4

diaries. *See* journals
Dimock, Wai Chee, 189–90, 198
Disappointed House, the, 39, 47, 49–51, 74–75, 82, 84–85, 115, 169
domesticity, 27, 39, 46, 49–51, 73, 84–85, 132, 136, 145, 151, 162–63, 167–69
domestic realism, 4, 8, 29, 35n1

Emily Climbs (Montgomery), 3, 10, 23, 27–28, 33–34, 39, 42–43, 45–47, 55, 59–63, 74, 76–78, 80–83, 95, 106–7, 109, 132, 135, 139–41, 147, 156n2, 161, 163–64, 166–67, 170–71, 178, 181, 185–86, 190–92, 195–96, 198–99
Emily's Quest (Montgomery), 9, 13, 23–34, 38–39, 43, 45, 47–50, 55–64, 74, 76, 79, 81–82, 85, 100n4, 105–7, 121, 127n7, 135, 141, 145, 147, 154–55, 167–71, 179, 182, 184, 190–92, 196–99
Emily trilogy: adaptation of, 12, 14, 122–26; translations of, 5, 12, 14, 105–10, 112, 114–15, 117, 121–26, 201n2; translators of, 14, 105, 108–10, 115, 117, 120, 122, 125–26
exile, 39, 41, 45, 47–49, 151, 156n3

failure, 13, 23–34, 137
father figures, 4, 26–27, 30, 33, 57, 63, 76–77, 79–83, 90, 92, 94–95, 97–98, 123–24, 130, 132–33, 135–37, 139–40, 147, 149, 150, 153, 162–63, 166, 169, 184, 192, 193, 197, 206–7, 209, 213–15
fear, 45–46, 54–56, 58–60, 61–62, 64, 94–95, 137, 139, 144, 148, 152, 161, 181, 185, 196
Flash, the, 9, 13, 38–42, 46, 47, 56, 65n3, 134, 179–82, 187, 189, 191–93, 197, 199–200, 206
fluid time, 190–92, 195–96
funerals, 26, 89–91, 130

ghosts, 15, 48–49, 74, 85, 94–95, 144–45, 148–50, 152, 154–56, 196

223

globalized reading, 198
gothic genre, 10, 25, 35n8, 74, 79, 84, 144–45, 149, 151–52, 154, 186, 206, 208, 216nn6–7

hauntings, 48, 50, 144, 152, 156
heteronormativity, 133, 148, 149
history, 5, 7, 13, 15, 25, 27–28, 79, 144–45, 149–50, 157, 161–71, 172n5, 190, 200, 215; historical past, 25–26, 28, 29, 31, 34, 150, 162–63, 165, 167–71, 209, 214, 216n8
hurt/soul-wounds, 55, 62

Ikematsu, Naoko, 112, 128
imperfection and perfection, 55–56, 59, 62, 64, 66–67
instrumentality, 13, 38, 44–49
interconnectedness, 55–56, 64

journals, 3–4, 10–11, 14, 23, 35n4, 73, 75, 77, 81, 87–80, 91, 93, 99, 130, 133–34, 138, 142n1, 165–66, 172n11, 176–77, 185, 192, 194, 201n4

Kandori, Nobuo, 110
kawaii, 108–10, 118, 122
Kent, Teddy, 5, 14, 25, 28–32, 47, 49–50, 51n3, 55, 57–59, 60–65, 74–75, 79, 84–85, 92, 123, 135, 141, 145, 154–55, 168–70, 179, 181–82, 185, 195–98
Künstler/Künstlerroman, 7, 11, 35n7, 88, 131, 161, 171n1, 190

Laurence, Margaret, 175–76, 179–80, 183–84, 186
life writing, 87–92, 95, 98–99
Little Women (Alcott), 8
loneliness, 39, 55, 57, 63, 156n3, 213
Lyonne, Natasha, 203

MacDonald, Ewen, 117, 176
MacLulich, T. D., 8–9, 11, 24, 31, 35n7, 36n10, 171n1
Mad Mr. Morrison, 78, 156n1, 181, 185

marriage, 8, 25–26, 29–32, 36n12, 47, 49, 51n3, 84, 97, 125, 136, 145, 148–49, 152, 168–69, 170, 176–77, 179, 186
material culture/material objects, 12, 14, 71–73, 75, 83, 85, 137–38
maternal figures, 131, 141
maternal legacies, 131, 139, 208, 212, 217n20
mothering/mothers, 14–15, 31, 48, 62, 80, 82–83, 87, 89, 92–95, 117, 126n1, 130–42, 142n1, 151, 161, 162, 169, 171, 177–78, 180, 182, 193–94, 203–4, 206–10, 213–14, 216n4, 217n5, 217n16, 217n20; mother-daughter relations, 130–31; queer mothering/queering motherhood, 132–34
Munro, Alice, 106, 175–76, 179, 180, 183–84, 186, 198, 199, 200, 201n3
Muraoka, Hanako, 105–8, 117, 121, 125–26
Murray, Archibald, 131–32, 136, 149–50, 152, 163, 207–8, 213

nonreading, 204, 211, 212–14, 217n17

objects, 14, 71–73, 75, 78–80, 83, 85, 137–39, 198, 206, 212, 216n8, 217n17
"Ode: Intimations of Immortality" (Wordsworth). *See* Wordsworth, William
orphan girl narratives, 6, 8, 131, 205

Page, P. K., 24, 198–200
personal space, 4, 13, 15, 23, 40, 46, 60, 76–77, 80–81, 84–85, 88, 96–97, 139, 140, 162, 164, 166, 170–71, 179, 191
pride, 27, 57, 61–62, 82, 107, 137
private space, 4, 10, 14, 48, 56, 65, 76–77, 82, 88–89, 91–92, 95–96, 98–99, 153, 162, 164, 167, 170–71, 211
public space, 4, 14, 56, 65, 66n6, 88–89, 91–92, 95–99, 125, 142n1, 162, 164, 166, 168, 171, 177

queerness, 15, 28, 34, 40, 64, 66n7, 132–34, 144–56, 157n4

recording, as action, 4, 89–90, 92, 94, 97, 131, 134, 164–65, 168, 170–71, 211
rereading, 16, 165, 204, 211

romance and Romanticism, 6, 8–9, 11, 13, 15, 17, 25, 35n1, 42, 47–49, 50–51, 57, 64, 77, 79, 145, 155, 156n1, 157n4, 161–62, 164–65, 171, 179, 182, 189, 201n1

rooms, 31, 49, 74, 82–83, 85, 87, 135–36, 138–39, 178, 207

Rubio, Mary Henley, 3–4, 7, 11, 25, 35n1, 36n10, 36n13, 41, 50, 73, 92, 121, 127n5, 182, 192

Russian Doll (Headland series), 16, 203–15, 216n4, 216nn8–9, 216n11, 217n20

second sight, 46, 95, 140–41, 182, 194

secrecy, 56–57, 88, 92

Secret Garden, The (Burnett), 6, 10, 16n1

sexuality, 10, 32, 33, 146

shame/humiliation, 55–60, 62, 64, 75, 90, 140, 153, 162, 193

social justice, 88, 91, 95

sources/records, 165–67, 171

Starr, Emily Byrd, writing career, 8, 81, 170

St. Paul, 182–83, 186

texts in motion, 190, 198–200

time loops, 204–6, 209, 213

traditions, 6, 8–9, 13, 15, 16n2, 27–29, 73, 138, 144, 161, 163–64, 168–71, 180, 182

unhappiness, 15–27, 92, 153, 155

Urquhart, Jane, 106, 198–200

Victorian era, 6, 13, 16n1, 23, 25–34, 35n5, 36n9, 42, 61, 80, 83, 167–68, 172n9, 182

vulnerability, 56, 59, 62–64, 76, 154

Vulvokov, Nadia, 203–10, 212–15, 216n4, 216n10, 217n16, 217n20

Waller, Alison, 204, 211, 216nn13–14

Waterston, Elizabeth, 3, 7, 35n7, 127n5, 166, 168, 171n1, 177, 179

Wordsworth, Dorothy, 181

Wordsworth, William, 9, 13, 38–45, 51, 56, 181–82, 186, 189–92, 194–95, 198–201, 206

www.ingramcontent.com/pod-product-compliance
Lightning Source LLC
Chambersburg PA
CBHW022015220426
43663CB00007B/1090